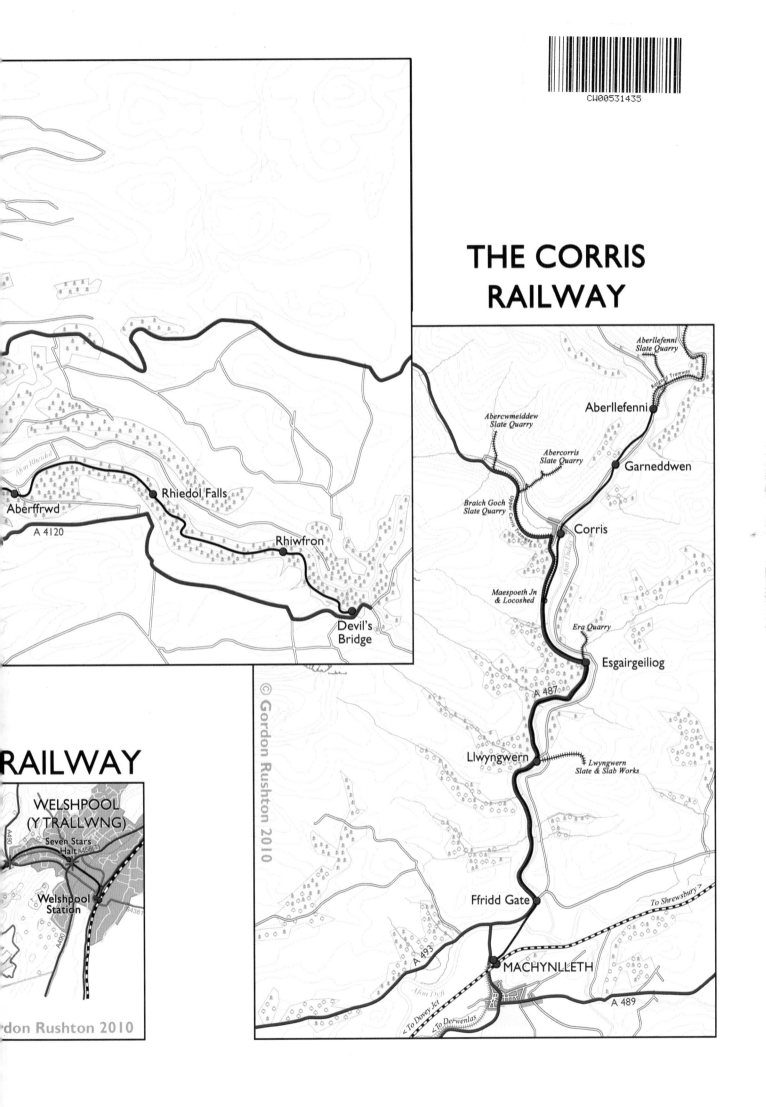

THE CORRIS RAILWAY

Aberllefenni
Slate Quarry

Abercwmeiddew
Slate Quarry

Abercorris
Slate Quarry

Aberllefenni

Garneddwen

Braich Goch
Slate Quarry

Corris

Maespoeth Jn
& Locoshed

Era Quarry

Esgairgeiliog

A 487

Llwyngwern

Lwyngwern
Slate & Slab Works

Ffridd Gate

To Shrewsbury

A 493

MACHYNLLETH

A 489

< To Dovey Jct

< To Derwenlas

Aberffrwd

A 4120

Rhiedol Falls

Rhiwfron

Devil's
Bridge

RAILWAY

WELSHPOOL
(Y TRALLWNG)

Seven Stars
Halt

Welshpool
Station

An Illustrated History of the
GREAT WESTERN
NARROW GAUGE

An
Illustrated History
of the

GREAT
WESTERN
NARROW
GAUGE

Peter Johnson

An imprint of
Ian Allan Publishing

An Illustrated History of the Great Western Narrow Gauge
Peter Johnson

First published 2011

ISBN 978 0 86093 636 7

Published by Oxford Publishing Co

an imprint of Ian Allan Publishing Ltd, Hersham, Surrey KT12 4RG. Printed in England by Ian Allan Printing Ltd, Hersham, Surrey KT12 4RG.

Visit the Ian Allan Publishing website at www.ianallanpublishing.com

Distributed in the Unites States of America and Canada by BookMasters Distribution Services.

Code 1107/B2

Front cover: **Narrow gauge the Great Western way. Take a locomotive, add brass number plates, a copper-capped chimney and a copper safety valve bonnet and it screams GWR. No 823, *Countess*, crosses Raven Square on the Welshpool & Llanfair Light Railway in the 1950s.** *Michael Whitehouse collection*

Back cover top: **No 8 heads a short train out of Aberystwyth c1964. It had been named *Llywelyn* in 1956 and painted in lined green livery in 1957. The faux-Cambrian carriage livery was replaced in 1968.** *Ian Allan Library*

Back cover bottom: **The Corris, Machynlleth, Aberdovey & Towyn Railway plan of 1852 showing the proposed connection with the Shrewsbury & Aberystwyth Railway.** *Parliamentary Archives*

Half title page: **Corris Railway No 3 with a passenger train near Llwyngwern, c1928.** *B. B. Edmonds*

Title page: **Vale of Rheidol Light Railway No 1, *Edward VII*, at Aberystwyth c1910. The loco livery is two shades of green and black. A 3d supplement was charged to travel in the third carriage, the semi-open.** *Kingsway/Author's collection*

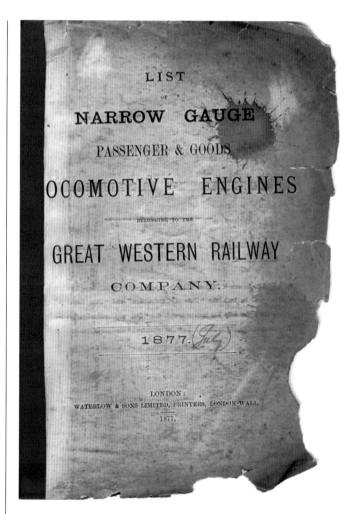

Produced in 1877, this list of GWR 'narrow gauge passenger & goods locomotives engines' related to the company's standard gauge stock. *Author's collection*

Contents

Introduction

In Great Western Railway terms a narrow gauge railway was initially a standard gauge, 4ft 8½in, line, reflecting the GWR's original Brunellian 7ft ¼in gauge main line. In 1892 though, the last of the broad gauge was converted to standard gauge and the GWR's services were operated on this gauge throughout. An early venture into less-than-standard gauge railways was its acquisition of the 2ft gauge Festiniog & Blaenau Railway, as a part of the development of the route from Bala to the slate centre of Blaenau Ffestiniog in 1880. This line was converted to standard gauge in 1883 and a small fleet of 2ft gauge wagons was built to carry slate quarried at Manod.

Between 1922 and 1930, however, the GWR became the owner and operator of three true narrow gauge railways, spread across three counties within a 30-mile radius of the market town of Machynlleth in Mid Wales. These railways, in order of acquisition, the Welshpool & Llanfair Light Railway, the Vale of Rheidol Light Railway, and the Corris Railway, although all narrow gauge, were very different in gauge, in character, in function, and in location.

The 2ft 3in gauge Corris Railway was the oldest. Originally the Corris, Machynlleth & River Dovey Tramroad, it used horses and gravity to carry slate when it was opened in 1859. Located mostly in Merionethshire, it was the shortest of these railways, its main line some 6½ miles long from Machynlleth to Corris with branches to the Morben wharves below Machynlleth, Upper Corris and Ratgoed. Following a change in ownership in 1878, the introduction of steam power, some reconstruction and fresh legislation, a formal passenger service was introduced in 1883.

In September 1883, the conversion of the 2ft gauge Festiniog & Blaenau Railway to standard gauge under the auspices of the GWR approached completion at Festiniog. *Author's collection*

A significant and unusual feature of the Corris was its operation of horse-drawn and later, motor coaches, for tourists visiting the nearby Talyllyn, the popularity of these services undoubtedly contributing to the railway's longevity. Financially, its apparent success was deceptive for despite paying dividends until 1905 it did not pay its way and required subsidies from its owner. The GWR did not want to buy the railway in 1930 but was persuaded to as part of a larger transaction. The passenger service lasted just until 1931 and, with the slate traffic already in serious decline, the railway was closed by the newly formed British Railways in 1948. Flood damage to the river bank had threatened to undermine the Dyfi river bridge and expenditure on the line was not deemed worthwhile. Thoughts of preservation crystallised with the founding of the Corris Railway Society in 1966. After much effort and persistence, a passenger service between the old loco shed at Maespoeth and Corris, a distance of less than one mile, was introduced in 2002.

The Vale of Rheidol Light Railway, 2ft gauge and incorporated in 1897, was initially a light railway in name only, for it was the product of an act of Parliament, not a light railway order. Powers to operate as a light railway were obtained before it was built, however. Opened in 1902, from the Cardiganshire coastal town of Aberystwyth the railway struck inland through the valley from which it took its name for nearly 12 miles, terminating at Devil's Bridge. Tourists visiting the famous waterfalls there was to produce much of the railway's traffic, despite the promoters' expectations of business from mines in the area. Independence was lost when the Cambrian Railways acquired control in 1913. The latter's ownership had lasted barely 10 years when the GWR took over at the railway Grouping in 1923.

There followed a period of investment quite unlike that ever made in any other narrow gauge railway at this time; new locomotives and carriages and a relocated station – the benefit

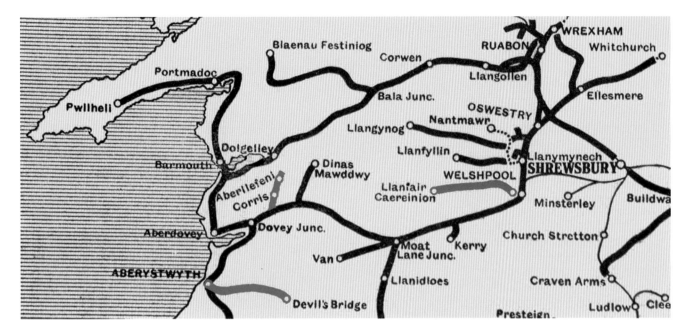

of being part of a large and substantial group. The VRLR became a part of British Railways in 1948, the state-owned concern managing to keep it going until 1989, when the line was sold, one of the first nationalised rail assets to be privatised. Since then the new owners have invested a considerable sum in the railway's infrastructure to secure its future.

In Montgomeryshire, the 2ft 6in gauge Welshpool & Llanfair Light Railway is significant in being the first narrow gauge railway to be authorised as a light railway under the auspices of the Light Railways Act of 1896. Its construction was untypical in being driven not by the requirements of mineral extraction but by those of agriculture, linking the market town of Welshpool with the village of Llanfair Caereinion, nine sparsely-populated miles away. Opened in 1903 and operated by the Cambrian Railways as a requirement of a treasury grant, the WLLR struggled to make its way. The GWR took over from the Cambrian in 1922 and acquired the WLLR company in 1923. In common with the nearby Corris Railway, the WLLR also lost its passenger service in 1931. It survived to be taken over by British Railways in 1948 and was not closed until 1956. Reopening by a preservation company started in 1963, 60 years after its opening.

After setbacks that could have defeated it, the WLLR has survived and grown to become one of the few railways that manages to operate without needing a bank overdraft.

Although two of these railways were not opened until the 20th century, they were very much children of the 19th century, where improved transportation made otherwise marginal enterprises viable. The GWR played an essential part in ensuring their survival into the 21st century, despite trying to avoid taking on the Corris at all, and only acquiring the others because they were a part of the Cambrian package at the Grouping. Although it might have been willing to acquire the VRLR without the Grouping, despite rejecting overtures to buy it in 1907, the same could not be said of the WLLR. The railways' continued existence is a consequence of changing times, where the part that steam railways marketed as tourist attractions can play in the economic viability of a locality, is as widely recognised as it is essential to the preservation of historic railways and their equipment.

The amount of historical material available, much of it not subject to scrutiny before, and limitations on space are responsible for ending the detailed examination of these railways' histories shortly after the time they ceased to be operated by British Railways. Subsequent events have been dealt with in summary. Perhaps there will be another opportunity to complete their stories in detail in the future. All three railways certainly deserve it.

Above: **An extract from the map used in GWR directors' reports from 1931, with the three narrow gauge lines highlighted.**

Left: **The GWR built 2-ton slate wagons to carry slate from Manod to Blaenau Ffestiniog, whence they were carried on standard gauge transporter wagons. This example is preserved at the Great Bush Railway in Sussex.** *Author*

Acknowledgements

It is doubly appropriate that publication of this historical exploration of the Welsh narrow gauge railways owned by the Great Western Railway should take place in 2011, for it not only coincides with the 40th anniversary of my first visit to Wales, on 4 July 1971, but also with my first encounter with these three railways. Whilst the prime purpose of the excursion was to ride on the Vale of Rheidol Light Railway, en route I saw the remnant of the Welshpool & Llanfair Light Railway's mixed-gauge siding at Welshpool and the Corris Railway's station building at Machynlleth. This excursion led to the expansion of my interest in Welsh railways and ultimately to this book.

As usual, the Parliamentary Archives have been the source of the Parliamentary plans. The opposed private bill committee minutes from the Corris Railway's 1879 bill turned out to be a rich source, with evidence of the railway's pre-steam operations. A copy of the GWR's Ministry of Transport draft order and associated plan relating to the relocation of the VRLR in 1925 are also deposited here.

At the National Archives, Kew, I saw Board of Trade, Ministry of Transport, Great Western Railway, British Transport Commission and British Railways records and the company minute books of all three railways. The Board of Trade records of dissolved companies was a particularly fruitful source for unpicking the origins of the VRLR and the acquisition of the Corris Railway by Imperial Tramways. More information on the origins of the CR and the involvement of the contractor Thomas Savin was uncovered in the Court of Chancery records. Newtown & Machynlleth Railway and the Aberystwyth & Welsh Coast Railway minutes contained references to the CR.

The effort required to examine the Cambrian Railways' officers' reports, more than 50 volumes, was fully justified, especially for the reports of the construction of the Welshpool & Llanfair Light Railway and its subsequent revenues and expenses. GWR records dealt briefly with the VRLR stock and, in more detail, with the acquisition of the CR. Several of the British Railways Board files that dealt with the sale of the VRLR were released following Freedom of Information Act applications.

Back issues of the *Manchester Guardian*, the *Times*, the *London Gazette* and the British Library's 19th century newspapers were viewed via the internet.

Richard Greenhough has been researching the Corris Railway for many years. I am grateful to him for allowing me to see copies of Imperial Tramways' annual reports and other documents in his collection. He was also good enough to read the manuscript and made several invaluable observations.

Many books and articles have been published about these railways, making the sourcing of older unpublished photographs more difficult. There are a few however, and I hope readers will appreciate the wide range of illustrations on offer. Michael Bishop, Alan Bowler, Alan Butcher, Robert Darlaston, Tim Edmonds, Adrian Gray, Paul Ingham, Ted Talbot and Michael Whitehouse kindly made their collections available to me. Over the years Paul has been training my eye to the finer detail of loco features that are useful aids to dating photographs.

Once again, I am grateful to Gordon Rushton for producing the endpaper maps in his inimitable style.

The award of a grant by the Railway & Canal Historical Society towards the expenses incurred in carrying out the research for this book was much appreciated.

Peter Johnson
LEICESTER, APRIL 2011

Miscellanea

Welsh place names

The anglicised versions of many Welsh place names have had the Welsh forms restored over the last 40 years or so. The archaic forms are used here where most appropriate. Exceptionally, Aberllefenny was adopted in place of Aberllefenni much earlier, from 1908 by the Railway Clearing House, which is reflected in the text. The use of Aberystwith for Aberystwyth was ended as early as 1867 in Bradshaw although perpetuated until 1892 by the Railway Clearing House; only the Welsh form is used here. For clarification the other places concerned are:

Aberdovey	Aberdyfi
Caernarvon	Caernarfon
Dolgelly/Dolgelley	Dolgellau
Dovey	Dyfi
Portmadoc	Porthmadog
Towyn	Tywyn

Counties

Cardiganshire	part of Dyfed
Merionethshire	part of Gwynedd
Montgomeryshire	part of Powys

Abbreviations

CMATR	Corris, Machynlleth, Aberdovey & Towyn Railway
CMRDT	Corris, Machynlleth & River Dovey Tramroad
CR	Corris Railway
GWR	Great Western Railway
MMR	Manchester & Milford Railway
VRLR	Vale of Rheidol Light Railway
WLLR	Welshpool & Llanfair Light Railway

Currency, weight and distance

£1 = 240d (pence) = 20s (shillings); 1s = 12d; 1 guinea = £1 1s
1 ton = 20 hundredweight (cwt)
1 mile = 8 furlongs = 80 chains = 1,760 yards = 1.60 kilometres; 1 yard = 3 feet = 0.91 metres; 1 chain = 22 yards

The value of money
Equivalent value of £1 in 2010

1850	£58.53	1920	£21.21
1860	£43.16	1925	£29.97
1870	£45.70	1930	£33.42
1880	£48.31	1935	£36.98
1890	£59.89	1940	£28.72
1900	£57.06	1945	£25.95
1905	£57.35	1950	£22.78
1910	£57.06	1955	£17.42
1915	£43.06	1960	£15.30

Data extracted from the currency converter on the National Archives website:
www.nationalarchives.gov.uk/currency

1

Corris Railway

The slate quarries of Corris and Aberllefenny were located five and six miles respectively to the north of Machynlleth, an ancient market town in the old county of Montgomeryshire, now Powys. The town sits just above the flood plains on the southern banks of the Afon Dyfi, River Dovey in English, 10 miles from the Cardigan Bay coast. The Romans settled in the locality and a market charter was granted in 1291. Here, Owain Glyndŵr was declared prince of Wales in 1400 and called a parliament in 1404. By 1851 the population was 1,665. In 2009, the Dyfi valley became the first UNESCO Biosphere in Wales, fulfilling conservation, development and logistical functions.

The quarries were set in the Dulas Valley, enclosed by mountains rising to 1,500ft and more. The main centre was at Corris, around the 100ft contour; there is little level ground in the locality to be dogmatic about its elevation. To the north west of Corris lies the Deri Valley, where the Braich Goch quarry tips once dominated the village. To the north east, further along the Dulas, lie Aberllefenny and Ratgoed and further quarries. As a quarrying centre, the Corris area was much smaller than Ffestiniog, Dinorwic, Nantlle or Penrhyn to the north.

The turnpike road from Dolgellau, the county town of Merioneth, reached the village via the Deri and, crossing to the eastern side, shared the Dulas valley with the river as far as its union with the Dyfi at Fridd Gate. From here it was the practice to take the slate across the river to wharves on the southern bank at Derwenlas and Morben, two miles from Machynlleth and the highest navigable point on the river. The slate was transhipped from there to small craft capable of navigating the river to the harbour at Aberdyfi, where it was transhipped again to coastal trading craft.

The river was first bridged at Machynlleth in 1533, the current structure dating from 1805. It seems likely that the quarry owners were responsible for building the new road down to the Dyfi sometime in the 1840s, bypassing Corris and applying a regular gradient that favoured the traffic. Between Maespoeth and Fridd Gate the alignment might have been that of the Roman road, Sarn Helen. It remained, though, a restriction on output, increasing the risk of damage in transit.

The first proposal for a railway to Corris came in November 1850 when the intention to deposit a bill was advertised. It could well be that that the quarry proprietors, who were the promoters, had been looking northwards and noticing how the Ffestiniog-area quarries had been able to increase their output and profitability since the Festiniog Railway had been opened in 1836. The road between promoting a bill and building a railway was to be long, tortuous and beset with disputes amongst the promoters.

The bill called for the Corris, Machynlleth & River Dovey Railway or Tramroad to construct and operate a 'line from the Aberllefenny slate quarries to the River Dovey, with branches'. The notice described it as 'a railway or tramroad commencing at or near the engine house at Aberllefenny slate quarries … and terminating at or near a certain house called or known as Panteidal, on the River Dovey … ', near the western end of the later Aberystwyth & Welsh Coast Railway's Aberdovey Tunnel No 1, together with branches 'from and out of the line of the intended railway or tramroad hereinafter described, commencing at or near a house called or place known as Aberllefenny … and terminating … at or near a certain house called or known as Tycam. Also a branch railway or tramroad … commencing in the township of Corris … at or near the fifth milestone on the turnpike road leading from the town of Machynlleth to the town of Dolgelley … and terminating at or near a certain house called or known as Tyddynyberth.'

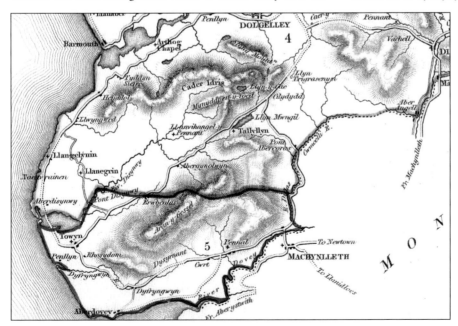

South Merionethshire location map, 1840, showing Machynlleth to the south east, Towyn to the west, and Dolgelley to the north. *R. Creighton, Lewis's Topographical Dictionary, extract/ Author's collection*

Measured from Aberllefenny, the deposited plans show a route of nearly 14 miles. Significant features were a viaduct 572 yards long taking the line over the Afon Pennal near Talgarth Hall, and a tunnel 68 yards long on a two-chain curve near Llugwy Hall, both on the northern bank of the Dovey. The branches were shown with lengths of 1 mile 6 furlongs 2 chains to Tycam and 2 miles 1 furlong to Tyddynyberth. The ruling grade to the former was 1 in 38 and 1 in 35 rising to 1 in 25 for the latter. On the estuarial section the gradient averaged 1 in 660 whereas on the valley section it was 1 in 113. The sharpest curves were of two chains, three along the river, one on the Tyddynyberth branch and two on the Tycam branch. As coastal craft were expected to be able to sail up to it, the terminus at Panteidal would eliminate transhipment to river craft, reducing costs and breakages.

Of particular interest, in contrast to the route adopted when the railway was eventually built, from the Dovey bridge as far as the location now known as Maespoeth, it followed an alignment on the western side of the road. The branches were more tram-like in their alignments and mostly followed the road exactly. The mixed nature of the alignments must be responsible for the 'railway or tramroad' uncertainty in the scheme's title. Finding routes that avoided existing structures, particularly around Corris, must have taxed the engineer, Gloucester-based Arthur Causton, who signed the estimate for £12,000.

Top right: **The Corris, Machynlleth & River Dovey Tramway plan of 1850.** *Parliamentary Archives*

Above: **The Corris, Machynlleth, Aberdovey & Towyn Railway plan of 1852 showing the proposed connection with the Shrewsbury & Aberystwyth Railway.** *Parliamentary Archives*

Right: **The Corris, Machynlleth & River Dovey Railway plan of 1857.** *Parliamentary Archives*

Far right: **The Corris Tramroad or Railway extension to Tir Stent, 1863.** *Parliamentary Archives*

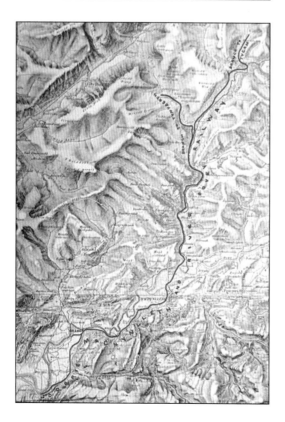

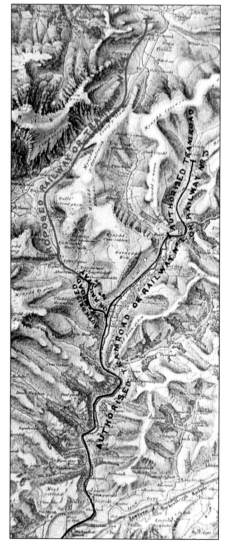

Due to unspecified disagreements between the promoters the bill was withdrawn, to be resubmitted in December 1851. On this occasion, the services of Henry Brookes, a Parliamentary agent, were used in preference to a Machynlleth solicitor. Several landowners objected to the bill, mounting a campaign that resulted in the promoters, one by one, relinquishing their involvement. Terms were eventually agreed and the bill was enacted as the Corris, Machynlleth & River Dovey Railway act on 1 July 1852, the last day of the Parliamentary session.

The promoters were the Viscount Seaham, Robert Davis Jones, John Rowlands, Francis Johnson Ford, John William Rowlands, and David Davis, also designated the first directors. Despite the title of the act, it still contained numerous references to tramroads and the company was to be incorporated as the 'Corris, Machynlleth & River Dovey Railway or Tramroad Company'. Constraints were placed on the limits of deviation where the line was to pass through land belonging to Seaham, the late Athelstan Corbet, Charles Thomas Thruston and Mary Matthews.

The nature of the railway, its purpose and method of working were described quite succinctly in article No 24 – 'The said railways or tramroads, being intended for the conveyance of slates, minerals, and merchandise, and to worked by horse-power travelling at low rates of speed only, it shall be lawful to construct the same upon a gauge of 2ft 2½in; provided always, that it shall not be lawful to use or employ any steam or locomotive engine on the railways or tramroads …' On any occasion that a locomotive was used in contravention of the act a penalty not exceeding £20 would be payable. Three years were allowed to exercise the compulsory purchase powers and five years for construction.

Brookes was to say that that the promoters' desire to use the narrow gauge resulted in the company's inability to use locomotives being imposed by the House of Lords' committee, also that it had been intended to carry passengers as well as merchandise, but an exemption from the 1846 Gauge Act was not obtained. As much of the route was in the parish of Talyllyn, adoption of a different naming convention could have seen the enterprise called the Talyllyn Railway.

After the act had been obtained, the Shrewsbury & Aberystwyth Railway Company issued its prospectus and it became clear that the CMRDR would attract 'pleasure and mercantile traffic' from Birmingham and the Midlands if it made a branch across the Dovey to join the SAR at Machynlleth, extended its line to Aberdovey and Towyn and could carry passengers.

Brookes claimed that he suggested promoting the ideas with a public meeting in Machynlleth, but disagreements again occurred and nothing was done. Concluding that the directors were refusing to act to bring the company into effect and conscious that the company's first ordinary meeting had to be held by 30 September, he considered himself its *de facto* secretary and representative of the company's solicitor, who was absent, and decided to act, on 13 September calling a meeting to be held on the last possible date.

Perhaps stirred on by Brookes's activities, the directors met for the first time on 29 September 1852, but John William Rowlands and Jones disagreed over the strategy for dealing with the deposit, leading to the meeting being adjourned.

At Brookes's meeting the next day, Seaham, Jones and Davies were re-elected directors and James Smith, Charles Brown Hornor, William Fenton and Edward Stanway were elected. Brookes was appointed secretary with authority to prepare share certificates and other documents. It was resolved to seek powers to amend the act, to extend the line to Machynlleth and Towyn, and to raise further capital and to commission the engineer to report on the feasibility of extending the line to Carnarvon.

A notice advertising the intention of depositing a bill for the Corris, Machynlleth, Aberdovey & Towyn Railway was placed in the *London Gazette* published on 23 November 1852. Two days after publication the original directors applied for an injunction to prevent Brookes from acting on the company's behalf, including 'soliciting any bill in Parliament', in their petition referring to the 'pretended meeting' and saying that three of the new directors were either not shareholders or held insufficient shares to qualify as a director, and had repudiated their appointments.

Above: **Corris Railway Company seal.**
National Archives

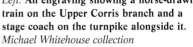

Left: **An engraving showing a horse-drawn train on the Upper Corris branch and a stage coach on the turnpike alongside it.**
Michael Whitehouse collection

Right: **This 20th century view of Corris shows the railway running from left to right with the extensive Braich Goch quarries ranged behind. The location of the station and the route of the Upper Corris branch are indicated.**
George & Son/Author's collection

Below right: **At Aberllefenny the main line to the Parliamentary terminus passed in front of the cottages on the left, serving the Aberllefenny slate quarry on the right. The Ratgoed route, which passed behind the cottages, is indicated where it crossed the main line, as are the slate works and the approximate location of the Parliamentary terminus.**
George & Son/Author's collection

The railway now proposed from Aberllefenny to Towyn would have been about 20 miles long, with the branch to the SAR at Machynlleth slightly more than half a mile long. It was to run from 'a farm house, called or known as Penrhyn, at a field numbered 64 on the plans of the Corris, Machynlleth & River Dovey Tramroad ... using the route of the said tramroad westward ... to a point called Panteidal ... and continuing ... past Aberdovey and terminating at the southern side of a road diverging westward from the village of Towyn to the seashore ... Also a branch railway, commencing ... at or near a farm there, called or known as Penrhyn, at a field numbered 64 on the aforesaid plans, and proceeding southward from the above point, crossing the River Dovey and the turnpike road from Machynlleth to the Dovey bridge, and forming a junction with the proposed Shrewsbury & Aberystwyth Railway in a field northward of the Machynlleth National School house and eastward of the turnpike road from Machynlleth to the Dovey bridge ... Also a branch railway ... commencing at or near a point upon the River Dovey shore, about a quarter of a mile east of a point of a rock at Aberdovey, called Penhelig Point, and continuing westward along the river shore on to a dock wall proposed to be erected to enclose Penhelig Bay ...'

Causton had re-surveyed the estuarine section, easing the curvature in several places at the expense of lengthening the tunnel to 158 yards and providing a second, 198 yards long. With 14 arches, spans up to 30ft wide and up to 20ft high, the viaduct, had it been built, would have been one of the most imposing structures on any British narrow gauge railway. The branch to the Shrewsbury & Aberystwyth Railway required a viaduct 402 yards long to cross the Dovey. The railway also intended to take powers to create an enclosed dock at Penhelig. The SAR's bill was deposited at the same time; both failed.

Whether the CMATR's failure was due to the injunction or for some other reason is not known, but the original directors still continued to take no action with regards to the 1852 railway. On 25 July 1855, the Earl Vane, previously Viscount Seaham, and his wife lodged a petition for an injunction against the company, claiming that it was acting illegally.

They alleged that shortly after the passing of the 1852 act, the undertaking was abandoned or considered to be abandoned and that the directors, including Vane, had never been re-elected, that no calls had been made to shareholders, and that the deposited monies had been 'misapplied or otherwise disposed of'. In May 1855, they petitioned, John Carnau Morris, Robert Davies Jones, John Rowlands and David Davies, who had interests in Aberllefenny or other quarries, announced their intention to act as CMRDR directors, and to build the railway from Aberllefenny only as far as Pumwern, on the Dovey's northern bank opposite Derwenlas.

Without the terminus at Panteidal, they continued, the railway would be useless for the purpose of transporting goods to and from Machynlleth, land transport being more convenient, claiming that the alleged directors intended to make the railway for their own benefit, not for that of the company or the public.

As affected landowners, the Vanes had received notices of the company's intentions in May and had refused to recognise their validity. After several exchanges and a court hearing, the company, with support from the under-sheriff of Merioneth, took possession of the land on 30 June, the day before the 1852 act's compulsory purchase powers expired.

The Vanes wanted a declaration that the company had no power to make a shorter railway and that the actions carried out in the company's name were illegal. They also wanted an injunction preventing the railway from being made to Pumwern

Top: **Upper Corris, with the Abercwmeiddew quarry incline and tips on the right. The quarry branch's divergence from the main line, which continued a little further, is between the cottages in the centre of the photograph.** *Frith/Author's collection*

Middle: **Braich Goch, on the Upper Corris branch, was the Corris Railway's biggest customer. This view of the quarry's stacking yard and mills shows a rake of the quarry's own slate wagons. Writing from Corris in 1910, the sender of this card said: 'Came by funny little railway, lovely scenery all the way ...'** *Commercial postcard/Author's collection*

Below: **The Dovey Valley looking eastwards towards Machynlleth from above Derwenlas. On the northern bank, Pumwern, the site of one of the Corris, Machynlleth, Aberdovey & Towyn Railway's proposed tunnels is indicated. There is no evidence here of the existence of the Corris Railway's Derwenlas branch.** *Jones 'Maglona' series/Author's collection*

13

Right: **A 1920s view of Machynlleth with the 1857 route to Derwenlas indicated. Passing to the west of the town, the railway ran close to the backs of properties on Brickfield Street before crossing the fields to follow the Aberystwyth road. The 1904 station is also indicated.** *W. H. S./Author's collection*

Below: **This intriguing photograph is probably the oldest extant of the steam-operated Corris Railway and might show a test train in 1879. It shows one of the locomotives as-built, with a 2nd class and a 1st class carriage; hand brakes were provided on each vehicle. Minimal protection was provided for the locomotive crew. The coupling has not been supplemented by the hook that was a feature of later operations, and the bufferbeam only shows slight sign of impact with wagons. The Hughes worksplate was to be superseded by a combined Falcon/CR numberplate.**
Paul Ingham Collection

only, for construction not to be started or continued, and for the land to be returned.

It was to be December 1857 before any more recorded activity occurred, when a fourth bill was deposited, producing another Corris, Machynlleth & River Dovey Tramroad Act on 12 July 1858. Of the 1852 act, the preamble merely stated that no part of the railway had been built and that the powers had lapsed. Later, the preamble of the 1864 act was to state that some land had been purchased in consequence of the 1852 act.

The act's description of the main line from Corris towards the Dovey was much the same as before, starting 'at or near the slate quarry yard and new engine house at Aberllefenny slate quarries', but this time the line crossed the river and terminated 'at or near an old pier or landing place called … Cae Coch or Red Quay, at Garreg, on the River Dovey', about 11¾ miles, plus three branches.

First, a short line from the Morben wharf to the south bank of the Dovey at Penfordddnewydd, the new road; second, a line commencing 'at or near the fifth milepost … and terminating at

or near the engine house at Tyn y berth [previously Tyddynyberth]', and third, 'commencing at or near the new engine house at Aberllefenny, and terminating at or near a certain house called or known as Ty cam [Tycam].'

The plans show that the greatest change from the previous proposals was between Maespoeth and the railway's Dovey bridge, where it had been moved to the east side of the road, following it for nearly four miles. The minimum radius was five chains, which also applied to the section south of the river. Here, the route was a mixture of roadside and cross-country. At 2 miles 5 chains, the Tyddynyberth branch was slightly shorter than before, and the route at Caewern had been realigned to avoid a double river crossing. The Tycam branch was unchanged.

Concerning the nature of the railway, article No 20 repeated article No 24 from the 1852 act referred to earlier, with two changes: the gauge was increased to 2ft 3in and the penalty for the use of locomotives was increased to £100. Apart from its later adoption by the Campbelltown & Macrihanish Railway on the Mull of Kintyre, the use of the 2ft 3in gauge for public

Just on the Aberllefenny side of Corris station, the railway crossed the river by a bridge parallel to the nearby road bridge, the location for posing this photograph between 1889 and 1893. Two four-wheeled carriages are shown with a bogie carriage and a brake van. The locomotive looks as though it has only been modified by the addition of a hook to the coupling. *WEH-Lyn Collection*

railways was to be restricted to an area within a radius of less than 20 miles from Corris. Its origin here is probably attributable to tramroads used within the quarries.

The promoters on this occasion were Thomas Frederick Halford, Frank Howard, Horatio Nelson Hughes, John Rowlands and John William Rowlands, who were nominated the first directors, only the last two remaining from the 1852 scheme. Hughes was a Liverpool merchant and ship owner who also owned the Ratgoed quarry. Causton now estimated the cost as £15,000 and that was the amount of the authorised capital in £10 shares.

After four bills and two acts, construction was put in hand and the line opened between Corris and Machynlleth in 1859. An account in the *North Wales Chronicle* of 9 April reported that 'Friday afternoon was celebrated as a holiday in the … neighbourhood'; the first day was 1 April. The line to the Morben wharves was still to be constructed: 'the full working of this line, on its final completion to the coast, will insure to the public a saving in carriage, of about 50% upon the present system of conveyance by wagons and carts.'

The CMRDT had been built cheaply, probably to reduce the land needed, without too much regard, it transpired, to the exactitudes of the deposited plans. It is likely that the line beyond Derwenlas was not built. The railway would refer to the Tyddynyberth branch as the Braich Goch branch, after the largest quarry that it served. To enthusiasts, it became known as the Upper Corris Tramway. The Tycam branch was always known as the Ratgoed Tramway.

There is no contemporary report of the railway as built although an early engraving *(see* p11) shows two horses hauling a train of nine wagons, possibly of three different types, downhill on the Tyddynyberth branch. There are reports that, like the Festiniog Railway contemporaneously, the loaded traffic was worked by gravity. Horses based at Machynlleth returned the empty wagons to the quarries. In 1872 the railway was to report that it possessed 'only a few slate trucks', a statement that

probably wouldn't have been inaccurate in 1859. Vignes *(see* Bibliography), who visited Wales in 1877, was unable to elicit any details of the railway's construction. Archaeology has revealed that the track was laid with lightweight bridge-section rail on slate sleepers.

By December 1862, the proprietors wished to resolve some issues that had arisen from five years' use of the tramroad, depositing a bill for fresh powers, including an extension. The *London Gazette* notice is not as accurate as the norm, headlining the proposal as an extension from Tycam to Tir Stent and Dolgelly, whereas it was an extension from Tyddynyberth to a junction with the then proposed Bala & Dolgelly Railway near Brithdir, about three miles from Dolgelly. Instead of just describing the extension, the notice described the entire route from 'a certain point in a field … Cae tri Bugail, and numbered 29 on the Parliamentary plan of the Newtown & Machynlleth Railway …'

The bill also sought powers to raise fresh capital, to enter into agreements with other railway companies 'in respect of the working, maintenance and use of the tramroad …', to convert the tramroad into a railway, to change the corporate name, to repeal Clause 19 of the 1858 act to permit the acquisition of land compulsorily, and Clause 20 to permit the use of locomotives. Charles B. Cooper had signed the estimate for £50,000.

This bill failed. The Aberystwyth & Welsh Coast Railway directors had resolved to object to it on 8 January 1863 – how much influence this had is unknown. Another bill was deposited in December 1863. The notice for it had been redrafted and the extension had been reduced in length. The engineer was George

Above: **No 2 at Machynlleth after it had been converted to an 0-4-2ST, equipped with vacuum brakes and fitted with a front spectacle plate. The vacuum ejector exhaust is plumbed into the smokebox; that on No 3 had a different alignment near the chimney. The cylinder lubricator is mounted on the smokebox front, just below the lamp bracket. The cabside plate records its visit to Loughborough in 1895. It is likely that its boiler had been renewed as its chimney and smokebox are obviously different from those in older photographs. The bufferbeam shows signs of wear.** *G. H. Wilkinson/Ted Talbot collection*

Below: **The plan of the Llwyngwern and Esgairgeiliog station buildings submitted to the Board of Trade by Dix in December 1883. It is dated 28 November.** *National Archives*

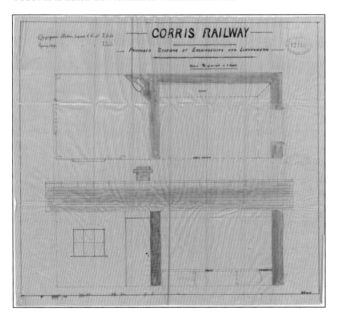

Owen, who signed the estimate for £24,000; he was soon to have the same function with the Cambrian Railways. The AWCR petitioned against this bill too, but withdrew its objection on learning that its contractor, Thomas Savin, had acquired control of the CMRDT and was willing to sell it to the AWCR. In June 1864, Savin chaired a general meeting approving of the bill and without further objections it was enacted on 25 July 1864.

With an additional £24,000 authorised capital and borrowing powers of £8,000, the 1864 act sanctioned four lines: from a junction with the Newtown & Machynlleth Railway to the new engine house at Aberllefenny slate quarries; from the fifth milestone on the turnpike to Ty'nyberth; from the new engine house at Aberllefenny to Ty Cam; and from the second

line, 'at or near Rognant House … terminating … in a field called Caerty, forming part of the farm of Bryncastell …' Owen's plan gives a distance of 5 miles, 7 furlongs and 2 chains for the last. Following the turnpike road, now the A487, but independent of it, the terminus was just a short distance from the Cross Foxes road junction.

The intended traffic was iron ore from a mine at Tir Stent. A report in the Welsh Mines Society newsletter (No 46) states that Tir Stent output was to be routed via the Bala–Dolgelley railway, opened 1868, an option in 1864 that might explain the lack of interest in investing in the route to Corris. The mine's output was later routed via an 18in gauge tramway to a wharf on the present A487 above the Cross Foxes Hotel.

With a gradient of 1 in 24 climbing from Tyddynyberth for five furlongs, followed by 1 in 62 for four miles rising to 674ft, and then falling to the terminus at 1 in 46 for just over 1½ miles, the extension would have been difficult to work with horses, requiring extensive reconstruction of the Tyddynyberth branch to improve clearances for locomotives. Features of the extension were two tunnels, 75 yards and 68 yards, on the 1 in 62 gradient, and a bridge across the turnpike.

The re-sanctioning of the existing lines was unusual; it was not included in the 1862 bill. The 1864 act's preamble explained the background. The CMRDR company of 1852 was referred to as 'the dissolved company' although the means by which it was dissolved were neither stated nor was it sanctioned by the act. The CMRDT company of 1858 was identified as the existing company. The 1852 company had bought land that had been taken over and used by the 1858 company, and although the two companies were 'the same or nearly the same', the land had not been vested in the 1858 company and 'it is expedient that [it] should be so vested.' It was perhaps to avoid any doubt that the 1858 company became the Corris Railway Company (CR) in the second clause.

It may be significant that the definitions extended the word 'railway' to 'include the tramroads of the company' to remove any uncertainty about the status of the branches. The 1852 company's property was transferred in Clause No 4, the extension approved in No 8 and the use of steam locomotives, at a maximum speed of 10mph, in No 14. The Dovey branches were abandoned by Clause No 26; the land not required there was to be sold within 10 years. The abandonment had not been proposed in the 1862 bill.

The railway was allowed to enter into agreements with the Oswestry & Newtown, Newtown & Machynlleth Railway and the AWCR. The preamble cited these and the Llanidloes & Newtown, Mid-Wales and Shrewsbury & Welshpool railways as being directly or indirectly connected with the railway and seemed to say that existing powers in the AWCR act of 1861 allowing agreements to be made between the AWCR and the second three, would permit agreements between the CR and the second three also.

Returning now to the intervention of Savin and the AWCR in the CMRDT's affairs, at the time of his bankruptcy in 1866, Savin had £13,000 of the CR's £15,000 issued capital (86.6%). Nothing is known of the circumstances or timing of his acquisition; it would have entitled him to a directorship but no records survive to show this except that a report of the statutory company meeting held on 8 June 1864 to approve the bill of the 1864 act in the *North Wales Chronicle*, stated he had chaired it.

The earliest reference to Savin having a connection with the CMRDT is in the AWCR minutes. On 25 April 1864, the AWCR directors resolved to buy the CMRDT from him for what he had paid, only to change their minds the next day. From December 1864, they were pursuing a working agreement with the CMRDT, then on 26 April 1865, resolved 'this company do purchase the Corris company for the sum of £21,000, payment to be made in preference shares of this company. That the debentures and all liabilities ... be adopted ... and that the additional rolling stock put on the line since it has been purchased by Mr Savin be taken from him at valuation.' Shortly to be merged into the Cambrian Railways, the AWCR said nothing more about the CR. Being tangled up in Savin's bankruptcy probably explains why the CR took no action to use its expensive new powers.

While Savin was still the principal shareholder, a child died playing on a train on the Derwenlas line near the AWCR overbridge at Machynlleth. The *Shropshire & Montgomeryshire Times* of 2 May 1865 reported the inquest jury's verdict of accidental death and its recommendation that 'Mr Savin, the proprietor of the line should be respectfully requested to have the tramroad properly fenced in.' Jones (*Tales of the Old Corris* – see Bibliography) quotes the report in full.

Savin's involvement probably explains the comment in the preamble to the 1864 act about the CMRDT being 'connected directly or indirectly' with the six railways mentioned earlier, and why it was a party to a scheme to amalgamate the Carnarvonshire, Nantlle and Beddgelert railways with the Cambrian Railways in 1865-7. He had substantial shareholdings in the Cambrian and its constituent companies and also in the Carnarvonshire Railway. Had the amalgamation bill deposited in December 1865 been successful, the restrictions on the CR's carriage of passengers and limiting its speed to 10mph would have been removed. The Cambrian resolved to withdraw the bill on 26 April 1866. A second attempt in 1866 expanded the proposal to include the Brecon & Merthyr Tydfil Junction, Mid-Wales, Neath & Brecon, Swansea Vale, Potteries, Shrewsbury & North Wales, Pembroke & Tenby railways and the Llanelly Railway & Dock Company. This also failed to make the statute books.

Before moving on, two agreements with the Newtown & Machynlleth Railway should be noted. On 23 July 1863 the NMR directors had sealed an agreement with 'the Corris Tramroad Company' containing terms permitting the CMRDT 'to convey slates &c into the Machynlleth station.' Then, on 23 July 1864, they sealed a conveyance for some CMRDT land.

Despite being authorised to use steam locomotives, the railway continued as before. The earliest information seen regarding its traffic comes from the Board of Trade's annual returns for 1872, when 15,669 tons of slate was carried, earning £1,648. With operating expenditure of only £662 and a

dividend of 5¾%, perhaps the directors could see no reason to make changes. It had taken a while to get to this position, although, in 1867 the executors of Jane Causton (Causton's mother?) had sued the company for the £500 Causton had lent to it against a mortgage deed in 1860. It had been repayable in 1863, but the company was without funds so the debt was transferred to her with agreement that it be repaid in 1866. She died on 15 March 1866, when the debt was inherited by her executors, Causton and others, who unsuccessfully sought repayment when it matured on 25 September 1866.

Greenhough *(see* Bibliography) identifies William Lawrence Banks and Charles Miller Layton as directors in 1867/8. Both were involved with several railway companies, mainly in Wales and the Marches. They had interests in common with James Fraser, an accountant, also a CMRDT director and its secretary from 1868 until 1871. According to Gasquoine *(see* Bibliography), Fraser also managed Savin's affairs in London.

An unexpected development was the carriage of passengers from 1874. The railway was quite open about this, returning 3,592 passengers carried 'in open trucks' for revenue of £90 that year. On 6 October 1874, Fraser had written to the Cambrian's Owen: 'We have started carrying passengers and goods up from Machynlleth to Corris and it is astonishing what a number will go up if we had any [sic] sufficient accommodation, as a beginning we would like to build a little warehouse and stable at Machynlleth and I am told that your company may be willing to let us have space at their yard for the purpose.' The increase to 11,830 passengers and £290 revenue in 1875 is indicative of the service being started part-way through 1874. Some rough arithmetic suggests that a fare of 6d was charged. Vignes was to imply that the wagons used by passengers were not slate wagons.

The lack of existing accommodation at Machynlleth is made clear by proposal to build a 'store and stable'; the horses used to return the slate empties hitherto must have been supplied and accommodated by contractors. Their involvement was mentioned in a report published in the *Oswestry Advertiser* of 25 July 1860 (reproduced more fully in Jones's *Great Western Corris* – see Bibliography) about a woman who was killed

Below: **A train bound for Machynlleth arriving at Llwyngwern, c1890. The van body on the platform was probably used as a store. The loco has no upper cab backsheet.** *Author's collection*

Right: **When photographed c1915 Llwyngwern's van body** *(see pp17)* **had been replaced by this corrugated iron shed. The orifice in the loco backsheet was a feature of the Corris locomotives. It gave the fireman more room to manage the fire. The close proximity of the wall to the train is obvious. Either the paint on the first carriage has experienced excessive weathering or two different liveries were in use.** *Author's collection*

Below: **No 2 at Aberllefenny between 1900 and 1915. The unusual arrangement for suspending the regulator handle and quadrant from the cab roof is noticeable. The vacuum brake pipe, visible here, was passed through the backsheet opening when hauling passenger trains from Machynlleth.** *Author's collection*

alighting from a moving train near Machynlleth. 'The contractors for the conveyance of slates and flags ... along the tramway allow their driver ... to convey passengers occasionally down on top of the load for a "trifling consideration" ...'

The carriage of passengers, albeit illegally, had probably started within days of the railway opening. The 1874 development was probably an attempt by the company to control, and make money from, the previously unauthorised activity. As a goods-only line, the railway was beyond the interest of the railway inspectors who must have been unaware of the note about passengers being carried in open trucks appearing in the Board of Trade's annual returns for several years.

Fraser, based in London, admitted that he was unfamiliar with the location so maybe what he said should be treated with caution. The implication, however, is that slate was transhipped to the Cambrian with minimal facilities and that no other goods were being carried, even from Machynlleth. Unlikely as it may seem, it was to be 1877 before the railway reported the carriage of any merchandise, 818 tons for revenue of £157.

With regard to Fraser's request, the Cambrian initially failed

to understand that the Corris required accommodation close to its own tracks and not remote from them. On 13 April 1875, Owen reported to his directors that the warehouse was required to store 'grain, flour and other commodities' en route for Corris and the stable for 'feeding at mid-day the two horses that work the passenger trains to and from the quarries, but these horses are stabled at the other end at night.' There was a further report but no comment subsequently so presumably the railway got the facilities it wanted.

Although the railway's original facilities went unrecorded, some details are known of changes made on the quarries' behalf. Braich Goch required more space at Machynlleth in 1869, leading to the Cambrian to use old rail to extend its lower-yard siding at a cost of £60. When the Abercwmeiddew Slate Company applied for wharfage in 1876 the Cambrian's traffic manager was not convinced that the company needed the space requested, but after taking up credit references the following year, the engineer submitted a proposal for a wharf 100ft long and 25ft wide that would cost £87 2s. The Cambrian also estimated the cost, £42, for extending the tramway, 'which

should be defrayed by the quarry proprietors.' On 22 March 1877, the traffic manager recommended that the Cambrian pay for the wharf and the quarry company pay for extending the narrow gauge siding to it. The quarry's name was often misspelled, incidentally, sometimes even on its own paperwork.

The railway was brought out of its equine stupor in 1878, after it had changed hands twice in two years. First, its share capital was acquired by the Tramways & General Works Company Limited (TGW), a company registered on 28 May 1877 with the objective of developing or modernising tramways; it already owned tramways in Middlesbrough, Dublin, Gloucester and Reading. Its majority shareholder, £7,000 of £9,414 shares issued by 5 December 1877, was the Continental & General Tramway Company, which had built and owned the Hull Street Tramways. One of Continental's founding directors in 1871 was Charles Edwards of Dolserau Hall, Dolgellau, which could provide a link to TGW's interest in the CR. The identities of the CR vendors are unknown; they are most likely to have been the directors and Savin's inspectors.

The second transfer occurred in July 1878, when the TGW portfolio was sold to Imperial Tramways Company Limited, a

Above: **No 2 at Machynlleth's original Corris Railway station, c1900. The box or bucket seen in most photographs of the locos' front ends contained sand for use on greasy rails.** *Author's collection*

Below: **Two locomotives and a train of seven carriages and a brake van cross the railway's timber trestle bridge over the Dovey, c1896-1906. In view of the restriction placed on double-heading over the replacement steel bridge it is unlikely that the engineer would have been too happy about this occurrence.** *Author's collection*

company registered on 20 June 1878. On 17 July, those companies and the CR made a legal agreement providing for the sale of the CR share capital to Imperial for £42,750. The agreement's preamble explained that the railway was unable to carry passengers, that it was desirable to relay the line between Machynlleth and Corris with steel rails, and to provide proper rolling stock. Also, considerable expenditure would be required to execute such work and to provide sufficient rolling stock, and that the CR's capital was fully subscribed while the CR had no power to raise more capital or to borrow money. It would be 'a great advantage' to the CR and the shareholders that it should be used for the conveyance of passengers by steam locomotives,

for which authority should be obtained forthwith.

Payment was to be in the form of Imperial shares at par, £25,000 to be issued to TGW when the CR shares had been transferred to Imperial, within 28 days of signing the agreement. Beyond the sale, the contract contained some unusual requirements.

Imperial was to apply for powers to use the CR for the 'conveyance of passengers by steam locomotion' in the CR's name as soon as possible, and TGW was to contribute £600 towards the expenses. TGW undertook to pay Imperial a guarantee of 5% interest on the purchase price from 1 July 1878 until parliamentary authority had been obtained or 31 December 1880. Any CR dividend of less than 5% would be offset against the guarantee. The CR would pay its directors a total of £150 annually.

Within four months of the agreement being signed, TGW was to relay the track between Machynlleth and Corris with 44lb steel rail and enable the CR to satisfy the Board of Trade's requirements to permit the carriage of passengers with steam haulage 'at ordinary speed'. TGW would also pay up to £500 for any extra works required to meet any Board of Trade requirements specified before 31 October 1879. Whilst the track was being relaid the CR was to provide 'all facilities' to the contractor, TGW, so that traffic 'shall be interfered with as little as possible'.

The £17,750 outstanding from the purchase price was effectively the construction budget. When Imperial's engineer, Joseph Kincaid, had issued certificates for work done and equipment supplied, Imperial shares to the equivalent value were to be issued to TGW, less 5% retention. Any residual credit remaining in the construction account when the works had been completed was also to be assigned to TGW in Imperial shares.

The agreement also called for the three steam locomotives and 10 carriages ordered from the Hughes Locomotive & Tramway Engineering Works Limited of Loughborough, Leicestershire, by TGW to be taken over by Imperial for the CR's use. Hughes had also been recently registered, on 13 June 1877.

The table (below), compiled from Stock Exchange Year Book data, shows how the CR's directors changed during the period of the takeover. John Marshall Gillies (chairman, London Tramways Company and director, Hughes Locomotive), Joseph William Grieg (chairman, North Metropolitan Tramways Company), Alfred James Lambert (director, TGW and chairman, Hull Street Tramways Company) and W. R. Bacon (experience of UK and US tramways) were also Imperial directors.

Kincaid was also the CR's engineer. He became a member of the Institution of Civil Engineers in 1879, worked on many projects in the UK and overseas, and in 1891 was to be referenced by Bristol Tramways as its consultant engineer.

Another 1878 development had occurred in September, when Owen reported to the Cambrian directors that the CR required a strip of Cambrian land at Machynlleth in order to install a run-round loop. He recommended approval as the CR would be a feeder to their company.

The arrival of the carriages was reported in the Aberystwyth Observer on 9 November 1878; they were 'constructed on the principle of the road tramway carriages', weighed about 1 ton, and the 1st class had cushions covered with green plush.

As agreed, in December 1878, a bill was deposited in Parliament. The only objector was Robert Davies Pryce, the Aberllefenny quarry owner, who is said to have thought that operating a passenger service would be detrimental to the railway's ability to carry his traffic. He was also a director of the Cambrian Railways and its chairman from 1884 to 1886; living at Cyfronydd, near Welshpool, he had inherited Aberllefenny through his mother. Witnesses were heard in the Commons on 8 May 1879. Pryce did not appear, neither did his barrister call any witnesses in his support.

The first witness was Joseph Richard Dix, the railway's manager who had taken up his appointment on 1 January 1879. He was unusual amongst English managers of Welsh enterprises in that he was to settle amongst the community and learn and speak Welsh. Born in Minehead to a railwayman father who became stationmaster at Machynlleth, Dix had also been employed by the Cambrian Railways before he joined the CR.

He told the committee that he had been acquainted with the locality and the railway for the past seven years and that there were about 12 quarries served by the railway, although they were not all working. Apart from experimental trips, the steam locomotives had not been used. He was familiar with the Festiniog Railway, knew that it carried passengers, and ran at speeds higher than 10mph.

Dix thought that the carriage of passengers had started because it was not expressly excluded by the 1858 act. When he joined the company he discovered that the 1864 act forbad the carriage of passengers, so he stopped it. The figure of 3,232 passengers carried in 1879 suggests that the service had been stopped in March or April. Passengers rode in 'rude boxes; you could not call them carriages; only boxes with a door at each side'; he confirmed that the vehicles had roofs.

The population was dissatisfied with the withdrawal of the service, Dix explained, and people could not be deterred from riding on the wagons despite an omnibus service being started in substitution. It would be cheaper to carry the passengers by rail than by road. He did not anticipate running separate passenger trains but 'I suppose we should put carriage on at the end of the mineral trains.' The quarrymen had asked for a workmen's train in the morning and in the evening.

His predecessor as manager had been [David] Owen. Trains from the quarries, Aberllefenny was cited, were worked by quarry employees. Pryce could continue to work his own traffic if the railway was empowered to run passenger trains. The railway owned three or four wagons for its own purposes; the slate was carried in the quarries' own wagons.

Pryce's barrister had to be reminded that the railway already had powers to use locomotives and that there was no point in asking questions about their use. There was some intensive questioning about the railway's proposed right to charge an extra 1d per mile for the carriage of goods in its own vehicles and, despite the chairman's protestations, about the population

Corris Railway company directors 1876-84

1876	1877	1878	1879	1880	1881	1882	1883	1884
J. Rowlands	J. Rowlands	J. Rowlands	J. Rowlands	J. Fraser	J. Fraser	W.R. Bacon	W.R. Bacon	A.J. Lambert
H.N. Hughes	J. Fraser	H.N. Hughes	J. Fraser	J.M. Gillies	J.M. Gillies	J. Fraser	J. Fraser	J. Fraser
J. Fraser	J. Garner	J. Fraser	J.M. Gillies	J.W. Greig	J.W. Greig	A.J. Lambert	A.J. Lambert	E.T. Gourley
J. Garner	C. Morrison	J. Garner	A.J. Lambert	A.J. Lambert	A.J. Lambert			W. Ward
C. Morrison		C. Morrison	C. Morrison	J.W. Maclure	J.W. Maclure			

No 3 with a short train at Aberllefenny, possibly in 1930. The carriage next to the loco has some differences to the others, noticeably the clerestory roof with ventilators and also a different style of grab handles. Might the window-side rails and long running boards have been used by the guard to move between carriages while the train was in motion? Only two of the carriages had clerestories.
Michael Whitehouse collection

of the district. On the numbers who might be prepared to travel, and being told that 50 people had complained about the passenger service being withdrawn, the barrister asked: 'Do you really mean to represent to the committee that there is any feeling at all in that part of the country that induced your board to ask Parliament to change the character of legislation simply to meet the requirements of the public on the grounds which you have stated, to meet the wants of the people who have complained?' 'I do not quite follow the question.' Dix replied.

Regarding the slate traffic, Dix said that Pryce's quarry currently sent a quarter of the railway's traffic, though perhaps only one sixth when all the quarries were working. Not unsurprisingly, he did not know how the locomotives were financed, or who had paid for them.

The second witness was William Bright, manager of the Abercwmeiddew quarry for three years. He did not speak Welsh so relied on English-speaking shopkeepers for information about the locality. He was in favour of the railway carrying passengers; 'It would be a very great boon ...' The quarry employed 120 men and produced 100–140 tons of slate in 28 days. It was a new quarry. Another 30 men would be employed shortly. Mr Spooner, 'one of the chief engineers in the neighbourhood', estimated that the quarry would be capable of producing 1,000 tons per month in three to four years. Charles Easton Spooner was the secretary and engineer of the Festiniog Railway Company (FR) who also undertook freelance work for quarries and railways in North Wales.

Responding to a question about traffic on market days, Bright said that he had 'had to sit in an open carriage with just a piece of wood put across', which sounds indicative of riding on the railway. Shopkeepers wanted steam trains, their coal would be cheaper and the men would like to 'get down to their homes quicker on Saturday and back on Monday' – the quarrymen living in barracks in the quarries during the week. He did not think that the railway was less fit than the FR for the carriage of passengers, but 'I know the Festiniog is a dangerous line to carry on, I should not like to go on it myself; it has such tremendous curves.' He had seen the trains at Portmadoc, but he must have been told about the curves. Until a few weeks earlier the quarry had hauled its own slate on the railway. Now the railway provided the horses and, using the quarry's own wagons, charged 3s per ton, a saving for the quarry.

The third witness was the vicar of Corris, Robert John Edwards. He had been at Corris for three years and at Carnarvon previously. He and the residents had always expected the railway to adopt steam traction and carry passengers. He only knew of Pryce objecting. He had been a passenger 'pretty frequently' but thought the cost would deter quarrymen from travelling daily, even if they had the opportunity to do so.

Following an adjournment, the committee concluded that the preamble was not proved. On 8 March 1880, however, examination of the bill was resumed in the Lords and, after hearing representations from the barristers, it was declared that the bill had become unopposed and could proceed. The *North Wales Chronicle* provided an explanation on 19 June 1880. The railway had renewed its application and a petition against it was withdrawn just before it was to be heard. The price the company paid for having the opposition withdrawn was the insertion of a clause so convoluted as to be almost meaningless. The essence of it was that so long as the railway did not use locomotives it could not carry passengers if doing so interfered with the conveyance of mineral traffic by the quarry owners or lessees using horses 'as freely they were entitled to prior to the passing of the act'. Intriguingly, there is nothing in the previous acts that specifically allowed working the traffic to be devolved by the railway in this way, although the 1858 act's Clause No 23, the 'power to take tolls', allowed up to 1d per mile to be charged if the railway's own 'horse or other motive power' was used. The royal assent was given on 9 July 1880.

After all that effort, the act was quite short, only 11 clauses. The restrictions on speed and the carriage of passengers were removed subject to the company obtaining Board of Trade approval for any train that it wished to run at speeds greater than 15mph. For passengers, the company could charge a toll of 2d per mile plus an additional ½d per mile for any carried in carriages owned by the railway. The maximum charge, however, was 2d per mile for travel in a 1st or 2nd class carriage and 1d per mile for 3rd class travel. Were the toll and the charge to be amalgamated? Was the company expecting carriages to be operated that it did not own? The charges did not apply to special trains.

Imperial's directors' reports show that TGW paid £1,662 10s against the guarantee in 1879 and £2,190 4s 2d in 1880. The parliamentary delay had knocked holes into the contract so TGW had paid for the first, 1878, bill and Imperial had paid for the second. Including the cost of the 1880 act, the CR's capital cost to Imperial had reached £43,984 2s 4d.

The Talyllyn service was an essential part of the Corris Railway's summer operations. In 1910, the railway had four of these waggonettes available. *George & Sons/Author's collection*

When news of the bill's success reached Corris, any rejoicing was not universal. On 13 July, Morris Thomas, druggist of Corris, perhaps one of the shopkeepers who Bright said was in favour of the railway, wrote to the Board of Trade, complaining that a high wall separating the railway from the turnpike would be essential for public safety. The railway, he wrote, 'runs as close as 2ft to the other for a distance of about four miles and there is only a wire fence in some parts and a bare hedge for six months in the year in other parts of the line to hide it from view on the turnpike road. The railway traffic will therefore be so open to the turnpike road that with the many sharp curves on the line it must be highly dangerous to the gentry, the farmers and public generally travelling with horses on the turnpike road. Trusting you will deem the above worthy of your consideration.'

The letter was copied to the railway company for comment. Steam had been used for the goods traffic since 1878 without any complaint and the company had no intention of starting the passenger service until the railway had been approved by the Board of Trade.

On 11 August 1880, Henry Sewell of Llwyngwern wrote that he and his family had to cross the railway on a level crossing 300 yards from his house, 'at which there is no person in charge. If the Corris Tramway is allowed to carry passengers by steam we shall be in danger of being run over in crossing the line as a train coming from Corris can only be seen a few yards off.' Saying that he had only recently moved into the area, he thought that there was no danger in using the crossing 'until the recent introduction of steam for working the line.' Sewell also complained about the proximity of the railway to the turnpike. He was told that the matter would be dealt with during the inspection.

The railway decided that it would be ready to start the passenger service on 19 September and gave one month's notice. Before the inspection could take place, however, on 7 September John Evans of the Lion Hotel at Machynlleth wrote to tell the Board of Trade of the hazards to be caused by the steam-hauled passenger trains. '... it will be extremely dangerous to my horses and conveyances and to the public generally going along the turnpike road ...' In addition to being told that the matter would be dealt with by the inspector, Evans was also told that the commissioners or trustees of the toll had a remedy in Clause 63 of the 1845 Railway Clauses Act, where if they thought that there was a risk of horses being frightened by steam locomotives they could apply to the Board of Trade for a certificate requiring the railway to erect a screen if such was found necessary.

The work being carried out on the railway obviously took longer than anticipated, for on 27 September, notice was given that it would be ready for use by passenger trains from 30 September and be ready for inspection during the following 10 days. Major Francis A. Marindin RE received his instructions the next day. The outcome could not have been anticipated.

His report was submitted from Machynlleth on 7 October. A length of 5 miles 25 chains had been altered and improved for passenger traffic. It was intended to work with one engine in steam and 'the only passenger traffic expected was that of the slate quarry villages.' The width between tracks at passing places was 5ft. Vignoles-section 44lb, flat-bottom rail in 24ft lengths was fixed to half-round larch sleepers with dog spikes. The sleepers were 4ft 4in x 8in x 4¾in, laid 3ft apart. There was one spike fixed in each sleeper on each side, placed alternately inside and outside the rails. The ballast was broken slate waste and river gravel. He drew attention to the steepest gradient of 1 in 35 and the several places with two-chain check-railed curves.

In addition to the termini he noted intermediate stations at Pandy and Esgairgeiliog, saying that they had loops that were not used. Pandy was the only station without sidings. The 'mineral line junction' and 'engine shed siding' at Maespoeth were also observed. There were no overbridges, but a 'timber viaduct' over the Dovey and five bridges over streams, three with stone arches, one requiring repair. The single level crossing on a public road had 'proper gates, a lodge and signals'. There were three locomotives, four 1st class and six 2nd class four-wheeled carriages. The 3ft 8½in wheelbase carriages had end doors and a brake.

Only Corris had a low platform. Machynlleth had only a

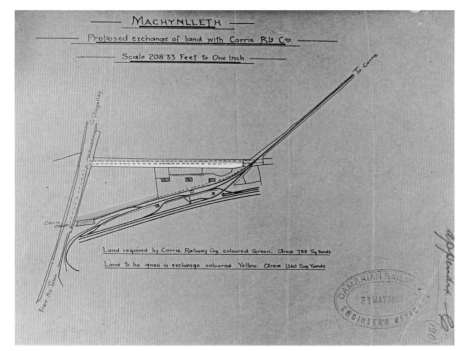

'bare shed, without any proper approach and with no urinals or conveniences.' The only building at intermediate stations was a signal hut. Corris had a covered shed and urinals but no separate accommodation for ladies.

There were a number of features that he particularly did not like. Lineside structures, including walls, banks, houses, trees, signal posts and telegraph poles, were in 'a great number of places' between 1in and 6in of the side of the carriages and engine. The facing point locks were unsatisfactory. Fencing in some places was inadequate. For these reasons the line could not be opened for passenger traffic without danger to the public.

Marindin went on: 'It is however

altogether more of the nature of a steam tramway than a railway, the authorised speed being only 3 miles an hour more, and the rolling stock of a similar character, and before reporting as to the additional works which should be required I submit that the question should be referred for the joint consideration of the inspecting officers.'

There is no record of the railway's response to this bombshell. The track had been relaid, three locomotives and 10 carriages purchased, an act of Parliament obtained and the inspector not only refused to approve the line for passengers, but refused to issue any requirements, deferring to a committee of his colleagues.

Before drafting their report, the inspecting officers called for details of Captain Henry W. Tyler's reports of his inspection of the FR for passenger traffic in 1864. They were particularly concerned to know whether there were any deposited plans for the FR and what the sharpest authorised curves were. As the FR's 1832 act pre-dated the requirement for such detailed plans there was no way of telling if curves as sharp as two and four chains that Tyler saw had been authorised by Parliament.

The inspecting officers' report was compiled on 23 October 1880. In summary they said that the railway could not be approved because of unauthorised sharp curves, the proposed

use of four-wheeled locomotives, the absence of clearances, and insufficient space between the lines where they were double. The issue with four-coupled locomotives arose because of concerns about the loss of stability if an axle broke the inspectors apparently unaware of the four-coupled locomotives approved by Tyler on the FR.

The company's rebuttal of the joint report was sent on 25 November 1880. Whilst the directors recognised the technical validity of the joint report, wrote the company's secretary from London, they believed special circumstances applied and that it should be approved. Occasional trains would be run, comprising two cars and a locomotive. The cars were similar to those used on tramways and the speed would not exceed that already approved for steam tramways. The curves and gradients complained of were less severe than those found on tramways, so the deeper flange allowed by the Corris rail and the check rails further diminished the risk of accident.

Four-wheeled locomotives had been approved for use on tramways and those used at Corris had been running without accident. Parallel tramlines were allowed to be only 3ft apart, rather than the railway's 5ft. The limited clearances elsewhere were accommodated by not having opening windows. It was proposed to fit light gates to the carriage platform to prevent

Right: **Also seen at the second station, this photograph shows the off-side of the train, not normally seen by passengers or photographers. There are detail differences between the carriages. The higher roof and outward-opening spectacles identify the locomotive as No 1.**
Paul Ingham collection

Below: **This splendid view of No 2 at Corris was too good to leave out. The two wagons of coal and the scales in the foreground could well be evidence of Dix's retail activities *(see p*p42).**
Michael Whitehouse collection

anyone from putting themselves at danger. As the one-engine-in-steam method of working would be adopted, the space at passing places was not relevant as trains would not pass each other. Trains would be run as on a tramway, stopping as required by passengers, and without having intermediate stations. 'In conclusion I would add that in the event of your board sanctioning the carriage of passengers on the line as at present constructed, my directors will undertake to work it strictly in conformity with any regulations with which the board may see fit to couple their sanction.'

The inspecting officers made a joint response, sent on 6 December 1880. It pulled no punches: 'We submit 1st that as this railway was not constructed in accordance with the plans deposited for making it as a tramway, which plans only authorised curves of 5 chains radius. 2nd that as by act of Parliament specially applied for, it has been transformed from a tramway to a railway, it is not, in our opinion proper that the requirements deemed necessary to provide for the safety of the public travelling on railways should be departed from and therefore for the reasons stated in our memorandum of the 23rd October last, we cannot recommend the Board of Trade to

sanction the opening of the Corris Railway for public traffic either as a railway or as a tramway.'

Beyond a formal acknowledgement the CR appeared to make no response. Its official application to open the railway not having been withdrawn, the Board of Trade continued to send a notice of postponement each month until eventually, on 21 October 1881, it wrote to ask if the company would withdraw the application until the railway was ready to be re-inspected. Earlier, on 12 March, the inspecting officers had written: 'On the question respecting the Corris Railway, we see no reason whatever for altering the opinion in our minute of 6 December last. To deviate from it would be to afford a precedent, certain to be hereafter quoted when similar irregularities are introduced by the company constructing any new line.' There is nothing in the file to indicate what triggered this assertion. In 1877, incidentally, Marindin had been unaware that a part of the North Wales Narrow Gauge Railways had been built on a different alignment beyond the limits of deviation at Plas y Nant. The notice was withdrawn on 2 November.

Kincaid, the engineer, wrote two letters on 18 January 1882, one to Marindin and one to the Board of Trade. He and Marindin

had met and exchanged correspondence, but the details were not recorded or retained. They had determined a strategy that Marindin thought would be accepted and now Kincaid had approval to make a commitment to the Board of Trade.

He undertook that all curves of less than five chains on the CR would be increased to five chains; all curves of five chains 'and under', a contradiction, would be check railed; a third pair of wheels would be fitted to the locomotives; a ladies' waiting room would be provided at Corris and the platform width would be increased; at Machynlleth a ladies' waiting room and approach from the main road would be provided; the space between double tracks would be increased to 6ft; facing points, other than those at the terminus, would be provided with patent locking apparatus, and obstructions on the eastern side of the railway would be removed so that none were closer than 2ft 4in at any point between 2ft 6in above rail height and the top of the highest carriage doors. Because it was impossible to improve

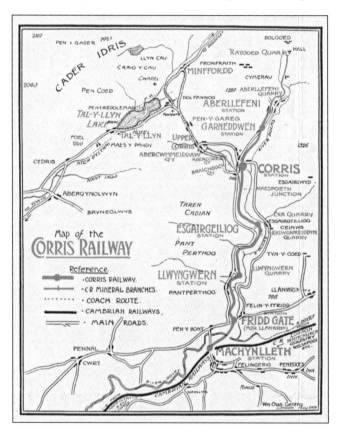

Map of the CORRIS RAILWAY

clearances between the railway and the turnpike, the fireman's side of the loco cab would be sealed, similarly the carriage doors.

This appeared to be satisfactory, Kincaid was informed, 'but the fitness of the line for passenger traffic must depend upon the report received from the inspecting officer.' Even now, getting the Corris Railway approved for passenger traffic was not going to be easy. On 3 July 1882 Kincaid wrote that the railway was ready to be inspected, the work having been carried out with one exception, the line's position between the river and road preventing the curve at Coedwig bridge from being increased to more than four chains. He hoped this would be acceptable.

Marindin returned to Corris and submitted his report from Shrewsbury on 18 July. He found that the requirements of 1880 had been met with the exception of the alterations to the curves. At Coedwig, the curve was actually only 1.87 chains while five other curves the railway had said were five chains were actually 3.5 chains, 3.2 chains, 3.2 chains, 3.7 chains and three chains. Being told that this was owing to a miscalculation on the part of the agent who laid out the curves he said he: 'did not consider it to be necessary to proceed any further in my inspection.'

Receiving the news, Kincaid had an air of desperation when he wrote on 25 July 1882: 'Owing to a serious blunder made by the local engineer ... many of the curves are under five chains ... These curves as laid cannot be further improved and I should not have undertaken the works required to enlarge them to five chains radius had I not been misled ...' He continued: 'Your requirements have been satisfied with the exception of the alteration of the curves and these have been improved to the utmost extent possible and I would submit that the Board of Trade having the power of permitting certain deviations from the parliamentary plans should now, in view of the narrowness of the gauge and the limited speed, refuse to sanction the opening of the line for public traffic, if the inspecting officer pronounces it, as laid, safe for passenger traffic.'

'My directors', he pleaded, 'would be quite prepared to affix to each engine a governor limiting the speed to any authorised maximum and to submit to any other regulations required ... Seeing the great expense which the directors have incurred ... that the inhabitants of the district are most desirous ... that Parliament has sanctioned ... my directors trust that you will see your way ...'

It was to no avail. On 9 August, the Board of Trade wrote to Kincaid that permission could not be given because the curves were so much less than those approved by Parliament. In his note on Kincaid's letter, Major General Charles Scrope Hutchinson suggested that the company could apply for fresh powers

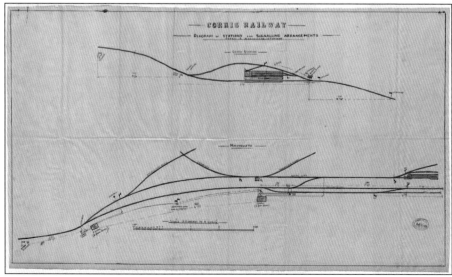

Above left: **Dated 1909, this map was an element in the poster produced that year. It was also reproduced in the railway's reports for several years (see pp45).** *National Archives*

Left: **A signalling diagram for Machynlleth and Corris produced in 1910 to support O'Sullivan's application to run two trains.** *National Archives*

Right: **No 3 appears to have had a new smokebox by the time this photograph was taken at Machynlleth in the late 1920s. It has no lamp bracket, and there is no sign of any bolt holes, and the smokebox door is different.**
E. A. Gurney-Smith/Author's collection

Below: **The Kerr, Stuart 'Tattoo' class 0-4-2ST was purchased in 1921, costing £1,825. It might not have been allocated a number officially until after the GWR took over. Here, it was photographed at Machynlleth with a train that comprised four carriages, two with clerestories, and the van. Assembled for the photograph are five employees, a vicar and his wife, and the fireman's girlfriend.**
Ian Allan Library

Right: **In contrast, this 1930s view of No 4 shows it with a goods train and fitted with a GWR side-mounted lamp bracket. The GWR modified its worksplates to serve as number plates.**
Paul Ingham collection

Left: **Although the line looks overgrown and neglected, the signalling remains in situ in this view of the Corris end of Machynlleth Station. The disc on the right indicates the location of a trap point.** *Paul Ingham collection*

Below: **A short mixed train on the second Dovey river bridge. It would be interesting to know what the braking arrangements were.** *Michael Whitehouse collection*

authorising curves of not less than two chains with a requirement to use a governor restricting speeds to 10mph. He remarked that on the FR there were two-chain curves and the speed was 15mph and that there were steam tramways with curves as sharp as one chain operated at speeds of 8 or 10mph that had not been objected to. Marindin agreed with his colleague.

There is no record of this strategy being communicated to Kincaid, but on 19 October he wrote that he had been instructed to prepare an application to Parliament and wished to know if the Board of Trade had any objection to this stratagem. He was informed that there would be none, provided there were no curves of less than two chains and that the speed of trains was mechanically governed to 12mph.

The bill was deposited in December 1882. While it was being processed the Board of Trade became concerned about two level crossings that had not been authorised. Although it decided that no further action was required, so missing the opportunity of having them validated by Parliament, their status was to be raised later. The act received royal assent on 18 June 1883.

By its terms, the Board of Trade was authorised to approve the works for the 'conveyance of passengers notwithstanding that the same may not have been constructed in some respects in accordance with the deposited plans relating thereto ...' subject to the minimum curvature being two chains and the speed limited to 12mph unless otherwise permitted.

Marindin was instructed to return to Corris on 23 June

1883 and wrote his report in London on 5 July. The permanent way was unchanged from 1880, but the curves had been altered and complied with the 1883 act. 'The engine in use is also fitted with a mechanical apparatus which prevents it from running at a higher rate of speed than 12mph.' The intermediate stations had been removed. There were two level crossings on public roads, one of which had been a private road in 1880. The crossings were provided with gates and lodges, one was interlocked with signals, the other required discs and lamps attaching to the gates, and a signal controlled by the keeper. With these requirements, and the fitting of the other two locomotives with governors, met Marindin wrote that 'upon the receipt of a satisfactory undertaking as to the method of working with one engine only in steam, the opening of this single line for passenger traffic may be sanctioned.'

The undertaking was made the next day. It had taken nearly three years, three inspections and an act of Parliament to get the railway approved for the carriage of passengers. So much for the agreement's four months. No doubt the directors, and Imperial, would have appreciated TGW's 'additional works' £500 if they had still been able to call upon it. During the remainder of 1883, 20,162 passengers were carried, a figure that doubled the following year.

Within a few months of opening, the company had reconsidered its position concerning intermediate stations and thought it should provide at least a shelter at Esgairgeiliog and Llwyngwern. On 26 October, Owen the engineer had written to the company that he 'cannot see that any difficulty should arise from the Board of Trade upon the company giving an undertaking to put up sufficient shelter by erecting waiting sheds. No platforms will be required and signalling is all that can be desired.' His letter was passed to the Board of Trade which consulted Marindin, who said that either the company should submit plans for approval or that it should construct the stations and submit them for inspection.

A plan was submitted on 11 December 1883, with a note explaining that Llwyngwern was on a gradient of 1 in 157 and a curve of 21.52 chains to the left, from Machynlleth, and Esgairgeiliog was on a gradient of 1 in 187 and on a curve of 13.53 chains, also to the left. Marindin decided that the buildings

Fridd Wood was a popular location for photographers, whether or not a train was present. *George & Sons/Author's collection*

could be erected without the need for loops or platforms, but that the company should 'provide the usual sanitary conveniences, which judging from the plans … have not been thought of.' He also required an inspection.

Apart from painting, delayed because of the weather, the stations were ready for Marindin by 26 February 1884. He again set off for Corris, reporting from Shrewsbury on 6 March. Esgairgeiliog had a siding facing down trains. The signalling was satisfactory and 'sufficient accommodation has been provided for the class of traffic on this narrow gauge line', which nicely escapes the point of whether these wayside stations had been provided with 'the usual sanitary conveniences'. Nameboards were required and had been ordered; on the understanding that they would be 'at once supplied' he could recommend that use of the stations be sanctioned.

In 1884 Imperial's capital expenditure was restated to include the reference to the CR's capital being purchased for £25,000 already mentioned. £1,239 5s 4d had been spent to meet the requirements of passenger traffic and £610 17s 3d on Parliamentary and engineering expenses, of which £200 was written off. Post-purchase expenditure came to £8,102 19s 5d. Even taking the guarantee payments into account the restated figures do not balance with the £42,750 purchase price first given.

Deposited sets of directors' reports for the CR are incomplete before 1885. Coincidentally, the earliest surviving minute book also dates from that year, when the directors were Lambert, Fraser, William Ward and Colonel Edward Temperley Gourley. The first was the chairman. Gourley, a ship owner and MP for Sunderland, and Ward had joined the board in 1883 and 1884 respectively. The secretary, Edward Miall Fraser, had been in office since 1871, except for 1881/2, and had conducted the correspondence with the Board of Trade after Kincaid ceased to be involved during 1883; he was James Fraser's son.

The directors' meetings were held in London at about two-weekly intervals with Dix only occasionally in attendance. After reviewing the financial position, the directors would deal with correspondence, mostly from Dix. Some of the meetings had only one or two items to deal with and must have been very short.

It would be reasonable to expect some formal structure to have been put in place to reimburse Imperial with the costs it incurred on the CR's behalf. No advantage was taken of the 1864 act's authorised but unissued capital. In 1885 the company deemed the authority expired and the opportunities offered by the 1880 and 1883 acts were not taken. Notwithstanding this, payments to Imperial were made at irregular intervals, presumably for management services and when the directors thought the CR could stand it. There is no obvious correlation between these payments and Imperial's accounts.

The accounting was not straightforward. The half-year to 30 June 1885 was not typical but serves as an example. On the capital account, £40 had been spent on new rolling stock and £260 17s 3d had been written off at 31 December 1864. On the revenue account a £450 (6% on £15,000) dividend had been received and the £260 17s 3d deducted. In the balance sheet, £143 8s 5d owed by the CR was shown as a liability.

The Board of Trade returns show that during the last seven years of horse haulage an average of nearly 17,000 tons of slate had produced dividends ranging from 4½% to 8½%. There were no dividends in 1879 and 1880, while for the following seven years a slightly reduced slate volume and passenger traffic from 1883 produced dividends in the range of 1⅛% to 5%.

Even with the steam locomotives in use, the CR had not turned its back on horse haulage because the locomotives did not venture onto the branches. In some cases, the quarries undertook their own haulage and in others they paid the CR for it. On 8 May 1885, the directors dealt with a notice from Abercwmeiddew terminating the company's haulage of its slate. A week later, Dix was authorised to negotiate to undertake Braich Goch's haulage for 2s per ton with a rebate of 1s per ton on any excess over 5,000 tons carried in six months. Over the years there were regular entries relating to horses, their equipment and accommodation in the reports; such expenditure was allocated to capital. On 27 August 1885, the directors approved Dix's request to buy a new horse for £30 and to sell one that was 'past work'. In December 'the horse employed at Machynlleth station had cut its foot severely, but was now recovering.'

It was November before any progress was made over the haulage. Braich Goch declined to pay 2s per ton whilst Abercwmeiddew agreed to pay 2s 6d, and to oil their own wagons. The latter, however, wished to have the terms embodied in an agreement but the directors resolved 'that no departure be made from the existing custom'. Dix was to continue negotiating with Braich Goch.

There was bound to be conflict with the quarries allowed to undertake their own haulage and this came to a head in January 1887. Dix complained that 'trains were frequently delayed by the irregularity of the Braich Goch Company's trains and that their manager claimed to have the use of the line for two hours in the mornings and two hours in the afternoons.' As unlikely as it seems, a timetable for August 1887 reproduced in Boyd *(see* Bibliography) show no advertised movements between the arrival of the 9.45am from Machynlleth at Corris at 10.10am and its departure at 12.50pm, and again after that train returned at 2pm until 4.40pm. Braich Goch's rights were to be investigated.

Another station was being considered in April 1885, when Dix reported that he had been negotiating for the small piece of land required at Fridd Gate. The owner was seeking £5 annually for the land and the adjacent house the crossing keeper was using. Dix was instructed to get the best price, and to get the house rent free for a year if the railway put it into good repair. Trains stopped there from 2 October and earned £3 0s 9d during the first month. The Board of Trade was not troubled on this occasion.

A programme of re-sleepering was in place in the mid-1880s. Whether this means that the steel rails installed in 1879/80 had been laid on old sleepers or the sleepers installed then had not lasted well, is not known. The engineer, Owen, inspected the line annually and reported on the areas that needed attention. In March 1885, Dix reported that he had sourced 5,000 larch sleepers for the main line at 1s each and 1,000 for the

branches at 9d. In June he estimated £900 expenditure on sleepers and had ordered £100 worth. On 31 July, he reported delivery of '800 out of the first 2,000 large sleepers' at a cost of £40. Gourley visited the railway in September and recommended that 'square creosoted sleepers' should be used on curves, at joints and in the middle of each rail length, also that a trial should be made of using galvanised and tarred spikes. Imperial allocated £100 for expenditure on sleepers during the second half of the year.

In May 1886, the section between Llwyngwern and Esgairgeiliog, about 1½ miles, was reported to be complete and there were 1,000 sleepers in stock. By July, half the line, 1,100 yards from Machynlleth, 2,300 yards from milepost 2 and 500 yards at Corris, would have been completed when the 650 sleepers in stock had been used. Faced with this information Dix was instructed to 'limit expenditure under all heads to what is absolutely necessary for the same passage of the traffic.' Dix reported the task complete except for 150 yards on 27 November 1888 while 500 sleepers were required for sidings at Machynlleth, Maespoeth and Corris.

With regards to rolling stock, in March 1885 Dix had reported discussions with the Falcon Works at Loughborough with a view to modifying the brake van for use on mineral as well as passenger trains. This was probably changes to its couplings and might explain the £40 spent by Imperial on otherwise unaccounted for new CR rolling stock already mentioned.

Above: **A train of empty wagons and a brake van hauled by No 4, on one of the sharper curves.** *H. B. Tours/Adrian Gray collection*

Left: **No 3 with a very short train at Llwyngwern. The GWR lamp bracket fitted after 1931 is clearly defined.** *Paul Ingham collection*

29

The CR was no different from any other railway when it came to passengers or local youth misbehaving. In June 1885, a passenger, Griffith Edwards, was brought to the directors' attention for jumping from a train in motion and on another occasion for wounding a sheep and driving it on to railway premises. In July, Dix reported that Edwards had been fined 1s and £1 10s costs. Dix was to have posters printed announcing the conviction and to exhibit them at stations.

More seriously, in May 1886 a child was killed when 'a lad, Joseph Hughes, letter carrier and two children got onto an empty wagon at Upper Corris and set it in motion down the line.' It had overturned at 'the quarry'; Braich Goch? Hughes broke his leg. The coroner's jury recommended that wagons should not be left unattended. The directors resolved that 'if possible' the wheels of wagons left on the line should be secured by a chain and lock.

The police were not above misusing the railway either. Reported on 3 June 1886, Sergeant Roberts 'borrowed' a wagon from Aberllefenny and travelled in it to Corris. Dix reported it to the chief constable, but 'did not think it advisable to take further action', a position the directors accepted.

Staff got into trouble as well. A platelayer was dismissed in October 1885 after he had been acting as signalman at Machynlleth and derailed a passenger train. Viewing with a 21st century perspective, the author wonders if he had been properly trained. If it was a train in service, which was implied, then the Board of Trade should have been informed. In November 1888, a trolley ran away at Maespoeth bank, smashing the gates at Pont Ifans and damaging those at Llwyngwern before it stopped at Fridd Gate. The two men using it were sacked.

More seriously in the directors' eyes, in December 1888, Dix detected that E. W. Evans, stationmaster at Esgairgeiliog, had received money without accounting for it on two occasions. The money was paid in and he 'severely reprimanded' Evans. The directors resolved that 'the manager be informed that the board take a serious view of such delinquency and had the circumstances been reported earlier would have directed the dismissal of Evans.'

The Talyllyn Railway had been opened between Towyn and Abergynolwyn to serve the Bryn Eglwys quarries in 1866. The quarries were working the same slate veins as those around

Above: **Maespoeth junction and shed in 1939. It is as well that the point is set for Corris, for the Upper Corris track is covered by brambles. The small range of buildings between the signalbox and the loco shed included a stable for ponies.** *Author's collection*

Right: **No 4 taking water at Maespoeth. The water tank was in the building's roof. The use of slate and wire fences was a feature of both the Corris and the Talyllyn railways.** *H. B. Tours/Adrian Gray collection*

Corris, about four miles distance in a straight line, and the two railways shared the same 2ft 3in gauge. In November 1885, William McConnel, then chairman of the TR, 'inquired the price of the spare engine'; Dix was instructed to say that it would not be sold for less than the original price, £700.

The reference to 'the spare engine' suggests that the CR's traffic did not require three locomotives in traffic, which the method of working, one engine in steam, and the contemporary timetables tend to support. It is most likely that normally one engine would have been in service whilst another was undergoing routine maintenance. It would only have been on rare occasions, holidays perhaps, that the weight of a train would have required two engines and then they would have been double-headed. It was to be 1951 before the TR received any 'spare' engines from the CR; in the meantime it had made do with the two it had been equipped with in 1865.

Disposal of the unwanted formation to Derwenlas and Morben seem to have passed unrecorded. When the Machynlleth district highways board wanted to extend the footpath from the town to the Dovey river bridge, through the CR arch under the Cambrian line to Aberystwyth, in November 1885 it approached the Cambrian for permission.

The weather and its consequences proved to be an on-going problem for the CR. On three days in the winter of 1885/6 trains were stopped by flooding at Machynlleth, with water 3ft 6in above the track on one occasion. During the same period a landslip also occurred at Coedwig curve. The retaining walls at milepost 3 and Pont Ifans required attention in April 1886. Dix estimated £40 to repair them but the directors wanted him to see if buttresses or timber shoring would be a more economical solution – Dix had them pulled down and rebuilt.

A storm on 15 October 1886 brought down 35 yards of embankment and retaining wall near the third milepost. The minutes reveal a conflict between Dix and Owen on a remedy, the former reporting that it would take two weeks to repair with trains were stopped in the meantime, the latter recommending a new wall on deeper foundations 'than the manager considered necessary and that he [Owen] must disclaim any responsibility for the stability of the work'. Dix was to confer with Owen and follow his instructions. After the secretary and Owen inspected the site on 27 October the latter said he was 'thoroughly satisfied with the way in which the work … had been carried out.' The line was re-opened on 3 November. Over the years there were to be several newspaper reports of flooding affecting services. On 11 February 1889, though, it was to be heavy snow that caused the disruption.

It is indicative of the fluctuating nature of the slate quarrying industry that the CR sometimes had problems getting paid and would resort to direct action to protect its interests. Two quarries made regular appearances in the minutes, Abercorris and Abercwmeiddew. In December 1885 the Abercorris company was £56 9s 9d in arrears, accumulated over six months. When one of its cheques was returned unpaid in July 1886 Dix was instructed to detain seven wagons loaded with slate. The CR seized another at Machynlleth when the quarry closed 'for want of funds' in November, and owed £31 5s 7d. The Cambrian seized a wagon as well. In January 1887, Dix was told to demand cash for any haulage until the debt was settled. When Abercorris' liquidator demanded the wagon's return a few weeks later, Dix told him that it had been taken before his, the liquidator's, appointment and stated that it would not be returned until the debt was cleared. In November 1887, Dix asked his directors for permission to use the wagon and was told to ensure the CR retained possession of it.

By February 1886, poor trading had forced the closure of Abercwmeiddew. It had been in arrears for some time and the CR had been insisting on cash in advance for several months; £63 5s 7d of the arrears was paid in June 1886, and the quarry reopened in August.

In January 1886, Dix had been concerned about the loss of benefit for the CR when he learned that photographs of Talyllyn displayed in the Cambrian Railways' 1st class carriages described the lake as being 'near Towyn'. His action in asking for the caption to be changed to 'near Corris via Machynlleth', was approved by the directors, but he was advised 'to adopt a more conciliatory tone when dealing with Mr Conacher', the Cambrian's secretary. By April he had obtained approval to display CR advertising boards at 12 of the Cambrian Railways' principal stations on the coast.

One of the reasons that Dix would have been concerned about the route to Talyllyn being misrepresented was the tourist road service that the railway ran there. The first mention of it in the post-1885 minutes was in June 1886 when Dix reported 'he had been offered a suitable brake for the Talyllyn traffic for £20.' Traffic figures were to be included in the reports from 1890. These reveal that the CR ran two services, posting, the hire of horses to travellers, and the Talyllyn coach operation. The latter was always the more popular of the two with numbers carried ranging from 1,989 in 1891 to 9,226 in 1902. Posting bookings ranged from 316 in 1890 to 1,068 in 1900. The brake and harness were bought for £20 10s and another horse for £25. In

Right: **On 5 August 1943, No 3 and its load of coal arrive at Corris. A GWR-style lamp bracket is mounted on the loco's backsheet.** *Paul Ingham collection*

Below: **Seen on 7 August 1925, Corris station was unusual on narrow gauge lines in having an overall roof. The carriage shed alongside made it look more imposing, but the facilities were minimal with only a bench for those who had to wait. The roof of the railway's stable block is visible above the goods stock standing on the avoiding line.** *Humphrey Household/Paul Ingham collection*

Right: **Transport contrasts in Corris. The Crosville motor bus on the Dolgelley–Corris route is a stark distinction with the horse-drawn ensemble in the station.** *Author's collection*

September 1886, Dix reported that the 'Talyllyn car' had carried 1,019 passengers and earned £46 15s 9d since 1 July. Another horse purchased for £15 was expected to be sold for £12 at the end of the month. In April 1887 Dix bought 'a car suited to the Talyllyn service' for £18.

Technology in the form of a Byng telephone system costing £3 18s 6d was installed between Dix's office and 'the station' in June 1886. The office was at the house where Dix lived, Arddol Terrace, in Bridge Street, Corris.

At some unspecified locations in Corris, wagons were taken off the railway to be unloaded (coal was cited in a *North Wales Chronicle* report), much to the distress of the Dolgellau highways board, concerned about damage done to the roads by the wheel flanges. Following a public meeting to debate the issue in September 1886, the CR was allowed to continue the practice. The directors 'resolved that the manager be informed of the satisfaction of the board at the result of his exertions.'

Nevertheless, the issue obviously continued to raise tensions in some quarters for on 7 January 1887 two cases were brought against CR employees at Towyn petty sessions. In the first case, Edward Thomas was accused of 'causing injury or damage to the highway' contrary to the Highways Act of 1835. The CR's counsel argued that the act justified the use and the case was dismissed. In the second case, Thomas and Hugh Thomas were charged with having used 'trams' on the roads with projections, the wheel flanges, contrary to Merionethshire by-laws.

The CR's counsel argued, successfully, that the by-laws were unreasonable and could not remove a right created by Parliament and the flanges were not projections within the by-laws' meaning. Perhaps tiring at the 'very long legal argument' the bench ordered that any future prosecutions should by undertaken by the authorities and not individuals. The *North Wales Chronicle* of 15 January 1887 reported that public support for the railway's position was demonstrated on the evening after the cases by Dix being carried through the streets of Corris. The minutes of 13 January had noted that 'the people in the village [are] subscribing to defray the company's expenses.' It might have been more productive if the highways board had simply billed the railway for any damage done.

Lambert, the chairman, and Ward visited the railway on 17/18 September 1886. They reported 'The widening of the line between Corris and Aberllefenny was in course of completion and it had been proposed to put down steel rails with the view of extending the passenger traffic to Aberllefenny. One of the engines needed repairs and a bogie was required for the third engine. Some new cars were wanted and those in use required overhauling.' Lambert was to investigate the prices of new cars, rails and sleepers. Meanwhile, arrangements had been made for F. Adams, the Reading Tramway's fitter, to repair the existing cars, one of the benefits of the CR being part of a larger group. Adams remained at Corris until 27 November, repairing wagons after he had completed the cars.

The comment about the 'bogie ... required for the third engine' is indicative of the loco's position as spare and implies that the other two locos already had bogies, more accurately pony trucks, fitted to honour the commitment made to the Board of Trade by Kincaid in 1882. £418 was to be allocated to expenditure on locomotive repairs in 1887. Lambert had found 150 tons of steel Vignoles 41¼lb rail at £3 10s per ton located at Rhymney by 7 October 1886. Fishplates and spikes were required too.

On 9 December 1886 Dix wrote to the Board of Trade requesting a meeting to discuss the removal of the mechanical speed governors fitted to the locos in compliance with the 1883 act. He met Marindin and explained that the devices were

regularly breaking and were not required on similar undertakings. Marindin cited the FR and the North Wales Narrow Gauge Railways when he reported on the request. Dix got the approval he sought, providing train speeds did not exceed 12mph, on 20 October.

By February 1887, work on the Aberllefenny extension was within a week of completion although the track had not been relaid. Dix suggested making an informal approach to Marindin to ensure that there were no difficulties meeting the Board of Trade's requirements. At the 10 March board meeting the estimate for completion looked a little optimistic. Widening Abercorris cutting, just beyond Corris station, would take two weeks more. Retaining walls at Garneddwen, 100 yards x 3 yards, and Caecoch, 50 yards x 4 yards also remained outstanding. Dix wanted to employ an additional 12 men to have the line ready to be opened by 1 July. The directors approved five men. Dix arranged for the supply of 6,000 half-round sleepers, 1s 3d, and 2,000 rectangular sleepers, 1s 5d, to be paid for in seven instalments at three monthly intervals.

One of the three overbridges between Corris and Aberllefenny, at Fronwen. *Paul Ingham collection*

Before the directors' meeting on 24 March Lambert had approved the employment of the 12 men Dix had requested.

Half the distance had been relaid, Dix reported on 31 May. The retaining walls at Fron wen cutting, near Aberllefenny and below Garneddwen, were nearly finished. Several adjoining landowners or lessees had been demanding additional level crossings, the land having been sub-divided since the line had been built; Dix was to make the best terms possible. Where the line crossed public roads at Corris and Garneddwen, keeper's lodges were required. Dix had rented a cottage at Garneddwen for £5 10s annually inclusive of rates and taxes, and had agreed to buy a plot of land at Corris for £5, for this purpose.

Two weeks later the relaying was within ½ mile of Aberllefenny. The line would not be ready until sometime in July. Level crossing gates would cost 15s each, the crossings £3 in total. By mid-July the relaying was nearly complete and 'the station was also well advanced.' Hot weather and a water shortage had caused the delay. Both station and relaying were complete by July 27. The level crossings and associated signalling were on the verge of completion and the fencing would take another week. A survey would be carried out to gather the data required by the Board of Trade in anticipation that the inspection would take place during the first week of August.

In the event, it was 9 August 1887 before CR secretary John W. Alison requested an inspection. Appointed to the task on 16 August, Hutchinson submitted his report on 31 August. The extension was 1½ miles long, the steepest gradient was 1 in 59 and the sharpest curve had a radius of 5 chains. The only works were three overbridges of 8½ft span, constructed with stone abutments and slab tops, and a river bridge of 12½ft span constructed with stone abutments and stone arch top and local stone retaining walls. With the exception of some slight settlement in one of the abutments of the river bridge these works appeared to have been substantially built and to be standing well. There were two public road crossings, provided with proper gates. One of these appeared to be authorised, he wrote, but the other, at 5m 4ch, of a side street in Corris, the road should have been diverted and a bridge built.

This crossing had existed since the line had opened, nearly 30 years, however, and no objections had been made. Houses had been built around it, and it would be costly and difficult to divert the road and build a bridge. By section 2 of the 1883 act the Board of Trade could approve the non-compliance with the plans and he recommended this approach, provided all trains approaching the level crossing from Aberllefenny were required to stop dead before passing over it. If the act was not considered to give this power, then the company must undertake to get the crossing authorised. The points of two sidings were locked with the train staff, and at Corris and Aberllefenny there were signals interlocked with the points.

The requirements were: at Corris, the normal position of the upper points should be for the siding, both sidings should have interlocked catch points; at Aberllefenny a starting signal interlocked with the facing points and trap points above the station were needed; a disc and lamp iron were required for the level crossing gates at 5m 54ch.

At the Board of Trade there was some doubt that the 1883 act could be used to approve the level crossing, the relevant clause being concerned with curvature, but eventually common sense

prevailed, 'the railway is of little importance … there is at present small traffic …', and approval was given on 7 September 1887. It should be noted that the line thus approved did not extend to the terminus of the Parliamentary line, nearly half a mile beyond Aberllefenny station. Against an estimate of £1,500, £1,556 18s 1d had been spent. Imperial wrote the expenditure down against revenue over three years and did not add it to the 'additional expenditure' fund. On 15 September, the directors instructed Alison 'to convey to Mr Dix the expression of the directors' satisfaction at the way in which he had carried out the reconstruction works.' On 29 November, Dix reported that the extension had earned £57 16s 5d from carrying 3,719 passengers.

The level crossing at Pantperthog, 300 yards below Llwyngwern station, brought the CR into dispute with the highways surveyor in September 1887. The surveyor complained that the railway did not keep a lodge and had a summons issued. The gate keys were kept at a cottage nearby but the surveyor wanted them kept at another cottage. The case was decided in the railway's favour, but the directors told Dix to find a solution that avoided the risk of a penalty in the future.

After less than five years in service, although it was nearly 10 years old, consideration was given to improving the passenger stock, a process that led to the introduction of bogie carriages. In October 1887, Dix started a dialogue with the Falcon Engine & Car Works, successors to Hughes, over the supply of new underframes for the cars. 'He was of the opinion that bogie cars would not be suitable.' By 3 November, Falcon had quoted £145 each for two vehicles and the next day G. F. Milnes of Birkenhead quoted £110 each for two 12-seat cars of 'tramway type'. Later in the month, Milnes quoted £180 for a 24-seat bogie car whilst Falcon had quoted £210 for a 30-seat car. Asked to quote for a 24-seat vehicle, the Falcon price was £190. Comparing the specifications, Dix thought the Falcon vehicle more suitable and in December 1887 the directors agreed to place an order.

Falcon visited Corris to check the measurements and in February produced a design that did away with the balconies and which had a single entrance in the centre, offering to supply

Three quarters of a mile from Corris, Garneddwen was a halt equipped with a small shelter and a bench. The level crossing was behind the photographer.
George & Sons/Author's collection

a 30-seat vehicle for £205 or a 24-seat vehicle for £195. The directors chose the cheaper option. In May 1888, Dix learned that Falcon was proposing to employ a combined centre buffer and coupling on the carriage despite his preference for ordinary buffers. Unable to persuade Falcon to supply buffers without charge, he decided to fit them himself for £2 or £2 10s.

A different approach was considered in June 1888, when Falcon offered to supply an iron frame with bogies on which two four-wheeled car bodies could be mounted. The cost of painting and other work would bring the price to £80. The directors wanted to know the price with a timber frame. The bogie carriage was delivered on 18 August 1888, when Dix reported that it ran very satisfactorily. A month later he added that passengers preferred it to the 'ordinary' 1st class carriages; the ride in a 3rd class bogie carriage would have been much better than that in a 1st class four-wheeler.

The big increase in the number of passengers carried in 1888, from 46,586 to 54,178, continued to keep minds focused on the carriage fleet. In October, Falcon offered another bogie carriage, with buffers, for £195, £203 if fitted as 1st class or £390 for two ordered together. Approval was given to order one carriage 'similar to the last' on 18 October, paying one third down and the remainder in six instalments over 18 months. For conversions, Dix proposed ordering two iron underframes but received approval to order one.

When the directors met on 1 November 1888 Dix proposed that the new carriage be fitted as 1st class, enabling 'the present 1st class' to be made into 3rd class. A compromise was reached, to make it a composite carriage. In August Dix had been instructed to have the existing carriages painted at a cost not to exceed £2 10s each. On 19 October he had reported that the painting had not been started and that he 'had had to discard one of the carriages as being not worth repairing.'

The conversion was delivered by 19 March 1899 'and was a decided success' reported Dix. Hearing this on 4 April, the directors resolved not to order 'a second' new carriage 'at present' and that 'two more of the old carriages should be mounted on a bogie frame.' Having received a quotation of £113 8s 2d for this conversion Dix wrote to the directors on 3 July, questioning 'the advisability of converting any more as the cost was so great.' A decision was deferred until the directors had visited. A few months later Dix had changed his mind, asking for another conversion on 12 December but, once again, a decision was deferred.

Gourley must have used his influence as a director of Sunderland Tramways in June 1888, when a lame horse was being sold and two more were required for the 'Talyllyn waggonette'. It was arranged for a Mr Morrison of Sunderland to purchase them. At a cost of £40, they arrived from Sunderland in July. How they coped with being spoken to in Welsh was not recorded. They were sold, without comment, for £27 15s in October. Its inability to obtain suitable animals in the locality was probably the reason for going to Sunderland and was the explanation given in June 1889, when Dix was given permission to obtain horses from Ireland – two were purchased for £62 9s including expenses. In October, Dix arranged for them to be wintered at a farm near Machynlleth until 25 March 1890, for £5 inclusive. They would be put out to graze, given shelter and hay during inclement weather and visited at least once a week.

Locomotive facilities at Machynlleth were enhanced in June 1888 when Dix had a tube well sunk at Machynlleth and obtained a water supply suitable for them. A galvanised iron tank cost £4 10s. At Maespoeth loco shed, the pipes had corroded through by July 1889 and approval was given for their replacement at a cost of £17 10s.

Little detail about the company's administration appears in the minutes, but in July 1888 the secretary reported that he had complained to the bank about its charges. The bank agreed to reduce them by half, to ⅛%. Dix's application for an increase in salary made at the same time was deferred until Lambert and Gourley could visit, when they agreed to pay him £200 annually from 1 July.

Waste being tipped from Cymerau threatened the stability of the Ratgoed Tramway in August 1888. Large boulders had fallen into and diverted the stream into the railway formation. Dix's protestations to the quarry manager were ignored, but the quarry's underground manager promised remedial action, clearing the stream during October.

Dix reported three incidents with passengers or would-be passengers in November 1888. On 30 October Reverend O. F. Williams, the curate in charge at Corris, jumped into a wagon attached to the 12.15pm to Machynlleth at Maespoeth; Dix recommended that consideration of the matter await a further report. He had also summoned two men for riding in 1st class accommodation with 3rd class tickets. Magistrates had dismissed the case but the men would have to pay costs, £2 8s 6d, to the company. On another occasion, three 'persons' connected with the Dulas Slate Company had stopped a train they wanted to travel on by holding up a red handkerchief. This, wrote Dix, being an offence punishable by up to two years' imprisonment, he had accepted an offer of £4 4s being donated to the Railway Benevolent Institute, and £1 1s to the company to cover its legal expenses.

The Dulas Slate Company was in financial difficulties by January 1889, owing the CR £16 13s 9d for carriage. Dix seized two loads of goods as a lien for the debt; when the CR accepted 10s in £1 a year later, no mention was made of the goods seized. After Abercorris quarry changed hands, was reconstructed and asked for a credit account in 1890, the directors checked the status of the proprietors. The slate trade was showing signs of picking up, reported Dix, saying that Braich Goch had started working full time.

A new venture for the CR was Dix's initiative to hold an eisteddfod in Corris on 10 June 1889, Whit Monday. The event attracted a large audience with 1,166 passengers being carried and £18 0s 10d taken in fares. In contrast, in August 1889, Dix reported that slate traffic was depressed because a strike in the Ffestiniog quarries had resulted in stocks there being sold off.

Lewis Lewis, a gatekeeper, had worked for the railway for 20 years in 1889. He was 77 years old and unable to perform his duties, reported Dix, asking if Lewis could be granted a small pension. The directors agreed to pay him 2s 6d per week for a year.

Richard Davies, stationmaster at Llwyngwern, appeared in court in February 1890. The report is quoted in full: 'This man has been charged by Colonel Morris's keeper with poaching while looking after some wood which he had bought from Mr Gillart's woodman. He had been summoned and fined 6d with costs. The manager had information that both the charge and the magistrate's decision were unjust. Colonel Morris wished that the man should be discharged. The manager, however, stated that Davies had been a good servant to the company and had been unjustly charged. Resolved that Davies be retained in the service.'

The number of platelayers the CR normally employed is not known. In March 1890, Dix reported that they had applied for a pay rise of 1s per week and to be allowed to finish at 1pm on Saturdays. Dix's proposal to give them the same pay and conditions as Cambrian platelayers was approved.

The directors had a fatality to consider when they met on 3 October 1889. A child, Laura Pugh Davies, had strayed on to the Braich Goch branch on 18 September and had been run down by two wagons 'rounding a curve'. Returning a verdict of accidental death, the coroner's jury recommended the branch be fenced off and the men in charge of wagons be enjoined to use great caution in descending the inclines, whether they meant inclined planes or steep gradients is not clear. The Board of Trade wanted to know if the recommendations would be acted upon. Dix arranged to fence the 'Braich curve'.

The CR's compliance with the 1888 Regulation of Railways Act was considered on 31 October 1889. Dix had arranged for tickets to be printed bearing the fares and considered it probable that the Board of Trade would not require the company to adopt continuous brakes. Dix was wrong in his assumption, so started a correspondence that went on intermittently for five years.

'Section 1(a) (the block system) does not apply to us', wrote Dix on 21 December, 'as we work with only one engine in steam or two coupled together. Section 1(b) (interlocking of points and signals) does not apply because our passenger lines were passed in 1883 and 1887 and the existing requirements complied with. Section 1(c) (continuous brakes) – none of our passenger stock is provided with continuous brakes but all our vans and carriages are fitted with hand brakes applying to all wheels and … enable our trains to be stopped … in the length of the train. As our line is a narrow gauge of 2ft 3in gauge I beg to ask that we may be exempted from having to adopt a continuous automatic brake.' Regarding mixed trains, he explained that all trains were mixed, 90% of wagons were private owner vehicles. Making the usual excuses about the railway's narrow gauge and low speed he asked for it to be exempted from the requirements.

A clipping from the *Oswestry & Border Counties Advertiser* of 6 November reporting the CR's success at carrying over 30,000 passengers during the year was carefully kept in the file; perhaps someone at the Board of Trade thought that it showed the railway was busier than it represented itself. There appeared to be no hurry, for it was not until 4 March 1890 that Dix's appeal was repeated by the secretary. The draft order was prepared the next day, allowing no exception for continuous brakes and a six-month extension of time to fit them. Mixed trains 'might be allowed on the same condition as on the Talyllyn Railway.'

Alison wrote again on 20 November, asking that 'as the company's passenger stock is in course of being remodelled and reconstructed I am directed to ask that the period for applying continuous brakes may be extended to three years from the date of the order' and with regard to mixed trains for the CR to be allowed to run three such daily between Machynlleth and Aberllefenny. The order was made the same day, allowing the three years without demur. The question of the mixed trains would be considered in due course.

Reporting the order's obligations to the directors meeting on 11 December 1890, Dix recommended 'the engine about to be repaired should be fitted with the automatic vacuum brake and that the six remaining old carriages be fitted on three new bogie frames at the rate of one new frame per year to be fitted with the brake apparatus; the cost of the brake being £50 per engine, £15 per carriage, £20 for the guard's van.' He recommended the vacuum automatic brake be adopted. The directors adopted Dix's proposals, but in January 1892, when they agreed to his request to order two sets of brakes for carriages, costing £12 each, he was asked to report on the relative qualities of the vacuum brake and the Westinghouse brake. Both complied with Board of Trade requirements, he reported; 30,339 vehicles were fitted with vacuum brakes and 15,164 with Westinghouse. The

£278 spent on rolling stock repairs in 1892, which was much higher than in either the preceding or following years, probably included brake equipment.

The decision to put the third locomotive into traffic had followed an incident on 25 September 1890, when a tube burst on the loco hauling the 6.40am train from Machynlleth, delaying traffic by two hours. Identified as 'engine No 2', the directors accepted a tender of £105 15s for its repair 'in accordance with specification' on 8 January 1891. It was sent to Loughborough, the CR paying for its carriage. On 10 March, Dix reported that repairs were in progress and that he would travel to Loughborough to observe its steam test. Locomotive repairs cost £655 in 1891, increased from £340 the year before, and were £502 in 1892.

Braich Goch's 'right of access' to the CR's main line was an unexpected victim of the 1890 order. Dix wrote to the directors on 3 December 1890 saying that having escaped an obligation to adopt the block system it was 'most desirable that the Braich Goch haulage should be performed by the company.' Braich Goch responded by asking if the CR would purchase its wagons and provide them for its future use and if the CR would enter into an agreement to allow Braich Goch to be restored to its existing position. Dix advised against such an agreement, saying that Braich Goch had no statutory right to perform its own haulage. He was told to ask Braich Goch to justify its position.

Perhaps before he had done so, Dix informed the directors that although the 1858 act did not directly convey any rights on Braich Goch, it did incorporate the 1845 Railway Clauses Consolidation Act and quoted from Clause No 92: 'upon payment of the tolls from time to time demandable all companies and persons shall be entitled to use the railway, with *engines* and carriages properly constructed.' The company had, however, obtained a legal opinion in 1887 to the effect that Clause No 9 of the 1880 act gave the company the 'right to prevent the Braich Goch Company from carrying their slates over any of the portion of the line open for passenger traffic.' The relevant section reads: 'In the event of the company conveying passengers on the railways … by means of steam or locomotive power, the company shall convey … upon the terms and conditions contained in the act of 1858, the articles, matters, and things set forth in that act: provided always, that the company shall not be required to find carriages or wagons for the conveyance of such articles, matters, and things.'

Meeting on 5 February 1891, the directors resolved to give Braich Goch notice that after 30 June its use of the main line would cease and that the CR would carry its traffic at the statutory rates. The letter was to be drafted for approval at the next meeting. Before that occasion, following an intervention by Dix, they had reverted to their previous position and he had told Braich Goch that the CR did not want to buy the wagons or enter into an agreement. When no reply had been received by 2 April 1891, it was decided to serve notice that Braich Goch should discontinue its main line haulage from 29 June.

Details of the subsequent correspondence between the parties was not recorded in the minutes until 25 June 1891, when the secretary reported that he had visited Braich Goch on 5 June and had reached agreement that the CR would undertake the quarry's haulage from 1 July at a rate of 2s per ton, bringing 42 years of private haulage between Corris and Machynlleth to an end.

Earlier, on 22 January 1891, Dix had raised the question of the private owner wagons in general, saying that the wheels of most of them were in 'a very bad state of repair' and recommending the quarries be served with a formal notice requiring the wagons to comply with defined standards from 1 July. The directors agreed that a notice should be drafted by the solicitor.

Between Corris and Aberllefenny, habitation was sparse and the views much more open. The slate and wire fences remain in situ as a reminder of the railway that once served the area.
Paul Ingham collection

The next time the CR heard from the Board of Trade was when it received a letter dated 20 December 1893, which appeared to ask the railway's position regarding the 1889 act (the file copy has not survived). Writing from Bristol on 19 January 1894, secretary Samuel White repeated the points made by his predecessor, adding that continuous brakes had been fitted to all the rolling stock except for two carriages that had been withdrawn for it to be fitted, and that 'it was not the practice of this railway to take advantage of the modification which permits one unbraked vehicle at the tail of the train.'

Reviewing White's letter the Board of Trade realised that the undertaking concerning the method of working should have been amended to say that the engine should carry a staff. 'The remainder of the reply is satisfactory.' The amended undertaking was to be given on 5 February 1894. Capital expenditure during 1893 was £155, for vacuum brakes, a charabanc, a horse, and additional stabling.

At Aberllefenny, construction of a siding to serve a new works for Ashton, Green, Matthews & Company had started in October 1889. Located at 6 miles 6.18 chains, it replaced an earlier siding at 6 miles 11.90 chains. The railway did the work at a cost of £91 paid for by the company. The Board of Trade was informed on 4 February 1890, when Dix explained that a trap point had been put in 1 chain from the points and that the siding was 'now level for 1.50 chains and then [on] a falling gradient of 1 in 25 from the main line.'

Railway inspector Colonel F. H. Rich submitted his report from Dublin on 7 August 1890. Because of the gradient the CR undertook only to insert and remove wagons when the engine was at the south end of the train. Subject to the point rods being secured by steel cotters or a nut and split pin, instead of split pins only, and the stock rail kept to gauge with a tie bar, he recommended the works be approved. The alterations were carried out by 19 August. On the 1901 Ordnance Survey map the site was called Matthew's Mill.

The Talyllyn and posting traffic did well in 1889, receipts for

the year reaching £110 10s 6d compared with £57 15s 3d, but when Dix suggested buying a 10-seat waggonette for the traffic the directors asked for details of the service's running costs. Producing a figure of £48, Dix received approval to purchase the vehicle. When it was not delivered until September 1890 he negotiated a reduction in price to £20. In June 1891, Dix bought the Braich Goch Inn's waggonette for £6; he had been in the habit of borrowing it at peak times.

The carriages came back on the CR's agenda at the end of 1889, when Dix's proposal to convert two more of the four-wheelers into a bogie carriage was rebuffed by the directors. However, when he returned to the subject in January 1890 he was successful. On this occasion Brush Electrical Engineering, successors to Hughes and Falcon, had offered to do the conversion, complete with fittings and painting for £87 19s including transport. Dix's estimate of an additional expenditure of £30 for unspecified alterations and repairs, the same job was implied, was also accepted.

In September 1890 it was the wagons' turn to make an appearance in the minutes. Several wagon wheels having become worn out, Dix had ordered six sets of wheels with axles from Hadfield of Sheffield at £7 19s 6d per set. He had obtained prices from other suppliers, but Hadfield's had proved the most satisfactory in the past, which may be taken to mean that they were not the cheapest. The railway had a need for trucks to carry timber, reported Dix. He proposed to build two for £10 each.

The encouragement of summer visitors to Corris was facilitated by an arrangement Dix made with the Cambrian Railways in February 1890 for through tickets to be sold at Aberystwyth, Borth, Aberdovey, Towyn, Barmouth and Dolgelley.

After buying horses from Sunderland and Ireland, in May 1890 Dix proposed buying one from Aberystwyth fair, a little closer to home. One of the horses had gone lame so another was needed for the Talyllyn traffic. He paid £30 for a bay mare. He was unable to sell the Irish horses in November 1890 so put them out to grass near Borth for 10s each per month, telling the directors that he expected to achieve the purchase price when he sold them in the spring. The bay was sold for £30 in June 1891. At the same time he told the directors that he would need to buy two horses for the summer traffic. In October he sold two at Machynlleth fair, one bought in 1889 for £26 sold for £15, and one bought in 1890 for £31 sold for £26.

Abercwmeiddew was in trouble again in April 1890, owing £47 8s 8d although £23 had been paid on account. Dix was to tell the quarry that without regular monthly payments the CR would cease to give credit. By May, the quarry had paid up to March. Dix was to insist on monthly payments.

Apart from the initial problems with retaining walls following the line's reconstruction for steam locomotives, its infrastructure was rarely mentioned. By September 1890, the timber beams of a bridge at Aberllefenny had become unsafe for traffic. They could be repaired for £25 said Dix, telling the directors that replacing the timber with iron would be considerably more expensive.

William Williams travelled from Llwyngwern to Machynlleth on 23 October 1890 and jumped off the train as it approached the station to avoid the fare. This was a double offence and the

directors supported Dix's recommendation to prosecute. When Williams offered to pay £1 and agreed to notices being distributed describing his offences, the summons was withdrawn.

Deterioration in the main line sleepers was reported by Dix in March 1891, barely three years after their installation had been completed. He proposed a programme of replacing 2,000 annually, paying 1s 6d for the first 2,000. As an experiment he had pickled 904 sleepers in carbolineum avenarius, a tar oil preservative, at a cost of 3d each and was satisfied with the results. The Ratgoed branch was in poor condition and required 2,000 sleepers which could be obtained for 11d each. The main line purchase was approved. Dix was to make enquiries about the suitability of using 9ft red Baltic sleepers cut in half. The directors were not fully convinced with the treated sleeper he sent to London for them to inspect, but obviously saw the benefit of treating the timber, resolving to obtain tenders for creosoted sleepers.

Six tenders for red Baltic sleepers had been received by 30 April 1891 with prices ranging from 11d to 1s 3¾d untreated and 1s 2½d to 1s 7¼d treated delivered to Machynlleth. 2,000 untreated sleepers were ordered from E. A. Jones of Wrexham at 11d each, A. J. Jones of Aberdovey undertaking to creosote them for 3½d each; 250 to be treated with carbolineum. The Ratgoed sleepers were delivered by July 1891.

On 14 September 1891 Dix reported the discovery of a leak in the boiler on 'engine No 3', 'several of the pipes in the smokebox required renewing'. The work was estimated to cost £10.

The Dovey bridge required attention, Dix wrote on 4 November 1891, as the ends of eight longitudinal beams were rotten. Replacements cost £10 and were installed on 6 November, the train service running to Fridd Gate while the work was carried out.

Dix was rebuked after telling the directors that he had

No 4 and its train in the loop at Aberllefenn on 9 June 1925. The loco ran for some time with a clamp on its cracked chimney. The flaps on either side of the saddle tanks were also a feature of the 1920s, designed to stop water overflowing from the tank getting into the motion. *A. W. Croughton/Michael Whitehouse collection*

No 3 at Aberllefenny in the 1920s. The glass in one of its spectacles is broken. When hauling passenger trains the vacuum pipe was fed through the hole in the cab backsheet.
R. G. Jarvis/Author's collection

accepted an offer from Ferndale Collieries to supply steam coal during 1892 for £1 3s 3d per ton. He was told 'in future to obtain the sanction of the board before making contracts.' At the next meeting, on 14 January 1892, his report that the previous price had been £1 4s 6d was accepted without comment.

When the line was blocked by snow for several days in January 1892 Dix received complaints about the delay to services from the quarry owners. His handling of them was approved by the directors.

In 1892 the company came under pressure from the Cambrian Railways to join the Railway Clearing House to benefit from revenue sharing on through traffic, with particular reference to the Post Office (Parcels) Act of 1882. The sharing arrangement for parcels was being reviewed and the Cambrian claimed that the CR would benefit by £32 per year. The secretary was deputed to attend a conference of general managers dealing with the issue and Dix proposed registering with the GPO to become a party to the act. The directors, however, resolved to enquire if the company might be able to make special terms with the GPO if it remained independent. The returns show that the railway had been paid for carrying mails since 1883 and had been paid £50 annually since 1888. On learning that there would be no benefit in remaining independent, on 26 February 1892 the directors resolved to register with the GPO.

A long-standing dispute over charges for using the Dulas Slate Company's bridge at Esgairgeiliog, which was crossed by the Era slate quarry branch, was revived in March 1892. The minute explained that the CR had originally been allowed free use in exchange for providing the siding to the slate enamel works. When the property changed hands in 1885 a wayleave was demanded, originally £5 but settled at £1 in 1886. Despite agreeing to it the CR appears not to have paid. Now the owner was demanding £10

and had blocked the bridge. Before responding, Dix recommended taking the point out, and the directors decided to investigate the likely effect on traffic at the station.

On 24 March 1892, Dix was instructed to establish whether, if the company paid £6 to cover the previous six years, it could have free use of the bridge for all traffic. He reported back that the owner claimed to have been in possession since 1884, he wanted £10 for eight years use and to be informed of the station's traffic with a view to regulating charges in future. The directors decided to take no further action.

There was perhaps an unintended consequence to this affair for the bridge's owner, who charged Esgairgeiliog villagers a toll for using it. Dix sold them some timber so they could build a footbridge across the river and avoid it. In June 1894 the new directors were to instruct Dix to agree to the owner's terms for using the bridge.

Dix continued the carriage conversion programme, no doubt in accordance with the resolution of December 1890. However, when he submitted a report in respect of a vehicle that had been completed in March on 11 April 1892, he was again rebuked for acting without the directors' approval.

The Cambrian Railways threatened Dix's equanimity over the Talyllyn traffic when he discovered that the larger company had advertised a coach to run from Towyn to the lake from 1 June 1892, and also wanted to run a service from Machynlleth to the lake, the latter in direct competition with the CR's well-established service. In response, Dix obtained Ward's approval to bring the CR service forward to start on 1 June as well. The Cambrian's traffic manager appeared to think that there was an agreement that the CR service would not start until 1 July and responded by limiting the through tickets from coastal stations to one train a day. Dix was instructed to meet the Cambrian and restore good relations. On 16 June, 'The secretary was instructed to intimate to the manager that the board are dissatisfied at hearing no further report from him as to this matter [arrangement with Cambrian Railways] and to desire that a general report be furnished for the information of every board meeting.'

By the time the board met on 30 June 1892, Dix was able to report that he had established a rapport with the Cambrian, through ticketing had been restored in full, and a circular tour from the coastal stations via Corris and Towyn had been arranged. If there was any benefit for the CR from the last it was not stated. June receipts for the Talyllyn coach had been £16 19s 9d. Two more horses might be required and one horse was sold for 15s in October. It had been used since 1885 but had developed a cracked heel. Two spare horses were being wintered in two fields for £5. Dix was instructed to rotate the horses in use.

Changes in the company's direction made during 1891 continued into 1892. Previously, the CR's board had remained unchanged since 1885. There was no comment after Lambert, the chairman, attended a meeting for the last time on 14 May 1891. Subsequent meetings were chaired by Ward, who signed the minutes 'chairman pro tem' until 23 July, the date of a general meeting, after which he signed as chairman. George White of Bristol was elected a director on 12 November 1891 and Ward was formally elected chairman on 26 November. Lambert had died on 22 September, aged 52. White had been secretary of the Bristol Tramways & Carriage Company since 1875 and was now the largest shareholder in Imperial. The changes he wrought there were carried through to the CR.

Hugh C. Godfray, not Godfrey, a solicitor, became an additional director in 1892, attending his first board meeting on 25 February although his election was not formally recorded. A more significant change occurred on 11 August when White and Godfray proposed that James Clifton Robinson be elected managing director of the company, a move that was followed by Ward's resignation as a director and White's election as chairman.

Gourley resigned on 19 September 1892 and Godfray was appointed the company's solicitor on 27 October. Consequences of the new order were that Dix lost his contact with the directors, dealing with Robinson alone, board meetings became less frequent, and the approval of cheques and proposed dividends were recorded in the minutes, which otherwise became much less informative, with comments such as 'Various traffic details were considered and settled' becoming commonplace. If they continued the payments to Imperial were no longer recorded. Since 1885, £2,950 had been paid, but this money has not been identified in the CR or the Imperial accounts. In 1892, the CR debt to Imperial was £611.

Robinson had a long career in tramways, working for George Francis Train on the first British tramway in Birkenhead in his youth. His obituary recorded that from 1875 to 1882 he had run Bristol Tramways for Kincaid (see p20). In 1892, he had just returned from a two-year assignment for the American Street Railway Association to become the managing director of Imperial Tramways.

In parallel with these changes, Fraser, whose involvement with the CR pre-dated 1874, was negotiating to sell the railway to the Cambrian. He reported on 16 November 1892 that his negotiations were continuing. Secretary Alison resigned on 23 November, 'as arranged with the directors of the owning company, the Imperial Tramways Company.' The meeting was adjourned to Godfray's office where it was resolved to transfer the registered office to Clare Street House in Bristol and to appoint Samuel White, George White's brother, as secretary. The Cambrian refused the offer to buy the CR and, in June 1895, a subsequent invitation to lease it. The company's attention then turned to the Great Western Railway as a possible purchaser.

Approaching the completion of 10 years of steam and passenger operation and an almost complete change of direction, it is appropriate to review the CR's performance. One thing that stands out is that the dividends were much lower than they had been before 1878, ranging from nothing in 1890 to 5% in 1885, the average being less than 3%. Passenger traffic had grown steadily from less than 50,000 in 1884 and regularly exceeding 55,000 from 1888. Merchandise was static through the decade whilst slate was roundly 16,000 tons per year, dipping to 13,546 tons in 1891. Costs however, were considerably increased, rising from £1,688 in 1884 to £2,847 in 1892, reflecting not only the cost of maintaining the locos and keeping the track fit for passenger trains, but also an increase in annual train mileage of nearly 4,000 miles over the period. The three years of posting and Talyllyn coach traffic and revenue available during this period are insufficient to make any generalisations about it.

Meeting still in London on 6 April 1893, with Fraser in the chair and with Godfray and Robinson present, Samuel White presented George White's and Robinson's report on rolling stock. They had authorised another carriage conversion, the 'alteration of one engine and one guard's van and the fitting of automatic brakes to the whole of the vehicles named …' Dix had been to Loughborough to arrange the 'extra repairs necessary, the repairs and alterations to the locomotive being completed at Corris, the manager having arranged to supplement his own staff with any assistance necessary to finish off that portion of the work.' There were to be no further reports about the rolling stock, leaving the stories of the locomotive overhauls and carriage conversions incomplete. In 1893, expenditure had been £435 on locomotive repairs and £201 on carriage repairs.

Authorisation for Dix to order uniforms, costing about £25, on the same occasion implies that they had not been a feature of CR operations previously. The smithy's bellows was to be renewed at a cost of £7 10s.

An accident caused by 'slippery state of metals and brakes failing to act' occurred on the Tyddynyberth branch in October 1893. The several wagons of Braich Goch slates involved would cost £17 or £18 to repair, Dix reported, adding that 'no injury was caused to any of the brakesmen attending to the wagons'. This is indicative of the wagons still being run to Maespoeth by gravity.

In 1894, the Board of Trade complained about the lack of a waiting room at Corris. On 29 June, Dix was instructed to acquire the necessary land. Two years previously, Dix had reported being given notice to quit the stables at Corris and suggested acquiring a plot of land next to the station and 'adding a waiting room to the station and building, a stable and coach house.' The directors had not been interested. There is no record of what happened to the horses after they had been evicted. Expenditure of £333 for new stables was added to the capital account in 1896.

Perhaps Dix had been told of the proposal to lease the railway to the Cambrian but when Robinson had told the directors on 2 August 1894 that he had expressed an interest in leasing the line himself, their response was brutal. 'The secretary was instructed to write to Mr Dix expressing the view of the board, that assuming from his application he was under the impression he could work the railway to better advantage, they expected him to exercise all his energies for the company's benefit.'

The directors were probably unaware of his patented device to stop a train automatically when a signal was at danger, as announced in the *Western Mail* on 8 May 1894.

The company's defence to a claim for damages and costs was unsuccessful, a Mr Williams being awarded £79 8s 2d, Robinson reported in November 1895. The case involved a man who was killed after jumping a fence on to the railway. The minute noted: 'It seemed an extraordinary decision … there was no chance of appealing successfully.' Neither the incident nor the serving of the writ had been recorded previously.

Another claim against the company involved some land at Pont Ifans. Ownership was claimed by Walter Hume Long, an MP from Wiltshire, at the end of 1897, the railway having been in occupation since 1859. After making an offer that would have inhibited railway operation if executed, he succeeded with a court action in September 1899. The company bought the land from Long, agreed a draft conveyance in May 1900 and in 1901 paid his legal costs of £247 1s 5d. In 1903, Long was to object to fences alongside the railway, requiring their removal or payment of an annual nominal sum. They were removed.

There is no evidence to suggest that the CR's owners still harboured any ambitions to extend the line. Dolgelley's light railways committee thought differently, however, its resolution to petition the CR to extend to the county town being reported by the *North Wales Chronicle* on 4 December 1897.

What turned out to be the final development in the CR coaching stock occurred in 1898, the acquisition of two bogie carriages from the Metropolitan Carriage & Wagon Company. The purchase and expenditure is not mentioned in any of the surviving records.

Stable at £7,732 2s 2d since 1886, the 'additional expenditure' item in Imperial's accounts did not appear as a separate item after Imperial was restructured on 28 September 1898. The 1878 company had been put into liquidation and a new company registered with the same name. Thereafter, the value of Imperial's capital assets and investments was amalgamated.

It had been Dix's practice to take leave at the end of April each year. In 1901, however, he was told that this was not convenient but 'later on the managing director would send one of his assistants to Corris to take charge during the manager's absence.' When he asked for an increase in salary in 1902 it was refused. After Owen had died in 1901 Dix took on the responsibility of signing the reports as engineer; he had signed as locomotive superintendent since at least 1885 and probably had done so since his appointment.

Samuel White was elected a director on 26 March 1902, resigning as secretary. He was replaced in that post by William George Verdon Smith, George White's nephew.

Repairs to the Dovey bridge, Dix having said it was in a defective condition in November 1902, and the replacement of Machynlleth station building in June 1903, were both approved without reference to cost.

Abercwmeiddew quarry took a unilateral decision to withhold some of the money it owed the company towards the

end of 1903, claiming that the charges were excessive. The quarry was told that the rates were defined by Parliament and 'that unless they adopt a more reasonable attitude, prepayment of any freight for conveyance must be insisted upon.' No more was said.

In December 1903, Dix told the directors of a large rock fall at Braich Goch, warning that slate volumes would be reduced as a result. A year later, White reported that he had been communicating with Dix on the subject of decreased traffic receipts and that Dix 'had promised to use his utmost efforts to try to substantially reduce the decrease before the end of the year.' Revenue for the year, at £4,000, was only £381 less than in 1902, whilst expenditure was reduced by £409. A 6% dividend was declared.

Two of the directors received honours in this period. George White became a baronet, adopting the designation 'White of Cotham House', in Bristol, in the birthday honours list announced on 24 June 1904, while Robinson was to receive a knighthood a year later.

Details of the 1902 repairs to the Dovey bridge were not described in the minutes, but in October 1905 Robinson 'reported the necessity for re-constructing the bridge over the river Dovey.' Tenders were considered on 16 May 1906 and contracts awarded to Dorman, Long & Company Limited for the steelwork (£412), and J. Chidlow Roberts for the coffer dams (£465). The work was carried out by the company under Robinson's supervision. In October, he forecast that it would be completed in two to three weeks. The lack of further comment suggests that that target was probably met.

In June 1904, the Cambrian dealt with a letter from Dix: 'Our station at Machynlleth, owing to a variety of causes, has been allowed to become very dilapidated. It was originally very badly built without any pretence as to design or elegance and quite in the wrong position. There is no space for proper platform accommodation, and sidings are very cramped and inconvenient. My directors have given me permission to erect new station buildings, but to carry out this properly and to remodel our platform and sidings it is desirable that we should have another portion of your field adjoining ... We have some land ... which originally formed part of our line to Derwenlas and which was abandoned on the opening of the Cambrian line. This latter piece of land is of no use to us, but as it adjoins your property my directors have agreed to my offering you this strip in exchange for the portion of the field now required ... I may say that the land is not fenced off, but if you agree to the proposed exchange we will put up a suitable fence or remove the present fence to the new boundary ...' The Cambrian accepted the proposal, as well it might; the land it received covered 1,360 square yards, whilst that given up amounted to 782 square yards.

There are no details available to identify the station building's architect or builder, but with those of the Festiniog Railway and the Isle of Man Railways, it is one of the most attractive narrow gauge railway buildings in the British Isles. A carriage shed was to be erected alongside in 1907.

The expenditure on the bridge and the station was not recorded against the CR's capital account, the last expenditure under this heading being recorded in 1901, as shown in the table.

Capital expenditure 1885–1901

1885		Cr	Dr
	Increase in value of horses		£4 5s
1886	Waggonette		£20
	Depreciation in horses	£10	
1887	Waggonette		£18
	Depreciation in horses	£9 10s	
	Horse sold	£20	
1888	Horse sold	£16	
	Depreciation in horses	£4	
1889	Dog cart and harness		£31 17s 6d
	Two horses		£48
	Depreciation in horses	£18	
1891	Waggonette		£6
1892	Two horses		£50
1894	Expenditure on horses		£57 12s
1896	Lines open to traffic, new stables, buildings etc.		£333 9s 8d
	Horses		£9
1897	Lines open to traffic, buildings etc.		£63 3s 2d
	Horses		£47
1898	Lines open to traffic, buildings etc.		£45 6s 6d
1899	Working stock		£6 3s 6d
1901	Lines open to traffic, buildings etc., working stock		£90

Occasionally, railway customers would request a reduction in their rates. Ratgoed's request considered on 19 October 1906 was refused. The application made by Aberllefenny coal merchant William Hughes for a reduction, considered on 17 December 1906, brought about Dix's dismissal from the company, for Hughes claimed that he was being overcharged because the manager was also trading in coal. Asked to explain himself, Dix admitted to being a shareholder in the Corris Coal Company; the extent of his participation was not recorded.

Having obtained further information from Dix in January, on 28 May 1907 the directors resolved to dismiss him, paying him £50 in lieu of three months' salary. At the same time they considered the application of J. J. O'Sullivan for the post and appointed him on an annual salary of £250. O'Sullivan had been the manager of the Cork, Blackrock & Passage Railway for 22 years. The delay between the issue being raised and the dismissal/appointment may be accounted for by the need to find a replacement. Hughes's request for a reduction in rates appears to have been overlooked.

Legally, 1908 was a busy year for the company, with three writs being served on it. The first claim, considered in February, was made by Williams, Jones & Company of Corris for the non-payment of invoices rendered for the supply of coal in April and June 1907, totalling £38 13s 1d. The directors, having discovered that Dix was a partner in the company, were reluctant to pay. It is not clear if the Corris Coal Company was a trading name for Williams, Jones or was a different company.

The second claim was Dix's own, considered on 27 April 1908. He wanted £25 for furniture that he said he owned and £7 10s for rent to the end of 1907. The company believed that it owned the furniture and asked for proof to the contrary and responded to Dix's claim for six months' notice to terminate the office tenancy by saying that it had been terminated by his dismissal. It agreed, however, that rent had been paid up until June and the office had been used until October, offering to settle for £5. Dix replied, via his solicitor, that he could substantiate both claims and would settle for £32 10s.

The third claim, discussed on 28 July, was from Roberts, the Dovey bridge reconstruction contractor, seeking £126 for additional items outside the contract. It had been brought in the High Court and sent for arbitration, being heard by Basil Mott on 9 July. He awarded Roberts £83 18s plus costs. 'It was believed that there good grounds for an appeal but in view of the comparatively small amount at stake it was not considered worth the company's while to incur the expenses of further litigation.'

With regards to Williams, Jones's claim, the company had obtained counsel's opinion and had been informed that whilst the company was liable to pay the £38 13s 1d it was entitled to counterclaim in respect of the profit Williams, Jones had made because of Dix's involvement in the business. In December 1908, the directors expected the hearing to take place in January 1909. However, the outcome is not known because no more meetings were to be minuted until 1929.

Dix appeared to have had little rapport with the directors under White's leadership. Even before that, most contact was by letter, but there was a directorial visit to Corris most years and he did occasionally attend board meetings. Despite telling him off occasionally, the pre-White directors would also acknowledge when they thought that he had performed well. He must have worked hard at running the railway for he had no clerical support. His account books and records had been subjected to unannounced auditors' inspections in 1898 and 1906, when everything had been found in order, so financial impropriety was not an issue.

Under White's chairmanship, he was refused leave and a pay rise. Robinson probably never visited Corris, although Dix did sign an illuminated address presented to Robinson and his wife on the occasion of their silver wedding anniversary in 1899. He had apparently been told in 1880 that he could take on external engagements. From a 21st century perspective it would seem that he had a claim for wrongful dismissal.

The company's only legal expenditure in several years was £50 in 1909 which could be the costs element of Roberts's claim, if the award was allocated to maintenance. Both Williams, Jones and Dix succeeded in their claims.

Dix's dismissal coincided with a change in the CR's fortunes. From 1893 until 1903 dividends had been 5% or higher. In 1904, 4% was paid, followed by 1% in 1905. Profits insufficient to pay a dividend were made in 1906-8 but in 1909 a loss was made for the first time. Thereafter minimal profits were made on only three occasions during the remainder of the company's existence. Given the CR debt being carried by Imperial, £4,756 in 1909 rising to £18,216 in 1930, the payment of dividends appears to have been a pointless exercise. It might have been a sop to Imperial shareholders which was no longer required under the White regime. With a degree of unwarranted optimism, Imperial always showed the CR debt as an asset.

The lack of directorial activity from 1909 may be related to Robinson's retirement during the year and his death in New York on 6 November 1910. He was replaced as a director by solicitor Hugh Greenfield Doggett but the managing director role was not continued. Apart from complying with their statutory obligations the directors seem to have given up on the railway.

Fortunately, O'Sullivan's letter book covering the period from 1908 until 1915 survives at the National Archives, giving an understanding of the railway from its manager's perspective.

Before dealing with that, a passenger traffic query of this era needs reviewing. A CR excess fare ticket for a journey made from Corris to Upper Corris on 12 August 1909 was sold on an internet auction site in March 2010. The CR ran no passenger trains to Upper Corris. None of the promotional material seen for the Talyllyn coach services suggests that short journeys might be made. Was the CR charging people to ride, in this case, on the Upper Corris empties? The ticket realised £37.

Returning to O'Sullivan's correspondence, in 1908 he had been keen to negotiate through rates to main line railway destinations. The quarries had been pushing him for reductions but any concession that he made would be insignificant without a contribution from the larger companies. He wrote to the LNWR and the GWR saying that the Cambrian had told him that it could do nothing without their agreement. As an example, he thought the rate from Machynlleth to Birmingham, 8s 9d per ton/108 miles, was biased against his customers when compared with the rates from Porthmadog, 9s 7d/155 miles, or Blaenau Ffestiniog, 8s 9d/119 miles. If the rate was calculated proportionately, then from Machynlleth it would be 7s 11d based on the Porthmadog rate or 6s 8d based on Blaenau Ffestiniog.

He had been told that Ratgoed and Cymerau would be developed if the rates were better and the new owners of Braich Goch, which was closed, wanted better terms. Persisting, he wrote to the Cambrian in September with a petition from the quarry owners, saying that if the Machynlleth rate was improved he was prepared to recommend a single rate, including transhipping at Machynlleth, for all the Corris area quarries, except Llwyngwern. Llwyngwern, being closer to Machynlleth, would not stand being charged a general rate that was appropriate for Corris and Aberllefenny. He proposed that the main line companies tried a 10% rebate for 12 months to encourage the business. It is unlikely that the GWR and the LNWR would want to disturb the status quo and equally likely that the Cambrian would be aware of this and its response to O'Sullivan was to fob him off.

In spite of its recent reconstruction the Dovey bridge still required close observation. Low water in August 1908 revealed that the stone protecting the northern side of the bridge piers was not performing as required, so O'Sullivan had CR personnel reinforce it with rough concrete. In December, scouring around the western sides of the piers occurred after flooding. On this occasion O'Sullivan had stone available for reinforcing as soon as the water level fell, although he thought that more concrete would be required.

Rhiw'r Gwreiddyn was a small slate quarry half a mile south of Esgairgeiliog. Despite that proximity, it was never rail connected, its output being taken to Machynlleth by road. In 1908, O'Sullivan informed Robinson that he had managed to get the traffic by carting the output to Esgairgeiliog, a measure that required double handling. To avoid this he had asked Kerr, Stuart, better known as locomotive builders, about supplying a 'road waggon' capable of carrying a CR wagon between the quarry and the railway. Such a wagon would also be useful at Machynlleth and Corris, he said.

Getting a price of £12, he ordered one, only to be told that the price should be £32. Obtaining quotes for similar vehicles

No 3 passes Aberllefenny loop with a well-laden train in 1939. The pit, the only one on the line, looks as though it has been used as a depository for locomotive ash. *A. E. Rimmer/Author's collection*

from Stagg & Botson, T. C. Aveling and Buck & Hickman, ranging from £28 to £35 3s 8d, he cancelled the order, telling Robinson that as the prices were so similar it was obvious that a mistake had been made and there was no point in trying to enforce the contract. He then obtained a road trolley from the disused Hendre Ddu quarry for £4 10s. He was building a wagon to carry the trolley, he said, and anticipated completing the project for about £12 in total.

Lineside timber at two locations was dealt with in December 1908, with 69 larch trees growing at the foot of an embankment bought for £14 10s to be used as telegraph poles and sleepers. Many of the line's telegraph poles, noted O'Sullivan, were in poor condition. He had also noticed that the site bought by the railway from Long at Pont Ifans in 1900/1 had been included in a plot offered for sale for timber. He had got the auctioneer to withdraw it, requiring Robinson to produce the deeds to support his contention that it was CR land.

The transfer of £1,976 to the capital account under the heading of 'lines open for traffic, buildings etc' in 1908 was no doubt a retrospective allocation in respect of the Dovey bridge reconstruction and the Machynlleth station building, which were not otherwise accounted for.

Some of the railway's money was kept in a bank account in O'Sullivan's name. Writing to Robinson about the accounts in January 1909 he explained: 'The balance shown on this account is in reality the property of the Corris Company though lodged in the bank in my name, and I propose leaving a signed cheque

in my safe so that the account can be transferred at any time without troubling my executors, should I unpreparedly and unfortunately be compelled to take a longer journey than I ever did during my railway career without a return pass.' His precautions were for nought, because in the event of his demise and the bank being aware of it, the cheque should have been refused. The directors obviously thought it was a suspect arrangement for on 2 April O'Sullivan informed Robinson that his account had been closed and a new one opened in the name of the Corris Railway No 2 account.

It was the practice of railway companies to exchange free travel passes for use by senior officers and directors. In February 1909, O'Sullivan informed Robinson that he had received passes from these companies: Cambrian, Brecon & Merthyr, Cheshire Lines Committee, Rhymney, North Wales Narrow Gauge, Bishop's Castle, Vale of Rheidol, Lancashire & Yorkshire, Talyllyn, Festiniog, Cork, Bandon & South Coast, Cork, Blackrock & Passage, Tralee & Dingle, and Great Western. His use of the last was restricted to the route between Aberystwyth and Carmarthen. Courtesy of the Cambrian, CLC and the LYR, he could have reached the English east coast, but he could not travel free to London. To use his Irish passes the Cambrian and GWR would have got him to Carmarthen from where he would have had to make his way to the Cork ferry at his own expense. Similarly, he would have had to pay for the journey across Ireland to reach the Tralee & Dingle Railway.

A fire occurred at Maespoeth shed on 8 May 1909. The carpenter arrived there at 7am and found one of the rafters alight. He managed to extinguish it before help arrived from Corris. It was believed that sparks from the loco that left the shed at 6.10am were responsible. O'Sullivan thought the damage would cost £5 to repair and solicited £2 compensation to replace the carpenter's damaged clothes.

The opportunity of acquiring some little-used rail the same

Beyond the passenger line, the Parliamentary line continued to Aberllefenny quarry. What might be called Ratgoed Junction is here, the tramway taking the left-hand line and passing behind the cottages. The main line continues straight on, to pass in front of them. Notice the single-bladed point, seen in March 1946.
Paul Ingham collection

section as that used on the tramways was taken by O'Sullivan in August 1909. The source was Cambergi quarry, near Aberllefenny and then closed. The railway had no stock and it was available for £2 10s per ton, 'practically old iron price'. The quarry had had a tramway about 4-500 yards long.

O'Sullivan put some effort in to marketing the railway's scenic attractions and commissioned a poster printed in two colours. The issue for Summer 1909, dated June, was illustrated by three engravings based on photographs and a map that highlighted the railway and the Talyllyn coach routes (see p25). The timetable showed connections from locations as far away as London, including both Euston and Paddington stations.

Despite the poster stating boldly, 'no Sunday trains', a Sunday service was started in August 1909. O'Sullivan had persuaded the Cambrian to offer through tickets to Talyllyn, telling Robinson that 'I have succeeded in getting in the thin end of the wedge with regards to Sunday passenger working.' He had obviously not settled in with the community in the way that Dix did. The Machynlleth Free Church Council soon objected, appealing for those responsible 'to reconsider the matter … to refrain from proceeding with a movement which is so utterly at variance with the long-established custom of the neighbourhood, and opposed to the highest interests and truest welfare of its people.'

It is unlikely that the council would have expected O'Sullivan's reply: '… at present I cannot see my way to comply, but if your council can succeed in getting the other companies to discontinue the running of Sunday trains and cheap excursion tickets to other places than Talyllyn lake, the owners of motor omnibuses and horse vehicles etc trading in competition with this company to abandon their services, assist the local quarry owners to increase their output and reopen the quarries now closed, I would be prepared to place the resolution before our managing director (Sir Clifton Robinson) for his favourable consideration. I may add that your aid in this direction would be appreciated, and would prevent the possibility of the line being closed for passenger traffic and only worked for mineral purposes, as the present revenue is only slightly in excess of the working expenses.'

In his covering letter to Robinson, whose name and rank he would regularly drop into his correspondence with others, O'Sullivan referred to the possibility of withdrawing the passenger service. It was a contingency that he hoped was remote but which he would consider if motor bus competition became more severe. He would have to see what savings would be made and if profits could be made on the mineral service at the current levels of income. He had made the comment, he explained, because he was aware that the community had become alert to the inconvenience caused by the closure of the nearby Mawddwy Railway, to passengers in 1901 and for all traffic in 1908; it was soon to be reopened.

He concluded by saying: 'I also had in view our proposed extension to Talyllyn Lake and Abergynolwyn to join with the Talyllyn line to Towyn.' O'Sullivan had promoted the idea of an electric railway linking the neighbouring lines to Robinson in July 1907 but there is no evidence that it was taken seriously; there was certainly no application for powers. The Cambrian was to decline to offer through tickets for Sunday services in subsequent years.

Producing the draft accounts for 1909 in January 1910 and seeing a loss of £210 led O'Sullivan to submit a detailed report to Robinson. Passenger traffic was affected by the weather and 'road motor coach' competition from Barmouth and Aberystwyth to the extent, he estimated, of £100. The local population was declining, leaving many empty properties and affecting local traffic. This also affected goods and parcels receipts as did competition from road carriers.

The slate trade was poor. Braich Goch was still closed, Rhiwgwreiddyn and Era were working in a small way; they could sell all their slate but lack of capital hampered development. Aberllefenny and Ratgoed showed slight increases. Output from Abercorris and Llwyngwern was down, in the latter case due to the bridge that connected the quarry to the railway collapsing. Although total tonnage was reduced by 177 tons, revenue was increased by £15 5s 3d because of the better rates obtained from Rhiwgwreiddyn and Era; their slate travelled a shorter distance.

Part of the Upper Corris branch was re-sleepered, the first time in 25 years that any work had been carried out on it. The Ratgoed Tramway had needed repairs and the main line had required 380 sleepers and fastenings. To economise on traffic expenses he had reduced staffing levels, decreasing wages by £192. On paper but not in fact, the loss was the railway's first.

The locomotives had been allowed to become run down. It had been difficult to keep them going in 1907/8 and although more expenditure had been required it should not be needed again for some time 'if the engines are properly looked after.' Work was done on all three loco boilers by Brush, Falcon's successor, apparently at Loughborough. Repairs on No 1 included a copper patch under the firehole door while they all needed copper stays and brass tubes replacing, and new steel plate in their coal bunkers. The boilers of Nos 2 and 3 were lifted out of their frames and a quantity of bolts replaced.

At Maespoeth extensive repairs were carried out on No 3, including repairing its pony truck, remetalling axle boxes and replacing piston rings and rods, valve spindles and quadrant blocks. Less extensive work was carried out on Nos 1 and 2. A figure of £507 4s 4d had been spent on loco running expenses during the year, compared with £414 7s 5d in 1908. On the capital account, £99 had been allocated to 'working stock', some of which would have been for upgrading a 3rd class compartment to 1st class and building a 'small iron wagon'.

O'Sullivan dealt with a letter from Dix on 2 February 1910, the latter having learned that retired railway officers qualified for privilege (quarter) fare tickets, requested ticket orders for himself and his wife to travel from Rhosneigr (Anglesey) to Afon Wen and Portmadoc on 8 February. O'Sullivan refused the request and informed Robinson: 'I enclose application received from Dix … If he was a retired officer in the ordinary way he would be entitled … I do not consider that he is entitled to any personal favours either from myself or the company.' A similar request to be made a year later was also refused, prompting Dix to request an explanation, but there is no record of any response.

The idea that Dix thought he should be treated as a retired officer raises questions about the way his dismissal was carried out. Robinson had been 'requested to formally dismiss Mr Dix', but on 1 July 1907 reported that he had sent his representative, accompanied by O'Sullivan, to take charge of Dix's records. In 1907 Dix was 58 years old; was he led to think that he had been compulsorily retired rather than dismissed? If Cozens' account (see Bibliography) was dependent on folk memory, as seems likely, then there was no recollection around the railway of Dix being dismissed when he was researching in the 1940s.

To deal with road competition for passengers O'Sullivan decided to run an extra train in connection with an extra on the Cambrian, writing to the Board of Trade on 21 February 1910 that he wished to divide the line into two sections, splitting it at Corris. He would then work the Machynlleth–Corris section

with the staff and telephone. Deputed to deal with the request, Colonel E. Druitt minuted that he could not understand it; whether O'Sullivan wanted to run one train after another combining staff and ticket working with absolute block and using the telephone instead of the block telegraph, or merely wanted to cross trains at Corris. It would be best if O'Sullivan met him with plans of the signalling arrangements or else Druitt would 'go over the line with him.'

The meeting took place in London on 2 April (a Saturday) and Druitt agreed to O'Sullivan's proposal. The line was already worked in two sections, Machynlleth–Corris and Corris–Aberllefenny. The first had a red staff with Annett's keys for Llwyngwern and Esgairgeiliog sidings and the key for the Maespoeth cabin, which was kept locked and the signals not used. The second had a blue staff with Annett's keys for Fronwen and Mathews Mill sidings, and the loop at Aberllefenny.

With Druitt's approval, the CR's operating rules were amended, dividing the line into three sections: Machynlleth–Maespoeth Junction; Maespoeth Junction–Corris, and Corris–Aberllefenny. The signals at Maespoeth and the Maespoeth Junction–Corris staff were not to be used and the key for the cabin was attached to the Machynlleth–Maespoeth Junction staff. Rules dealing with the train staff and signalling by telephone were added.

Maximum loadings were now defined for a single locomotive: four carriages and a van, and for two engines coupled together: eight carriages and a van. The rule about train working, 'the number of coaches to be decreased as the traffic gets light daily, and when possible one coach only to be worked without the van' was maintained.

The working timetables for 1909/10 show the locomotive leaving Maespoeth at 5.20am and the departure of the first train from Corris to Machynlleth at 5.35am. Trains were shown as 'mixed', 'pass' and 'G&P', the last without explanation, possibly passenger trains carrying merchandise. In 1910, the 9.5am and the 2.15pm from Machynlleth to Aberllefenny and the 8pm from Aberllefenny to Corris were indicated thus. Only the 5.35am and its return from Machynlleth to Aberllefenny was timetabled to run mixed. The service was arranged so that it could be worked by a single locomotive.

O'Sullivan told Robinson that the new arrangement meant that he could run more trains, or specials, when required. In addition to the extra train being run on the Cambrian, a motor

tour to Dolgelley was to be operated that the GWR was expected to promote in Bala, Corwen and Llangollen.

It was clearly time to modernise the Talyllyn coach service with modern motor coaches. He told the Cambrian's agent that the distance from Corris to Dolgelley was 12 miles: 'I think with a good coach we could do it in an hour.'

He was right to be cautious about the motor vehicles. Bristol could not supply him. A London company had its vehicles on hire to the War Office and could not make one available until 17 August 1910. A Sheffield company refused to make an agreement because it though it would not be paid if the weather was poor and the service unprofitable. For this year, O'Sullivan had to continue using horses.

In June 1910 he had sold a mare for £4 10s; she was five years old when purchased in 1892. He did not propose to buy any more horses if he could get charabancs. A horse called Captain was to be sold for £9 in January 1911; he had a cataract in one eye and O'Sullivan thought that he would sell the horse before his other eye was similarly afflicted.

At 31 December 1910 the CR owned the following road vehicles: 2 charabancs; 4 waggonettes, 1 dog cart; 2 brakes; 1 landau; 1 cart and 1 road trolley. It also owned 11 horses. In addition to the rolling stock that featured in the statutory returns, the railway owned three platelayers' trolleys. How the charabancs listed here, in O'Sullivan's annual return, fitted in with those he was trying to hire earlier in the year is not understood.

The slate traffic showed no improvement. Braich Goch was still not at work and in July 1910 the lessee at Llwyngwern went bankrupt owing the CR £5 1s 9d for one month's traffic. O'Sullivan told Robinson that he held five wagons and a slab truck as security, they were in fair condition and worth considerably more than the debt.

On 31 March 1911, O'Sullivan thought that he would try his luck with securing a royal visit to the CR with a letter to Lord Herbert Vane-Tempest. Following the forthcoming investiture of the Prince of Wales at Carnarvon on 13 July the King and Queen were to be his lordship's guests at Plas Machynlleth for the weekend. Offering to lay on a special train, O'Sullivan wrote: 'I am building a nice new carriage, and would push on its completion, so as to have it ready ... I could take them up to Corris or Aberllefenny and back in about an hour and a half, and would not object to doing it after church on Sunday if you thought well of it.' He also offered the use of two new motor charabancs if required. Lord Herbert obviously did not 'think well of it' although the royal party was to partake of a motor drive to Corris and Talyllyn, returning via Towyn and Aberdovey.

The new charabancs were those to be hired from, and newly built by, the Bristol Tramways & Carriage Company for the summer season. O'Sullivan's user-requirement was quite demanding: seating capacity 20 minimum, speed 19mph, capable of climbing gradients of 1 in 7 to 1 in 14 and with sufficient brake power to park on those gradients. The 'new' carriage was probably the first to be rebuilt with a clerestory roof.

In the years until the outbreak of the war, O'Sullivan put a lot of effort into promoting the road services and the company reaped some rewards from them. 'So far, the motor coaches are a complete success' he informed White on 13 September 1911. In addition to the Talyllyn service, circular tours were run in conjunction with the Cambrian and the GWR, with the CR's charabancs making the link between Corris and Dolgelley, and excursions were run from Aberystwyth.

The vehicles used were usually new 22-seat charabancs that travelled to Wales by rail. To get an operating licence from Aberystwyth Corporation he had to resort to subterfuge because the council would not give him a licence as the manager of the Corris Railway. He therefore applied in his own name as a resident of that town. Garages were rented in Dolgelley from 1912 and in Aberystwyth from 1913.

In 1913, two charabancs were driven to Wales for use on the Corris/Dolgelley services. To the £52 18s 11d profit they made, O'Sullivan added £58 railway revenue. Aberystwyth services made a profit of £236 17s 3d. O'Sullivan's table (below) contains more information for 1913.

With two exceptions, all of O'Sullivan's correspondence with Bristol from 1911–15 dealt with the guide book or the road services. The exceptions were an attempt to persuade White to join a consortium investing in the quarries, on 10 August 1912 and a brief note on 11 January 1913 commenting on the reopening of Abercwmeiddew, and reviewing the state of the quarries. The last letter, dated 15 September 1915, dealt with the termination of arrangements for renting a garage at the Waterloo Hydro Hotel in Aberystwyth because the vehicles had been commandeered for the war effort.

O'Sullivan's attempts to expand the CR's tourist market in December 1911 had brought him up against intra-railway politics. He had visited Charles L. Conacher, the Cambrian's traffic manager, hoping to secure that company's participation in a tourist brochure. Conacher made clear his opinion that the Cambrian already produced an adequate supply of such literature and that the CR's efforts were resented. The Cambrian also objected to the prospect of the CR issuing tourist tickets to Corris from other parts of the country; O'Sullivan realised that the other companies would not support the idea either. The CR had been publishing guidebooks since the mid-1890s and was to publish another during 1912.

Reviewing the period from Dix's dismissal in 1907, it appears that O'Sullivan could have done more to reduce costs, at least by reducing train mileage. Although the number of passengers carried fell by 4,000 in 1907, passenger train mileage increased by nearly 10,000 miles. In 1898, the railway's best year, 14,300

miles were run to carry 83,044 passengers. In contrast, 25,718 miles were operated to carry 60,164 passengers in 1908, O'Sullivan's best year. Goods train mileage, on the other hand, did reflect the traffic more accurately. When mineral traffic fell to a third of what it had been in 1905/6 the mileage was halved and remained at that level.

During the war the CR saw little change. Unlike the main line companies it was not taken over by the government and the requisitioning of the motor vehicles forced those who wanted to travel to use the trains. In 1915, the 38,229 passengers carried were just over 10,000 less than in 1913, while 4,668 tons of slate carried represented a reduction of 2,312 tons compared with 1913. By 1920, losses had risen to £4,208.

On 22 June 1917, F. H. Withers, now company secretary, asked the Board of Trade for permission to cut out some of the statistical minutiae from the annual reports, citing the need to save labour and paper. 'The cost of issuing such elaborate accounts is out of all proportion in the case of a railway with a total revenue of less than £2,000 for the year.' And for a company with only one shareholder, he might have added. He received the approval he needed after a civil servant had recommended: 'This unimportant, uncontrolled, narrow gauge railway may probably be allowed ...'

Two deaths in 1916/7 brought changes to the CR's management and direction. First, Sir George White died on 22 November 1916 and was replaced by his son, Sir George Stanley White, the second baronet, as a director, and by Samuel White as chairman. As a mark of mourning, the Bristol office used letterheads printed with black borders.

Then O'Sullivan died on 20 April 1917, aged 68. His responsibilities as manager were taken on by Withers. The records are incomplete for these years; the most likely sequence of events was that Godfray resigned earlier in 1917, leading to Verdon Smith's election to the board and Withers' appointment as secretary. Godfray had probably resigned because of ill health; he was to die after an operation on 21 May 1918. Previously, Doggett had died in the spring of 1915 and been replaced by James Henry Howell.

In Corris, Withers' agent was a D. Thomas, appointed principal clerk. This arrangement lasted until March 1921 when D. J. McCourt was appointed manager.

In contrast to the experiences of other railways, the CR's post-war passenger traffic came back to its 1910 levels, around 50,000 passengers. There was more variation in goods traffic, but it was to be 1927 before it fell below 6,000 tons, the level of 1912. The fare increases imposed on railways in 1917 were responsible for fare revenues increasing by around £400 annually but, of course, inflation had increased costs. Mileage, though, started off at 15,150, 5,000 less than in 1913, but steadily rose, with only two exceptions, to 22,457 by 1929.

The fall in slate traffic, 1,000 tons less in 1926 than in 1925, and then another 1,000 tons less in 1927, apparently followed an attempt to raise the rates. Braich Goch responded by buying a steam lorry to transport its output to Machynlleth. The Upper Corris branch consequently fell out of use in July 1927.

The CR's loss carried forward into 1922 was increased by

Vehicle	Route	Miles	Receipts	Passengers	Receipts per passenger	Receipts per mile
AE 2767	Aberystwyth, several routes	6,024	£622 5s 7d	7,515	19.8	24.7
AE 2553	Corris, Dolgellau	1,767				
AE 3180	Talyllyn, Abergynolwyn	2,154	£430 13s 5d	4,596	22.5	19.3
AE 3184	Talyllyn, Abergynolwyn	1,363				
AE 3184	Aberystwyth	289	£289 8s	271	21.9	20.5

£1,703, mostly a consequence of the purchase of a new locomotive, an 0-4-2ST obtained from Kerr, Stuart, delivered in June. The accumulated losses had reached £6,830, subsidised by Imperial. There was also an overdraft; £536 in 1922. Imperial showed the debt at £12,773.

The possibility of a change in the CR's control was first considered in January 1924. It appears that Verdon Smith, acting for Imperial, had approached the GWR and offered to sell the CR for £10,000. In return, Imperial would undertake to cease to run road services in Wales. The GWR inspected the line and found it, permanent way and rolling stock, in good order. Observing that the railway had powers to run road services, it noted that it owned two 32-seat charabancs and a six-seat motor waggonette, eight horse-drawn vehicles, two horse-drawn goods vehicles, and five horses. More information about the company's financial position was required to establish the value of an offer. This point was repeated at the end of the year, but nothing came of the proposal.

In July 1928, the CR and GWR entered into a non-compete agreement, whereby the times of the CR's omnibus service between Aberystwyth and Machynlleth would not conflict with those of the GWR, and both companies agreed not to undercut each other's fares.

The relationship became much closer after the GWR was approached by the accountant Sir William McLintock Bt with a proposal that it acquire the late Sir George White's controlling interest in the Bristol Tramways & Carriage Company early in 1929. In addition to owning the Bristol tramways the company also operated an extensive bus network in competition with the GWR and the London, Midland & Scottish Railway. On offer was 53% of the voting capital, 72% of the issued capital, held by White's trustees. An intriguing aside revealed that while the company had been paying 7% dividend for several years it also had considerable undeclared profits, which affected its valuation. McLintock's successors are part of today's KPMG financial services group.

At a meeting with McLintock on 4 February 1929, the GWR's assistant general manager John Milne made it quite clear that his company was not interested in the CR 'at any price'. By the end of the meeting he had agreed to recommend the purchase of the CR for £1,000 in conjunction with the purchase of the Bristol shares. This position was confirmed formally on 22 February.

Meeting on 6 February, Sir Felix Pole, the GWR's general manager, and McLintock agreed that the GWR would take over the CR from 1 March 1929 and that Imperial would discharge the CR's liabilities when the purchase was completed.

The first CR directors' meeting recorded since 1909 that took place on 27 February 1929 was undoubtedly a response to this proposal. On that occasion, Imperial's £15,000 ordinary CR stock was transferred from nominees to the company itself. An unexplained transfer of CR debentures made on the same occasion probably had the same outcome. For this meeting, Verdon Smith was chairman and his co-directors were Sir George Stanley White and Sydney E. Smith. Samuel White had died on 29 November 1928 at the age of 67. The fourth director listed in the 1928 annual report was Sidney E. Baker, a solicitor.

Although no money had changed hands and much needed to be done to put the takeover into effect, McLintock was anxious to complete the transaction, saying that the GWR had been effectively in control of the CR and responsible for its expenses since 1 March. The GWR, of course, could not take over a railway without the approval of Parliament, but it could make an investment, so on 18 July 1929 it agreed that the purchase money would buy the shares and the debentures rather than the railway. The records do not reveal the circumstances of Imperial

agreeing to advance £600, to be refunded by the GWR, so the CR could be kept going from 5 April.

The takeover strategy was in place by 17 September 1929. With the four Imperial directors remaining in office for the time being, and retaining their qualifying shareholdings, £13,000 ordinary stock would be transferred to the GWR on payment of £808 6s 5d. The transaction was itemised thus:

£15,000 ordinary stock	£7 6s 5d
£5,000 debenture stock	£200 0s 0d
Repayment of advance made by Imperial to the CR on 5 April 1929	£600 0s 0d
Remainder of debt due to Imperial by CR	£1 0s 0d
Total	£808 6s 5d

To reach this valuation, McLintock had actually worked backwards, starting by taking the value of stocks and stores, £1,100 15s 6d, adding the amounts due to the CR (£576 12s 2d) to the agreed purchase price of £1,000, and subtracting the current liabilities of £2,369 1s 3d, giving £208 6s 5d. He then suggested how it should be allocated. With the nominal payment of £1 to Imperial, the CR's accumulated losses of £15,844 7s 4d would be written off.

The stocks were transferred to Sir S. Ernest Palmer, a GWR director, and F. R. E. Davis, the GWR's company secretary, jointly as nominees of the GWR. The GWR's cheques were posted to McLintock on 19 November 1929, and Imperial's receipt for the reimbursement of the advance and its statement assigning the debt were issued the next day. The transfers of £13,000 ordinary stock and £5,000 debentures to the GWR were registered by the CR directors on 26 November 1929.

The first recorded GWR involvement with CR operational matters occurred on 19 December 1929, when the GWR's locomotive committee agreed to the reconditioning of CR No 3, 'the cost of the work to be borne by the CR company.' This arrangement was not mentioned in the correspondence dealing with the sale. No 3's loco history sheet shows that it had been at Swindon since 28 November and was returned to work on 22 April 1930, the overhaul being costed at £512. The loco's boiler history shows that since 1926 it had used a boiler built for No 1 in 1914; the GWR put it back to work with second-hand tubes.

The Great Western Railway Act of 1930 received royal assent on 4 June that year. In addition to authorising the transfer and the vesting of the CR in the GWR, it also ruled that CR officers would not become officers of the GWR and that the CR company would discharge any obligations due to them.

John Milne, now the GWR's general manager, wrote to his heads of departments on 11 July 1930 instructing them to 'take the necessary steps to bring this undertaking within the organisation …' and informing them that it had been agreed that the services of McCourt, the CR's manager, 'should be dispensed with' and that ganger Thomas Griffiths and porter J. Jones would be retired before the GWR took over.

The last recorded business of the CR directors had taken place on 13 March, when the last general meeting had been held, the only one recorded in the minute book. At the end of June, a GWR officer collected the CR's deeds from Bristol.

Regarding McCourt, little seems to be known about him; an Irishman, he lived in Machynlleth whilst running the CR; what he did subsequently is unknown. Whilst his dismissal on the GWR takeover may appear harsh, it might be that he had another job to go to, perhaps with Imperial or Bristol. The list of insurances in force when the GWR took over, incidentally, included one for a motor car that he had used.

In the short term, the GWR made a loss on the Bristol purchase. Not wishing to own more than 50% of the company, it sold the surplus shares over three months from April 1930 at prices several shillings less than the £1 10s it had paid. At the end of the year, though, it was to receive a 10% dividend on its holding.

On reflection, Imperial had been good to the CR. Given the same results it could not have maintained its losses had it been dependent on the goodwill of a group of ordinary shareholders. It was sufficiently well equipped for the services it offered and the paucity of tales about derailments or breakdowns, despite the on-going battle to replace sleepers, suggest that maintenance was more than adequate. There was one consistency through the Imperial years that dated to the CR's earliest days – the auditor's report on the company's final accounts was signed, just as all those preceding it, by J. Fraser, the practice started by James Fraser, the only individual to be involved with the original CMRDT and the Imperial era.

The CR was deemed to be included in the GWR from 4 August 1930, the date its account with the National Provincial Bank at Machynlleth was closed and its balance paid to the GWR's account with Lloyds Bank at Oswestry. For administrative purposes it was placed within the GWR's Central Wales division, which also had responsibility for the Vale of Rheidol Light Railway and the Welshpool & Llanfair Light Railway.

Notwithstanding the earlier expenditure on No 3, 4 August 1930 was also the date that it and the Kerr, Stuart were taken into GWR stock as Nos 3 and 4. The latter had probably been unnumbered previously. A local scrapman disposed of Nos 1 and 2 at Maespoeth.

In the meantime, on 24 July 1930, the GWR's engineers' department had recommend £2,000 be spent on general repairs to the CR. What was done was not recorded. Later, on 27 November 1930, the traffic committee resolved that the CR's passenger service should be withdrawn from 1 January 1931. There was no explanation for this decision but the massive fall in passenger numbers and revenue in 1930 (19,502/£390) compared with 1929 (52,455/£1,080) must have been relevant, as was the introduction of the GWR's competing road service. The possibility of the 1930 figures being for a part year cannot be ruled out.

Notwithstanding No 3's visit to Swindon it was not given any of those features traditionally associated with that place, brass numberplates or safety valve bonnet, for example, and in that way the Corris locomotive fleet, such as it was, was treated differently from the remainder of the GWR stock. The carriages built by Metropolitan in 1898, Nos 7 and 8, were sold into non-railway use at Gobowen and the remainder were condemned at Swindon on 22 December 1930.

Corris Railway carriages absorbed into GWR stock

Corris No	GWR No	Type
1	6215	Composite
2	4993	3rd
4	6216	Composite
5	4991	3rd
7	6217	Composite
8	4992	Composite

At a meeting of the GWR's law, parliamentary and estate committee held on 12 February 1931, it was agreed to buy the freeholds of two plots at Corris previously leased from the Marquis of Londonderry. The purchase, for £420, included the

right to take water which had previously cost £1 annually.

Under the new regime, the GWR's stationmaster at Machynlleth oversaw the CR's day-to-day operation. It must have looked very neglected on 15 July 1931, when a visiting enthusiast wrote a postcard home wondering if it had been closed completely. Although the CR traffic and revenue data was no longer required to be separately accounted for and published, the Corris Railway Society was, with support from WLLR members, able to obtain records from the Cambrian's Oswestry headquarters before it was closed in the 1960s.

There were only three quarries using the railway, Aberllefenny, Ratgoed and Cymerau, the first supplying most of the traffic, 2,219 out of 2,442 tons in 1934. It was owned by A. Hamilton Pryce, whose father had objected to the CR carrying passengers in 1879. The GWR reduced the rate from 5s 5d per ton to 3s 9d and then to 3s 3d, initially linked to an obligation to ship a minimum of 36 tons per week. There was still a small amount of coal and merchandise traffic to be had but the greatest issue was road competition.

A Caernarvon-based wholesaler who took 20 tons per week from Aberllefenny had a same-day service when he sent a lorry to collect and deliver it. The best the railways could do, in a co-ordinated attempt to get the traffic in 1936, was three days. Thanks to the intransigence of the quarry employees who undertook the transhipment at Machynlleth, some 36 hours of the journey were spent within 10 miles of the quarry.

In 1935, Pryce had sold a seven-year lease on Aberllefenny to Henry Haydn Jones, the local MP and owner of the Bryn Eglwys quarries and the Talyllyn Railway. Edward Thomas, Jones's manager, told the GWR that the CR rate should be minimal or even eliminated if it meant that the traffic was secured for rail throughout, but to no avail. Nevertheless, the CR remained in business and even increased its traffic in 1940 and 1941, carrying slate to repair bomb-damaged properties. Then the government decided that repairs should be deferred until the war ended and that was the beginning of the end for the CR. Until then, the only noticeable way that it had been affected by the war had been in 1941, when the Upper Corris branch had been lifted for scrap.

With 1,000 tons lost in 1942 and again in 1943, when it just scraped over 2,000 tons, operations were reduced to just three days a week in October 1943. A strike in 1947 brought about the loss of the Aberllefenny traffic, the GWR being deterred from closure by the Machynlleth stationmaster assuring Paddington that prospects would be good when the quarry reopened.

It was perhaps fortunate that the locomotives were not too taxed by the work expected of them and they rarely troubled their owners, for if there had been a catastrophic failure the railway's future would have been at risk. It was 25 June 1940 before No 4 required sufficient attention to warrant a visit to Swindon, where an intermediate overhaul took 71 days. Earlier, light repairs had been carried out on it over a 45-day period from 19 August 1930.

No 3 was returned to Swindon for an intermediate repair taking 49 days on 17 September 1942, the last time that any Corris loco made the journey to Wiltshire. Subsequently, work was carried out at Machynlleth, on No 4 from 4 December 1944, 93 days, No 3 from 3 July 1945, 22 days, and No 4 again from 9 December 1947, 43 days. After less than four months back in traffic it was taken out of service on 6 May 1948.

Whether the work carried out at Machynlleth was undertaken on Corris metals or whether the locos were put on a wagon and taken over to the standard gauge shed is not known. Taking the number of days out of traffic in the GWR era, No 3 (216 days

Right: **After the Corris Railway was closed, the locos were stored at Machynlleth until they were sold to the Talyllyn Railway in 1951. They were photographed on the TR's wharf on 21 April that year.** *Hugh Ballantyne*

Below: **Maespoeth shed in 1955, when it was occupied by the Forestry Commission.** *Robert Darlaston*

against No 4's 252 days) seems to have benefitted from its initial trip to Swindon but it might not have been used as much as No 4. The mileage recorded for No 3, 64,341 miles, is unlikely to be that worked since 1878. Since 1930 it represents just 3,500 miles annually. The 198,566 miles recorded for No 4 could easily be its mileage since new, 7,354 annually, twice as much as No 3. If No 4's recorded mileage was accrued only since 1930, then it averaged 11,031 miles annually, three times that of No 3. Either way it is no wonder that it required more time out of traffic and failed to see the end of the Corris service.

In the end, though, it was the weather that did for the CR. Heavy rain during August 1948 aggravated the scour near the Dovey bridge, leading to a decision to stable No 3 at Machynlleth in case the bridge was damaged. The out-of-service No 4 had been moved there in July. Following more rain, the service was suspended after 20 August.

The newly-formed Railway Executive proposed to close the line between Machynlleth and Aberllefenny, requesting the approval of the British Transport Commission on 29 September 1948. The flooding had caused erosion to within 3in of the rails. Keeping the line open would require expenditure of £2,000 to repair the erosion plus £5,400 to renew three other bridges.

Revenue in 1947 had been £252 (907 tons) against expenditure of £2,939. The traffic would be worked by road to Machynlleth at an estimated cost of £120 annually. Allowing for some unspecified civil engineering maintenance and renewals required before the closure process was completed, there would be a net annual saving of £2,204 if the line was closed. The net cost of recovery of permanent way, equipment and rolling stock was estimated at £1,441.

Regarding the Ratgoed Tramway, worked by 'gravitation and horse', it was the only means of access to the quarries that it served. If the executive continued to work it, annual maintenance and renewals would cost £380 against revenue of £27. It was proposed to make an arrangement with the quarry owners for them to operate and maintain it until the legal implications of abandonment had been considered, and then to sell it to them if practicable.

The commission approved both the closure and the Ratgoed recommendation when it met on 28 October 1948. Earlier, having read of the CR's closure in the 3 September issue of *Railway Gazette*, the Ministry of Transport had written to ask for confirmation, as it 'might be possible to carry out certain improvements to the trunk road by the use of the railway land.'

The track had been lifted between Aberllefenny and Corris when the 1948 Ordnance Survey was made although Boyd *(see* Bibliography) stated that demolition was not started until 16 November 1948. In 1949, 10 tons of rail were sold to the Talyllyn Railway. Boyd further stated that demolition was completed during 1951. The stationmaster at Machynlleth is said to have turned a blind-eye to instructions to send the locomotives to Swindon for scrapping, they were condemned on 25 October 1948, and kept them covered up until they were sold to the Talyllyn Railway on 1 March 1951.

On 28 March 1952, the Railway Executive asked the BTC to approve the Ratgoed Tramway's closure. Revenue in 1951 had been £2 11s 4d, of which £1 2s had been for transporting the machinery from the recently closed Ratgoed quarry. The quarry's owner had no further use for the line and did not wish to

Left: **The Aberllefenny quarry tramway continued in use until the 1980s, a tractor providing haulage to the Aberllefenny slate mills. This was the scene on 5 September 1962.** *J. N. White/Ian Allan Library*

Below: **The construction of a new Kerr, Stuart 'Tattoo' 0-4-2ST pays homage to the last locomotive supplied to the Corris Railway and serves as an illustration of the railway's achievements since its revival was started. Completed in 2005, No 7 was photographed at Maespoeth on 11 April 2009.** *Author*

buy it. There had been no objections to the closure proposals. Annual savings on permanent way repairs were estimated at £30 and recovery of track materials was expected to yield a surplus of £275. Approval to the closure was given on 8 April 1952.

Even without the damaged bridge, the CR would still have been an early candidate for closure. Milne's initial reaction, 'not at any price', was surely the right one for the GWR. It is unlikely to have recouped the CR's minimal purchase price and certainly would not have recouped its expenditure on No 3 authorised in 1929 and the £2,000 spent on the track in 1930. As it was, the CR carried on playing a useful role for the communities and quarries in the Dulas Valley, albeit one that was increasingly usurped by road transport, for the best part of another 20 years.

Had it lasted another 10 years or so, the CR would have been a good candidate for preservation on closure. In the event, it was 1966 before a society was formed, initially to record the railway's history. A museum was established in the former

parcels office in Corris in 1970 and subsequently expanded into the adjoining former stable. Plans for reviving the railway with a 2½-mile line from Corris to the Forestry Commission picnic site at Tan y Coed, near Esgairgeiliog, were drawn up in 1981, when the former loco shed at Maespoeth was acquired. Fulfilment of the society's ambitions has been a long process. A passenger service between Corris and Maespoeth was started on 3 June 2002 and a new example of the CR's Kerr, Stuart locomotive entered service in 2005. Elsewhere, the Machynlleth station building survives in commercial use and sections of abandoned trackbed are still to be seen, especially between Corris and Aberllefenny. The last two locomotives were popular additions to the Talyllyn Railway fleet and were joined by a brake van and several wagons sold by BR. The TR also acquired one of the carriage bodies sold by the GWR in 1930 and restored it to service in 1961. The remains of the second are on display in the CR museum.

2

Vale of Rheidol Light Railway

Without the main line railway, Aberystwyth would have been a typical Welsh west-coast market town with a small harbour. Even on modern roads, the 75 miles to Shrewsbury or Swansea will take the better part of two hours. The opening of the Aberystwyth & Welsh Coast Railway in 1864 brought access to markets that were not dependent on droving or the tides. It also brought tourists and its existence must have contributed to the decision to found University College Wales there in 1872.

Located at the confluence of the Ystwyth and Rheidol rivers, evidence of human activity dating to the Mesolithic and the bronze and iron ages has been found in the area. Edward I's castle, built in 1277, was attacked by Parliamentarian troops in 1649, its remains a local landmark. Victorian hotels were joined by a cliff lift on Constitution Hill, to the north of the town, in 1896.

Inland, before lowland slopes become hills and mountains, the land is agricultural, predominately for grazing sheep and cattle. Through it, heading eastwards, the Rheidol strikes a winding course, the valley closing in about seven miles from the coast. In the upper valley the area is littered with defunct mine workings, lead, zinc and copper amongst them, but, unlike many similar locations in Wales, no slate.

Additions to the landscape in the 20th century were the Rheidol hydro-electric power station, opened in 1964 and the largest hydro station in Wales, and the planting of many of the upper slopes with conifers.

At the head of the valley, the Rheidol is joined by the Mynach which, over thousands of years, created the spectacular 300ft waterfall at Pontarfynach – Devil's Bridge. To this natural phenomena had been added the man-made spectacle of three bridges crossing the Mynach Gorge, one above the other. The origins of the oldest, lowest, bridge are unknown; it might have been built by the monks at the nearby Strata Florida abbey in the 11th century. The second, middle, bridge was built in 1708, and the former Cardiganshire County Council built the third in 1901. Legend has it that the first bridge was impossible for man to build so therefore the devil had built it.

A network of minor roads meeting in the locality, the output from the Cwm Rheidol lead mine, the largest and most productive in the area, and the needs of the Hafod estate, the principal landowner in the region, combined to make Devil's Bridge a focal point for transport. There was only a small, widespread, community.

Tourism was established early in the 19th century and a notable visitor, the poet William Wordsworth, was inspired to compose a sonnet about the experience in 1824. The Hafod estate's Devil's Bridge hunting lodge became a popular hotel during the second half of the century.

Meeting in London in February 1895, the Royal Commission on Land in Wales and Monmouthshire heard evidence in favour of local authorities to participate in the promotion of light railways to improve access to rural areas. H. Enfield Taylor of Chester reeled off a long list of places that he thought would benefit, including 'from Aberystwyth, up the valley of the Rheidol, to the foot of the falls at the Devil's

Bridge, with a lift for passengers and goods to the summit, and a branch to the great mining district centring on Goginau'. The last, now known as Goginan, has many disused mines in its vicinity.

It may be that this comment triggered the development of what became the Vale of Rheidol Light Railway, but there had been earlier schemes proposed for serving the area. The Manchester & Milford Haven Railway branch from near Devil's Bridge to Aberystwyth was the first known, in 1845. In development proposals for what became the Manchester & Milford Railway were very fluid; it obtained powers for a branch to Aberystwyth from Devil's Bridge in 1861 which was abandoned within two years, and then obtained powers for a branch to Devil's Bridge from Crosswood in 1873. These schemes were for standard gauge lines.

The intention to deposit a bill for the Vale of Rheidol Railway was announced on 24 November 1896. The impetus came from mine owners, the Hafod estate, some farmers, and others who were interested in the development of Aberystwyth generally.

Two 2ft gauge railways were proposed; No 1 from the north-eastern corner of enclosure No 72 abutting Smithfield Road in Aberystwyth and terminating at the eastern boundary of enclosure No 98 in the parish of Upper Llanfihangel y Creuddyn, Devil's Bridge. Railway No 2 commenced at the southern end of the quay of Aberystwyth harbour and terminated at a junction with railway No 1 at the north-western corner of enclosure No 73.

'It is intended', stated the notice, 'to work the aforesaid railway as a light railway and to apply the provisions ... of the Regulation of Railways Act 1868 ... as to the crossing of roads on the level, limiting the speed of engines, and otherwise in such manner as the bill may prescribe.'

In opting to take advantage of the 1868 legislation the promoters were being overtaken by events, for, from January 1897 they could have used the 1896 Light Railways Act to obtain a Light Railway Order to achieve the same purpose. The legislation was an attempt to overcome the 'one size fits all' approach to railway regulation that had been applied to British railways since the Railway Clauses Consolidation Act had been enacted in 1845. Applying the same conditions to any railway, whether it be a high-speed main line or a country byway had the effect of discouraging development in remote rural areas due to the costs imposed. The 1868 act empowered the Board of Trade to issue a licence authorising the construction and operation of a railway as a light railway providing axle loads did not exceed eight tons and speed did not exceed 25mph.

The Board of Trade remained reluctant to relax the 1845 standards, however, and little use was made of the 1868 legislation. One of the issues remained the expense of obtaining compulsory purchase powers despite attempts to reduce costs by introducing simplified procedures in 1864 and 1870.

The 1896 act was introduced to address these issues and to permit local authorities to be involved financially in the promotion and operation of light railways. The Board of Trade was partially bypassed by the establishment of the Light Railway

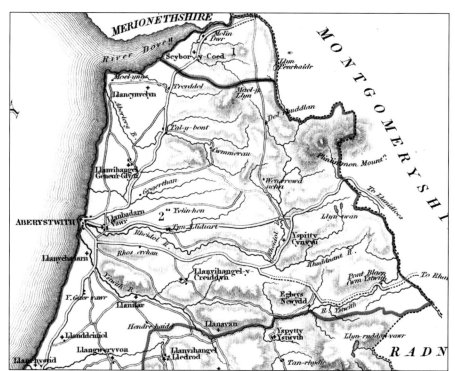

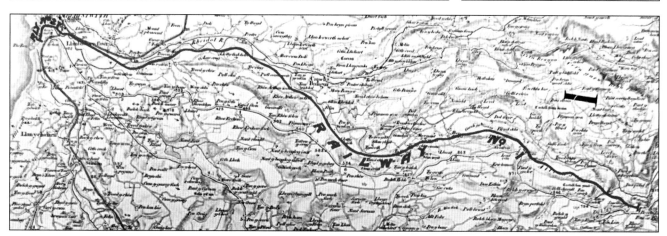

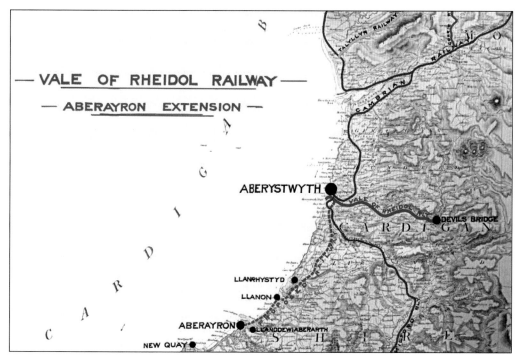

Right: **The first train to Devil's Bridge, on 5 November 1902.** *Author's collection*

Below: **The VRLR gradient profile.** *National Archives*

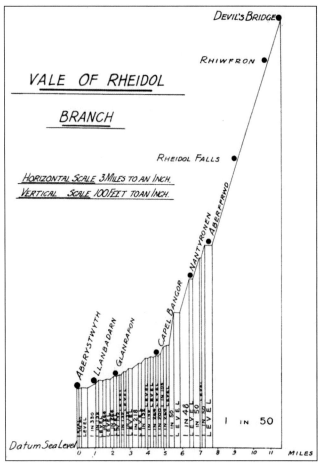

DEVIL'S BRIDGE

RHIWFRON

VALE OF RHEIDOL

BRANCH

RHEIDOL FALLS

HORIZONTAL SCALE 3 MILES TO AN INCH.
VERTICAL SCALE 100 FEET TO AN INCH.

ABERFFRWD

NANTYRONEN

CAPEL BANGOR

ABERYSTWYTH
LLANBADARN
GLANRAFON

1 IN 50

Datum Sea Level

0 1 2 3 4 5 6 7 8 9 10 11 MILES

Commission whose members were appointed by the president of the Board of Trade. The commissioners would assess the merits of an application and, if it warranted, submit an order to the Board of Trade for confirmation. When confirmed, an order had the same status as if enacted in Parliament.

There were no direct objections to the 1896 Vale of Rheidol bill, but there was a problem with the route proposed for the harbour branch crossing the foreshore at Aberystwyth. The Board of Trade exercised powers given to it by the Preliminary Inquiries Act of 1851 and the Harbours Transfers Act of 1862, and appointed vice-admiral Sir George Strong Nates KBC, FRS to inquire into the likely effects on navigation. The result was a requirement to have the construction details approved by the Board of Trade and permitting the route's deviation to the north of the authorised route to skirt the land at the high water mark.

The act received royal assent on 6 August 1897 and the Vale of Rheidol (Light) Railway Company was incorporated. The gauge could be increased up to 4ft 8½in at any time with the prior approval of the Board of Trade. The capital was £39,000. Three bridges over public roads were sanctioned, at Llanbadarn, Nantyronen and Aberffrwd. Three years were allowed to exercise the compulsory purchase provisions and five years for construction. The promoters were John Francis, Walter Taylor and Hugh Lowe.

The engineers were James Weeks Szlumper and William Weeks Szlumper; half-brothers with Polish ancestry, they had signed the estimate for £32,000. The surveyor of Cardiganshire since 1853, J. W. Szlumper had houses in Aberystwyth and Kew, had been knighted when elected mayor of Richmond in 1894, and had been appointed sheriff of Cardiganshire in 1898. He had been assistant engineer on the Manchester & Milford Railway in 1859, becoming engineer in 1861. He had previous experience with narrow gauge railways, having been engineer to the North Wales Narrow Gauge Railways since 1891 and the Lynton & Barnstaple Railway since 1895.

Capital for the new line was hard to come by so it might be relevant that within a short time the light railway legislation had been invoked to obtain an order for an extension, 16½ miles to the coastal town of Aberayron. Reviewing the application, the light railway commissioners deplored the use of the 'very small gauge', there was no need for it as the railway was routed on its own land and not in the road. The 2ft 6in gauge line from Welshpool to Llanfair had been sanctioned 'and if this gauge could be adhered to for the hilly parts of Wales, some of them may perhaps be connected with one another hereafter, and then it would be a great advantage if they were all of the same gauge … If the conditions of the already-sanctioned Vale of Rheidol Light Railway are similar … it would be a great improvement to construct both lines with a gauge of 2ft 6in instead of 2ft.'

The commissioners noted a curious feature in the draft order concerning the capital and revenue. The Aberayron capital and Devil's Bridge capital were to be kept separate but their revenues and expenses would be pooled. The net revenue would then be shared, not in proportion of capital but in proportion to the lengths of the two lines, with the result that the shareholders of the line constructed more cheaply would get a better return. They thought the estimate of £54,567 was high 'for a line of this very small gauge.'

They concluded their review with the observation that the proposal was probably not the best way of serving the area. The first four miles duplicated the Manchester & Milford Railway's route from Aberystwyth. A junction at this point would save four miles and the remaining 12 miles could probably be built for the same amount as the current proposal 'and in this way the district would get a standard gauge line at about the same cost as a miserable little 2ft gauge line.'

The Manchester & Milford Railway did, of course, object on the grounds that the proposal was unnecessary, competitive and would cause loss and injury to it. Nevertheless, following an inquiry, the Vale of Rheidol Light Railway (Aberayron Extension) Order was made on 13 August 1898.

On 21 December 1899, the company announced it would seek further powers in Parliament, notably extensions of time for compulsory purchase of land and to complete the 1897 works, and to work both the Devil's Bridge and Aberayron lines by electricity. Without meeting any objections, the Vale of Rheidol Light Railway Act of 1900 gained royal assent on 30 July. Two years were given to purchase land and the time to complete the Devil's Bridge line was extended by three years, to 1905. New capital of £12,000 and borrowing powers for £4,000 were also sanctioned.

With the act in place it was possible for the company to move on. The most likely explanation for the tardy progress would be difficulty in attracting investment. The directors met for the first time on 10 January 1901. The board comprised the promoters Taylor, Francis and Lowe together with Henry Herbert Montague Smith and W. T. Madge. The last two appear to have been appointed just before the meeting started and both had London addresses. Francis was local, a magistrate living in Borth. Taylor and Lowe were not at the meeting and nothing is known about them; their involvement was to be brief. Lowe's resignation was dealt with during the meeting, when he was replaced by Robert William English Parker. Smith was elected chairman; a 1903 article in the *Railway News* said that he was involved with promoting tube railways in London and that the promoters had approached him to use his contacts to move the project forward.

The Szlumpers, present at the meeting, were appointed the company's engineers and a draft agreement with them was approved. Arthur J. Hughes of Aberystwyth, also present, was appointed local solicitor with an obligation to conduct negotiations for the land required, acting for the company locally until the railway was opened, and paying survey fees, for £250. He was to 'take all necessary steps' to acquire the land needed 'without delay'.

Smith reported that he was authorised to apply for 350 £10 shares on behalf of Works Syndicate Limited, paying for the shares in full provided that one other director nominated by the syndicate in addition to himself was elected to the board, that Lumley & Lumley be appointed the company's London solicitors, and that the syndicate have first call on any debentures issued.

The syndicate had been registered for the purpose of raising capital for new developments in 1891. With Smith abstaining, his proposal was accepted. Parker, a contractor, was the other syndicate nominee. Syndicate shareholders included Sir Douglas and Francis Fox and James Henry Greathead, the civil engineers. The choice of solicitor is explained by the £3,000 investment registered to Walter Lumley. By 1897, the syndicate had raised £7,006 capital. Nothing is known of any other investments.

Back to January 1901, when the VRLR shares were allocated, Smith had 325 and Francis, Taylor, Lowe, Parker, Madge and Hughes had 25 each, J. W. Szlumper had 20, and W. W. Szlumper had 10.

Having released the syndicate's £3,500, payments were approved: £1,552 10s 10d to Hughes for expenses in connection with the act and the order; £900 to W. W. Szlumper for costs incurred to date; £990 to W. William Bell, parliamentary agent's charges for act and order, and £10 to petty cash; total £3,452 10s 10d. It is likely that the holders of the non-syndicate shares had only paid a nominal deposit for them at this date.

John Richard and Arthur Henry Pethick, two of four contracting brothers from Plymouth who wanted to build the railways, were also present at the meeting. Their offer of 21

There are many similar views of trains in the upper Rheidol Valley. This one has the advantage of showing the railway's contour-hugging sinuous route and the river below. *Author's collection*

December 1900 was read and Smith and the Szlumpers deputed to arrange terms with them. The other brothers were Benjamin Herbert and Nicholas Frank.

The final matter dealt with on this occasion was the parliamentary deposit of £1,560, paid by the promoters. The directors resolved to secure the release of the deposit, free of deductions and with interest, in order that it could be repaid as soon as possible.

Meeting next on 15 February, the directors allocated shares totalling £4,560, with the four Pethick brothers taking 1,125 each. Lowe's shares were transferred to Charles E. Cottier, Pethick Brothers' solicitor.

Pethick Brothers' tender to build the Vale of Rheidol Light Railway for £45,000 was accepted and the contract was signed on the same date. The shares they had agreed to take were therefore 10% of the contract price. They would anticipate selling them at a profit when the railway was completed. A separate item allowed Pethick Brothers to use second-hand rail already in stock, providing it weighed more than the 42lb/yard specified.

At the company's first general meeting held on 28 February, A. H. Pethick and W. W. Szlumper took the opportunity to put their stamp on the board, opposing Parker's re-election by nominating Francis J. Ellis instead. Parker was ejected with five votes against and only one in favour. Cottier was also elected a director. Judged by his regular attendance at meetings, W. W. Szlumper appears to have been more actively engaged in the construction than Sir James, perhaps because the latter was occupied by his concurrent position as the Brompton & Piccadilly Railway's engineer.

Work was started without ceremony on an unrecorded date. On 1 March 1901, however, Charles David Szlumper, Sir James' eldest son and the resident engineer, wrote to Thomas E. Owen seeking 'a couple of smart men' for survey work to start on 4 March, so presumably construction followed the surveyors. Szlumper specified that the 'smart men' should be able to speak English.

Despite the assumed support of their nominees, it was not long before the contractors were in dispute with the company. By 26 April 1901, £3,600 due from them under the terms of the 21 December agreement had not been paid and a report on progress obtained by Szlumper varied greatly from one submitted by the resident engineer. After the threat of legal action, the money was paid by the end of June, and on 11 July was allocated to the share accounts of the brothers equally, a transaction which demonstrates that the contractors had agreed to underwrite the shares. This was a money-go-round. Pethick Brothers would buy the shares, presumably with borrowed money, and the company would pay Pethick Brothers.

Another matter dealt with on 26 April was a letter from the Midland Railway Carriage & Wagon Company of Shrewsbury, offering for sale 'some trucks on hand, made for the Plynlimon & Hafan Railway Company.' The amount of £137 10s was to be paid for them on 24 September.

The directors visited Aberystwyth for the first time on 29 May 1901, examining the works in progress. While there, they agreed to form a finance and general purposes committee, comprising Smith, Francis and Madge, any two to form a quorum. The committee was to deal with all matters relating to the railway's construction, equipment and payment therefore. It met for the first time on 19 June 1901.

On that occasion, payment of £3,000 to Pethick Brothers was approved following presentation of Szlumper's first certificate and orders for 'trucks, carriages and engines' sanctioned. Some landowners and their tenants were not being as cooperative as they might have been and it had been

necessary to pay both parties merely to gain access. In one case, land owned by Emily Jenkins was occupied by the Reverend Thomas Jenkyns; she was paid £400 and he received £350.

Reporting an inspection that he had made the previous week on 11 July 1901, Sir James Szlumper explained that although a 'fair amount of work had been done' he regretted that at the current rate of progress, and bearing in mind that the working days would be getting shorter, it would be impossible for the line to be completed by the specified date, March 1902. Certificate No 2 (£2,400) was paid on the same date.

Submitting certificate No 3 (£1,200) on 14 August, the Szlumpers reported that little work had been carried out since the last meeting. In their opinion this was because the contractors did not have enough men on the work. John Pethick, who was present, said that they had tried to employ more men and were paying higher rates than normal in the locality, but the situation would not improve until the harvest was completed. He insisted that they would meet the contract deadline of having the line ready for inspection by 31 March 1902, a position he repeated, in the face of the engineers' continued doubts, on 30 October. Certificate No 4, for £1,200, had been submitted on 3 October.

In August, J. B. Sunders had been given the order, valued at £1,167 8s 4d, to supply and install the railway's signalling, and Midland Railway Carriage & Wagon was to supply two timber trucks at £59 each and three passenger brake vans at £79 each.

By 12 December 1901, Pethick Brothers' share accounts were in arrears to the extent of £22,860. Certificate No 5 (£1,500) had been submitted a month earlier and paid, and was followed by No 6 (£1,240) in December. Having bought 'plant and material' for the railway the contractors asked for an extra certificate to be issued, in order that they could be reimbursed. The request was passed to the directors who approved a certificate being issued for £7,000. The contractors also asked for more trucks, an order being placed with Midland RCW for five to be delivered before the end of the year.

Looking to the future, the directors resolved to appoint a traffic superintendent, choosing *Railway News*, the *People* (once each) and the *Western Mail* (twice) in which to advertise. All applicants were to be Welsh speakers, the successful candidate being offered a salary of £200. On 18 February 1902, the appointment of James Rees was approved subject to a satisfactory medical certificate being submitted and a fidelity guarantee of £250 being obtained. The appointment would take effect from 1 May 1902, acceptance that Pethick Brothers would be unable to complete their work by 31 March.

In choosing Rees, the directors thought that it was important for the post holder to have a good knowledge of the area and the traders and of others who might use the railway. He lived in Aberystwyth and worked for the Manchester & Milford Railway. While waiting to take up his appointment he was expected to report on staff requirements, wages to be paid, train working '&c &c'.

Pethick Brothers were paid £9,000 against certificate No 9 without comment on 18 February 1902. Given that it was the depth of winter it seems hard to believe that they had achieved this amount of work since December. One certificate appears to have been missed or misnumbered.

Funding arrangements for the locomotives were put in place on 26 April 1902. Davies & Metcalfe Limited of Romiley had agreed to accept part payment in the form of two £500 Lloyds 4% bonds payable on 15 July 1903.

Davies & Metcalfe had been founded as the Patent Exhaust Steam Injector Company in Aberystwyth in 1879. The directors were David Davies MP, Edward Davies, Edward Hamer, James

Metcalfe, James Szlumper and William Blakeway. The injectors were designed by Metcalfe, who had served his apprenticeship with the Manchester locomotive builders Sharp, Stewart & Company and had worked there as a draughtsman in the company's injector division before moving to Aberystwyth as the MMR's locomotive superintendent in 1869. Hamer was the MMR's general manager. The Davies's, father and son, had provided the working capital. Some small-scale production had been carried out by the Rheidol Foundry in Aberystwyth, with larger production runs carried out by Sharp, Stewart. Metcalfe had left the MMR to form Williams & Metcalfe at the Rheidol Foundry in 1882. PESIC had bought Sharp, Stewart's injector division when that company relocated to Glasgow, started the Romiley factory in 1889, and adopted the Davies & Metcalfe name in 1902. Apart from the VRLR order, Davies & Metcalfe built no other locomotives. Aside from work undertaken for the VRLR, the only other locomotive work carried out by the company was the overhaul of the North Wales Narrow Gauge Railways' single Fairlies in 1902 and 1903.

Smith spent five days in Aberystwyth over Easter, 27-31 March 1902, telling his colleagues on 26 April that he had gone over the works with Sir James and that 'progress was not as satisfactory as desired.' Pethick Brothers was to be told to do whatever was required to have the line ready for inspection by 22 May. This had little effect and on 14 May the engineers told the directors that without another engine the line would not be ready for the summer. The contractors had not been able to find another loco and had sought to make an agreement with Davies

& Metcalfe to use one of the company's locos. The directors agreed to this providing Pethick Brothers gave an undertaking that the line would be ready by 1 July. Szlumpers' certificate No 10 for £2,000 was approved and paid. The first loco, *Prince of Wales*, was apparently delivered in May.

Ellis and Cottier proposed that the company borrow £1,000 on the directors' personal guarantees, the money to be paid to Davies & Metcalfe in exchange for the Lloyd bonds, these to be held by the directors until they had been repaid. By 9 June 1902, a £5,000 overdraft had been arranged with the National Provincial Bank of England, for a period of 12 months.

There were signs that the railway would soon be opened. Acetylene was ordered for lighting, a water supply was to be arranged at Devil's Bridge, a local contractor was to erect a carriage shed at Capel Bangor, leaving the question of who would pay for it in abeyance, and Pethick Brothers were to excavate a pit for a weighbridge to be paid for as an extra. R. Roberts & Sons was to be paid £31 2s 6d for the shed and Henry Pooley & Son £56 for the weighbridge.

Reviewing the situation on 9 June 1902, the directors formed the opinion that the engineers had not taken such steps as the contract permitted to ensure that the railway had been completed by 31 March, and that the interests of the shareholders were suffering as a result.

On 25 June, the engineers reported that they had inspected the line and thought that it would be completed by 12 July. On hearing that Davies & Metcalfe had written to say that the second loco, *Edward VII*, would be ready by about 16 July, the

Vale of Rheidol Light Railway share capital

	Date	Amount created	Amount received	Calls in arrears	Uncalled
Ordinary £10 shares	December 1901	£51,000	£26,890	£13,910	£9,250
Ordinary £10 shares	June 1902	£51,000	£44,140	£6,860	
Ordinary £10 shares	December 1902	£51,000	£51,000		
4% debentures	December 1902	£16,900	£16,900		

Capital expenditure 1901-2

	June 1901	December 1901	June 1902	December 1902
Construction contract, on account	£9,363 2s 4d	£16,540 0s 0d	£16,016 10s 0d	£12,288 11s 3d
Locomotive account			£1,000 0s 0d	£1,755 0s 0d
Land purchase		£375 16s 1d	£76 14s 2d	
Rent of office, expenses		£263 18s 7d	£279 14s 2d	
Engineering fees		£763 0s 0d	£300 0s 0d	£787 0s 0d
Rolling stock – trucks		£137 0s 0d	£137 10s 0d	
Signalling & Telegraphs			£450 0s 0	
Travelling expenses		£13 14s 0	£26 16s 10	
Printing, stationery and stamps		£5 8s 6	£8 5s 5	
Law charges		12s 6d		
Auditors		£5 5s 0d	£5 5s 0d	£5 5s 0d
General charges, including expenses to date of opening				£358 3s 0d
Interest on paid-up capital		£76 18s 1d	£87 8s 6d	£60 3s 3d
Legal expenses, stamps and brokerages				£1,721 4s 3
Traffic superintendent's department expenses			£45 8s 10d	
£9,363 2 4	£18,182 2s 9d	£18,433 11s 11d	£16,975 6s 9d	
Less interest received		£4 19s 9d		
		£18,177 3s 0d		

Above: **The detailed livery carried by the VRLR's second loco, *Prince of Wales*, is shown to advantage as the loco is prepared for its next journey to Devil's Bridge.**
K. A. C. R. Nunn/Paul Ingham Collection

Right: **The livery was simplified somewhat in later years. *Edward VII*'s driver oils round preparatory to working a short train. One of the wagons converted for passenger use is stabled in the headshunt.**
Author's collection

directors asked for overtime to be worked to complete it sooner.

Expenditure to June 1902 exceeded the available capital of £44,140 by around £2,000, a position that was eased by the £5,000 overdraft, and which would be improved further when the £6,860 arrears in calls for the shares were paid. No doubt the contractors were responsible for most, if not all, of the arrears. Attention was turned to the company's £17,000 unissued 4% debentures, Cottier saying that his firm (Lane & Cottier, stockbrokers?) had clients who might be interested in buying the issue if terms could be arranged. His co-directors agreed to accept not less than £90 per £100. Cottier, however, was mistaken about his firm's clients' interest in the debentures, for by 21 October, it had withdrawn from attempting to place them.

A resolution to apply to the Light Railway Commissioners for fresh powers, primarily to extend the time for completion of the Aberayron extension and to work the Devil's Bridge line as a light railway had been approved on 8 May 1901. The company also wished to replace certain bridges with level crossings and to obtain authority for the county council to invest in the extension. An inquiry had been held in Aberystwyth on 21 October, when Hughes, the solicitor, recited the company's case, adding that the extension was unlikely to be built without a Treasury grant. W. W. Szlumper was examined about the level crossings and offered to keep two of the bridges on the Aberayron line.

There were no objections at the inquiry, but on 14 May 1902, the promoters of a standard gauge line from Aberystwyth to New Quay submitted a petition against the order to the Board of Trade, claiming, inter alia, that the company would never be able to raise the required capital, that a narrow gauge line would not adequately benefit the locality, and that their standard gauge proposal would be better. Although they were ruled out of time the company was instructed to respond to the petition and to give proof of its financial ability to carry out its undertakings.

The company's hopes of obtaining funding from other sources were soon dashed. The Treasury ruled that it was not an 'existing railway company' as defined by the Light Railways Act and the county council disputed the company's claim that it had agreed to make an advance, saying that it had merely agreed to the company obtaining the power for it to do so. Notwithstanding those points, the company asked the commissioners to put the order to the Board of Trade.

The point about the 'existing railway company' was to do with the company's desire to obtain a Treasury grant as permitted by Clause No 5 of the Light Railways Act. This enabled the Boards of Agriculture or Trade to certify that a proposed light railway would benefit agriculture, the first, to be a necessary means of communication between a fishing harbour or village and a market, or necessary for the development or maintenance of some industry, the second, to qualify it for a free grant or loan from the Treasury.

There were several provisos, one being that the proposed railway must be constructed and worked by 'a railway company existing'. To determine if the VRLR met this criterion, Major E. Druitt was sent to make a preliminary inspection of the Devil's Bridge line. Another proviso was that the land must be provided free of charge. To undermine the company's position in this regard, a solicitor wrote, after the inquiry, that his client and other landowners intended to claim full compensation and damages for severance. Losing the Clause No 5 free grant, the company said that it would apply for a loan under the terms of Clause No 4.

Druitt made his inspection on 18 July, six days after the engineers had told the directors the line would be finished. He found that the formation had been completed throughout with rails laid up to 10 miles 33 chains. Track laying had just started from Devil's Bridge. Ballasting had been completed for 5½ miles and partially carried out for a further five miles, although the track still needed lifting in places. He had been told that the second-hand flat-bottom rails weighed between 52lb and 56lb per yard. The sleepers were 4ft 6in x 9in x 4½in uncreosoted Baltic fir or larch laid at 3ft 6in centres. The rails were spiked to the sleepers with iron spikes and base plates. At the joins 4in coach screws were used. There were too few sleepers in some locations. Drainage, especially in cuttings, was insufficient but would be attended to with the ballasting. Fencing was nearly done. Five stations were located at the termini and Llanbadarn, Capel Bangor and Nantyronen.

The line was to be worked on the Tyers electric tablet system, Capel Bangor being the passing place. Aberystwyth, Capel Bangor and Devil's Bridge were provided with signals and ground locking frames. At the other places the point levers were controlled by the section tablet. All the stations were lit with acetylene gas and had shelters. Telephone communication was to be provided between the stations, and the telephone poles had been erected for 9½ miles with the wires run out for five miles.

There was one underbridge, across the Rheidol. It had eight timber trestles and timber longitudinals. There was one overbridge where the line was crossed by the MMR. There were a few culverts. Some of the cuttings needed trimming to give adequate clearances for the carriages. The line had been built with level crossings without gates and with cattle guards. He thought that they were safe, the roads being little used, and saw no need for gates.

The locomotives and carriages had been delivered and were equipped with vacuum brakes. The carriages had centre buffer couplings and 'appear very suitable for the line.'

The railway, he summarised, appeared to be well constructed as far as it was finished, but a good deal of work was still required in platelaying, ballasting and drainage, before it could be approved for passenger traffic.

Faced with Druitt's report, the Board of Trade could find no further excuse for delaying to confirm the amendment order, and it was made on 1 August. Three more years were allowed to complete the extension land purchases and four more years for its construction. The county council was authorised to advance up to £18,000 for the extension and to borrow money for the purpose. The 1897 railway was allowed to be constructed and worked as a light railway, with its bridges replaced by open level crossings.

Green (see Bibliography), incidentally, claimed that the railway had been subject to deception and that some of the rail weighed as little as 32lb per yard. With a locomotive axle loading of 4.4 tons higher maintenance costs might have been expected if this was the case; it was to be 1906 before any new rail was bought. The North Wales Narrow Gauge Railways, not known for spending money unnecessarily, required 41lb rail for an axle loading of 2.8 tons. Green also referred to an account of this inspection that states that several derailments occurred in Druitt's presence.

The Board of Trade file containing correspondence concerning the VRLR's construction and inspections is missing or miscatalogued. The preliminary inspection report is in the Aberayron extension file and fortunately a separate file of transcripts of inspection reports contains Druitt's reports dated 14 August and 25 November 1902.

On the first occasion he was accompanied by Smith and one of the other directors, and by the engineers and contractors. Although he did not comment on it, he saw little progress compared with his July visit. Railway No 2, the harbour branch, was not inspected as it was not to be used by passengers. The junction between the two was worked by a single-lever groundframe unlocked by the Aberystwyth–Capel Bangor tablet.

The railway was 11 miles 59½ chains long and rose 669ft. The sharpest curve was three chains radius and the steepest gradient 1 in 50, in one place for a distance of nearly four miles, with some sharp reverse curves. The last seven miles was cut into the valley side, in some places precipitous. The highest embankment was 68ft and the deepest cutting 39ft. The Rheidol

The Bagnall 2-4-0T *Rheidol*, with its original diamond stack chimney and wooden dumb buffers, waits to leave Aberystwyth with a train of just a single carriage and brake van. The loco was No 3 in VRLR stock. *Author's collection*

No 1 on shed. There is a carriage in the fitter's shed, and to the right of that building, behind the loco, is the fitter's and plumber's shop. *K. A. C. R. Nunn/Paul Ingham Collection*¶

river bridge was formed of timber trestles, seven 16ft spans. Both it and the MMR's overbridge had sufficient theoretical strength.

The passing loop at Capel Bangor was worked by a nine-lever ground frame with two spare levers. The down home signal required moving so that it could be seen for 440yd. The siding at Nantyronen was also worked by a single lever locked by the tablet. Devil's Bridge had sidings worked from a five-lever ground frame and a crossover for the loco run-round worked by hand.

The first five miles of track were in good order but the remainder was unfinished, sleepers insufficiently packed and rails not set to line. Broken stone ballast needed breaking up and some sleepers were 'much below specified width' and in some places too far apart. On curves of less than five chains radius the sleepers should be not more that 3ft apart. On all curves on high banks and 'where the side of the valley is precipitous' check rails were required.

Clearances in the cuttings were still inadequate. The trap points in the engine shed siding and at Nantyronen needed to be double-bladed and made to run off at a sharper angle or moved further from the junction. Carriage running boards fouled the running line when stabled in the loop at Aberystwyth, which needed to be slewed. Druitt was particularly unhappy about the way the culvert at Llanbadarn had been bridged; it was a poor piece of workmanship and should be altered.

The railway was unfinished, he concluded, and it would be unsafe for the public to use it. The company withdrew its statutory notice of intent to open to passengers on 10 September.

Meeting on 21 October, the directors instructed the engineers to give the contractors a list of outstanding work and to enforce the contract. Had there really been nothing done since Druitt's visit in August? Certificate No 12 was approved and a cheque for £2,500 issued. Additional work sanctioned included ordering a bridge from Dorman, Long & Company, to cross the line at Devil's Bridge, for an estimated cost, including installation, of £70. A long list of payments approved included more signs of the impending opening: six station clocks, £16 10s; cylinder oil, £11 0s 11d; grease, £4 2s 1d; typewriting machine, £13 0s 0d and uniforms, £11 16s 6d.

Green stated that the first train to Devil's Bridge ran in October, for the directors. Two more ran on 5 November 1902, one for the directors and dignitaries, the other for employees and families; the first of these was reported in the *Manchester Guardian*'s 7 November edition. The railway was expected to be opened for traffic 'shortly'. In addition to capturing the

'enormous' summer passenger traffic to Devil's Bridge, the railway was expected to serve 'the more useful purpose of expediting the transit of lead ore from the mines, all of which are within a radius of four miles of the terminus.'

Writing on 11 November, the Cambrian's general manager, Charles Sherwood Denniss, explained that Rees had asked him about an exchange siding, saying that the Cambrian should pay all the costs if it wanted VRLR traffic as the VRLR could already exchange traffic with the MMR. A siding would cost £150; he did not recommend it as the VRLR's future was uncertain – he gave no explanation for this assertion.

By 11 November 1902, Smith had dealt with 'numerous' complaints made by the contractors that the locomotives were damaging the track. To determine if they had any foundation he had obtained a set of drawings and submitted them to Messrs Hawkshaw & Dobson for an opinion, Hawkshaw being president of the Institution of Civil Engineers. No obvious fault was found in the drawings, the rails were more than adequate and the locomotives' wheelbase was only 6ft and curves of three chain radius could be traversed. It might have been worthwhile turning down the flanges on the centre wheelsets if this had not been done. 'It is possible that the permanent way may require fresh alignment as it is often found that the curves are distorted by slewing and are actually sharper than originally set out.'

There appeared to be some issue with the carriages. Smith reported a meeting with the Midland Railway Carriage & Wagon Company and the engineers were 'requested to report at an early date upon the carriages and whether they had been placed in a condition to enable them to work satisfactory [sic] ...' Subsequently, Williams & Metcalfe's account for 'making the necessary repairs' to 'trucks' for £81 was passed to the maker.

Considering a possible opening date, assuming the forthcoming inspection was satisfactory, the directors resolved to open immediately for goods and to defer opening for passengers until 1 January 1903.

Smith reported that he had met the county council's finance committee concerning the £700 cost of re-surveying the Aberayron extension. Subsequently, the council had agreed to contribute £600 and he had provisionally committed the company to the remainder, making it clear to the council, he told his fellow directors, that Devil's Bridge capital and revenue could not be used on the extension.

On 17 November, Druitt was instructed to return to Wales, submitting his report on 25 November. He had tested the Rheidol river bridge, which he had not done previously, and was satisfied with the results. One of the trestles had showed signs of scour. Installation of the tablet instruments and telephones had been completed and his requirements of 14 August complied with except that four curves still required check rails. Imposing a speed limit of 10mph between Nantyronen and Devil's Bridge, except on the curves between 8¾ and 9 miles which was 6mph, he recommended that approval be given to opening the line to passenger traffic.

Following representations from Rees, the traffic superintendent, and subject to Druitt's requirements being met, Smith had agreed to the railway being opened to passengers from 22 December 1902, he told his colleagues on 5 December. The engineers' certificate No 13, for £2,460, was approved and paid.

The directors were still keen to place the debentures; there were bills to be paid and the overdraft to be cleared. Once again, Cottier said that his firm had clients who he thought would take them at 4% repayable in 1908, offering to try to place them, provided the firm received a 10% brokerage fee and he was paid his incidental expenses. These terms being accepted, he agreed that if his clients wanted to go ahead he would furnish their names and a £2,000 deposit by 8 December, and the remainder by 12 December.

The cheque for £13,210 was actually handed over when the directors next met, on 16 December, Cottier having previously informed Smith that the investors were John Richard Pethick, Nicholas Pethick, Benjamin Pethick and John Pethick. So now the Pethick brothers owned the majority of the company's shares and all of its debt. Did the directors see it coming?

Then Pethick Brothers submitted a claim for extras amounting to £5,323 16s 9d, offering to withdraw it if they were relieved of their obligation to maintain the railway immediately and the final certificate, representing the retention, 10% of the contract, was issued. The directors pointed out that the contract provided for the maintenance and the retention and the request could not be accepted unless the company's interests were protected.

Following 'considerable discussion' agreement was achieved: the certificate would be issued; when it had been paid the £1,900 due on Pethick Brothers' share accounts would be paid; the company would be given a full receipt for all work carried out under the contract, including the extras; Pethick Brothers would be relived from the maintenance liability forthwith; Pethick Brothers would transfer £2,000 of stock without charge as directed as a consideration for being released from the contract, and three items still outstanding would be referred to Sir James Szlumper for arbitration, his decision to be final.

Construction expenditure is shown in the table (below). Capital expenditure to the end of 1902 reached £62,953. With £51,000 ordinary stock and £16,900 of debentures issued the company was in a position to redeem the £5,000 overdraft. By 21 October 1903, £1,200 of the £2,000 shares surrendered by Pethick Brothers had been sold, £300 to them, realising £1,117 10s which was allocated to the 'contractors' maintenance of permanent way account'. During 1903, some of this money was spent on maintenance, leaving £271 15s 10d which was allocated to the maintenance reserve. The remaining £800 was registered to two directors as trustees, and the dividend accruing to it was paid to the maintenance reserve too.

The contractors had used a Bagnall 2-4-0T. Built to 750mm gauge in 1896 for export to a sugar plantation in Brazil but not delivered. In 1897, it was sold to the nearby 2ft 3in gauge Plynlimon & Hafan Railway, the source of the wagons referred to on p56, and named *Talybont*. This line was closed in 1899 and the locomotive returned to its maker where it was regauged for sale to Pethick Brothers, who renamed it *Rheidol*, in July 1900.

On 17 February 1903, Smith informed the finance committee, which had not met during 1902, that the contractors had offered to sell 'Loco *Rheidol*' to the company for £350. Bagnall had quoted £97 10s to repair it, he said. When the committee agreed to buy the loco on 24 March the price had increased to £400, £100 payable when the repairs had

Construction expenditure

	31 December 1901	30 June 1902	31 December 1902
Contract – payment on account	£16,540	£16,016 10s	£12,288 11s 3d
Works			
Locomotive account		£1,000	£1,755
Land purchase	£375 16s 1d	£76 14s 2d	
Rent of offices	£263 18s 7d	£279 14s 2d	
Engineering fees	£763	£300	£787
Rolling stock – trucks	£137 10s	£137 10s	
Signalling and telegraph		£450	
Travelling expenses	£13 14s	£26 15s 10d	
Printing, stationery and stamps	£5 8s 6d	£8 5s 5d	
Law charges	£0 12s 6d		£1,721 4s 3d
Auditors	£5 5s	£5 5s	£5 5s
Interest on capital	£76 18s 1d	£87 8s 6d	£60 3s 3d
Traffic superintendent's department expenses		£45 8s 10d	
General charges, including expenses to date of opening			£358 3s
Land and compensation			
	£18,182 2s 9d		
Less interest received	£4 19s 9d		
	£18,177 3s	£18,433 11s 11d	£16,975 6s 9d

been completed, and two equal instalments at three month intervals. Some accounts of this loco's history, incidentally, state that it was renamed *Rheidol* when purchased by the company. Smith's reference to it by that name is clear evidence that it was so named before the company bought it. The total cost of repairing the loco was £191, including £75 for fitting the automatic vacuum brake.

There was some disturbance of the directorial status quo when the general meeting was held on 26 February 1903. Cottier's proposal that Ellis be re-elected was countered by W. W. Szlumper's proposal that Arthur Henry Pethick be elected in his stead. The motion being carried, Pethick was elected. Perhaps Ellis knew this would happen as he had not attended the meeting. At a directors' meeting held after the general meeting the secretary was instructed to ask him to return 'the gold pass' so that it could be given to Pethick.

The company's determination to proceed with the Aberayron extension was confirmed by the creation of an 'independent committee' to deal with all matters relating to it on 19 May 1903. How independent it could be when it comprised four directors, including the chairman, is impossible to say. Advertisements seeking tenders were placed on 11 March. £3 3s was payable for copies of the bills of quantities and the specifications and tenders had to be returned by 6 April. The council agreed to advance £18,000 subject to the remainder, £66,000 being subscribed, and appointed David Charles Roberts its nominee director. By 29 October, however, the prospects for raising capital seem very familiar: '... bearing in mind the extraordinary financial conditions existing at the present moment in the City and the impossibility which has existed during the last four months of getting public subscriptions to any enterprise ...'

Other business dealt with on 19 May included the resignation of Francis, one of the VRLR's instigators. He was replaced by Joseph Mellowes of the Eclipse Glazing Works in Sheffield.

The directors made no immediate comment about the success, or otherwise, of their new railway, that was left to others. A report in the *Railway News* dated 24 January 1903 explained that before the railway, a visit to Devil's Bridge by charabanc could take over five hours and cost more than 5s, the road by-passing the best of the scenery. Now, not only did the 12-mile single journey take less time, about an hour, and cost less, 1s 6d return, but the passengers got much better views. It was an up-to-date line, 'only one class has been catered for, everyone gets there in the same time for the same money.' The stations had corrugated iron buildings containing stationmasters' and ticket offices, and waiting rooms.

Harold Macfarlane, an enthusiast, visited the line in May 1903, travelling with Rees, and had submitted his thoughts and observations to *The Railway Magazine*. There were six trains daily and two on Sundays, the last still an uncommon feature of train operation in Wales. During Easter week over 1,000 passengers a day had been carried. The railway did good business, he wrote, with merchandise, carrying groceries and parcels, garden produce, eggs and chickens. Three mines were sending 15-20 tons of lead ore per day and one had had erected an electric aerial ropeway across the valley to deliver its output to the railway at Rhiwfron. Exchange facilities existed with the MMR, and the increased volume being exported via the harbour because of the railway was responsible for the projected expenditure of up to £15,000 on improvements there.

'Strolling' back to Aberystwyth along the track, Macfarlane found the bracing air made him 'ravenously hungry, and the pleasant olive green-painted stations, though restful to the eye, boasted no refreshment rooms at which he could appease his appetite.' Passengers had to wait three years before they could obtain refreshments on railway premises.

As built, the railway was a mix of the well-specified and the basic. Two locomotives and 12 carriages were enough for two trains, with nothing in reserve. The purchase of *Rheidol* was fortuitous. The only intermediate loop, at Capel Bangor, was soon found to be in the wrong place. Where they existed, station facilities were rudimentary, timber-framed, corrugated iron-clad buildings. There was nothing at all imposing about either of the railway's terminal stations. Considering the nature of the traffic and that there were no inclines involved it seems remarkable that the VRLR never had any bogie wagons.

The half-yearly report to 30 June 1903 showed the some three-quarters of revenue had come from passenger trains, £1,157 16s 8d against £373 5s 10d for merchandise and

In this later view of Aberystwyth harbour seen from Pen Dinas, the loco shed is on the extreme right, as indicated. Also indicated are the route of the VRLR harbour branch near its terminus and the Constitution Hill cliff railway that was opened in 1896.
Frith/Author's collection

minerals. An operating profit of £320 17s 1d did not quite equal the debenture interest of £338. No dividend was paid; during construction 3% dividend had been paid out of capital. During the six months, and one week of 1902, 23,363 passengers had been carried and 13,432 passenger train miles run. Goods and mineral trains had accounted for 3,354 train miles.

During the second half of the year, the peak tourist season, despite poor weather the results improved considerably. An operating surplus of £1,574 3s was enough to pay the debenture interest in full, to pay a 3% dividend and to place £350 to reserves, leaving £170 13s 4d to be carried forward. Although 79,709 passengers had been carried and 17,576 train miles run, merchandise and mineral traffic was only slightly improved, producing £434 5s 5d revenue for train mileage reduced to 2,569 miles. Heavy rain in September, incidentally, had damaged railway embankments and had led to traffic being partially suspended, reported the *Manchester Guardian* on 10 September. Such reports were to occur regularly.

A regular feature of the reports under the train mileage heading was an entry for 'ballasting trains', this being 3,448 miles up to 31 December 1903, no doubt initially reflecting the maintenance avoided by the contractors. The report ledger has several entries for wages incurred on 'extra ballasting' in May and June 1903.

The acquisition of the locomotive *Rheidol* was useful in connection with the goods traffic routed on to the harbour branch,

Smith reported to shareholders on 8 February 1904, adding that the level of traffic would soon require more wagons. Saying that the passenger traffic could be 'more economically and rapidly carried on' with another station, he added that 'the additional stopping places recently provided' had been worthwhile.

The only additional stopping place recorded had been installed with a siding for the Rhiwfron traffic, 10¾ miles from Aberystwyth. Druitt had reported on it on 26 August 1903. Like the other sidings, it was controlled by a single lever locked by the tablet.

The siding installed at Plascrug to exchange traffic with the Cambrian was not inspected. Despite Denniss's earlier dismissal of the proposal he had been instructed to agree terms with the VRLR in February 1903. After some correspondence, Smith sent a sealed agreement which Denniss rejected for being arbitrary, one-sided and generally unsatisfactory. The VRLR did put in a siding at a cost of £47 10s for the turnout and groundframe, but faced with the Cambrian's refusal to use it without an agreement, Smith wrote to Denniss on 28 November 1903 and threatened to have it removed. A contribution of £26 was made to the Cambrian's expenses and the Cambrian directors resolved to seal the agreement on 20 January 1904. This item and other post-completion capital expenditure are shown in the table (*below*).

Following a very well-attended general meeting on 24 February 1904, the directors met regularly during the year,

	1903	1904	1905	1906	1907	1908	1910
Works	£277 3s 5d						
Law charges	£250						
General charges, including expenses to date of opening	£1,055 5s						
Land and compensation	£34	£127 3s	£19 17s		£94 15s 3d	£88 10s 2d	£76 17s 8d
Working stock	£3,845 11s 9d						
Devil's Bridge – erecting girder bridge	£16 16s 7d	£2 3s 4d					
Nantyronen – water tank	£8 15s 6d	£14 13s 3d					
Plascrug – Cambrian siding, contribution to cost	£26						
Rhiwfron – points and levers fixed at siding	£8 7s 6d						
Aberystwyth – telephone equipment and works	£38 3s 11d						
Purchase of locomotive *Rheidol*	£591						
Retentions, locomotives and carriages	£271 11s 8d						
Additions to carriages	£1 3s 1d	£8 3s 2d					
Engineering settlement £40							
Aberffrwd – passing place and station		£255 7s 10d					
Glanrafon – stopping place		£2 11s 2d					
Sundry equipment		£35 8s 6d					
Seats for station platforms		£9					
Lamps for Aberffrwd		£1 11s 6d					
Weighbridge at Devil's Bridge			£54 5s				
Foundations for weighbridge at Devil's Bridge			£15 15s 7d				
First class seating for carriages			£45 11s 8d				
Six box wagons			£252				
One ton derrick crane for Devil's Bridge				£20			
Further first class seating for carriages				£22 15s 10d			
	£6,423 18s 5d	£496 1s 10d	£387 9s 3d	£42 15s 10d	£94 15s 3d	£88 10s 2d	£76 17s 8d

conducting a great deal of business. The results of their discussion are summarised, first dealing with the directors and the company's administration.

At the general meeting, Madge had been due for re-election but when he was proposed by Smith he said that he was not anxious to be re-elected. His place was taken by Nicholas Pethick. At a board meeting on 25 February, Smith announced that as the railway had been built and opened and a dividend paid, he wished to be relieved of the responsibility of being chairman. He would continue as a director, though, representing the second-largest shareholding. Arthur Pethick was elected chairman. Mellowes, elected only the previous May, also resigned and was replaced by Sir James Szlumper. Ill-health was to bring about Smith's resignation on 15 June, when he was replaced by another Works Syndicate nominee, Archibald Robert Fowler.

Cottier's declaration that from 25 March the board's expenses would be saved, was followed by the transfer of the registered office from 28 Victoria Street to 115 Victoria Street, both in Westminster, prompting the secretary's resignation because of the inconvenience. Smith had been paid £250 a year for the use of his office.

The services of C. D. Szlumper as resident engineer had apparently been terminated later in 1903; after he had signed the half-year report's engineers' certificates on 22 July. No explanation was offered for him submitting a claim for £55 10s or for the directors being unwilling to meet it, but on 25 February 1904 the newly elected director Szlumper, his father, offered to pay £10 of the claim personally if the company paid £40, a proposal that was accepted.

Szlumper also accepted the proposal when the board met again on 29 February, when the possibility of appointing him the company's engineer was discussed. He took up the position from 25 March on a salary of £80 per annum payable quarterly. Before a decision had been taken he had been asked to report on Rees's proposals to install a passing place at Aberffrwd, as forecast by Smith, and a platform at Rheidol Falls. Previously, Rees had been instructed to stop a train comprising a locomotive and six carriages there in fine and wet weather to see if it could be restarted. '... if this was not possible it would be useless having a station at this place.'

Nothing more was said about Rheidol Falls at board level although its existence was reported to shareholders in the half-yearly report. Closer to Aberystwyth, a platform with minimal facilities was opened at Glanrafon on 7 May; it cost £2 11s 2d. The directors were informed that Aberffrwd was complete on 2 June; Druitt's report was dated 9 June. The ground frame had 10 levers, including two spare. He required only lighting and a fence to be satisfied; the latter was installed after the platform had been widened. The tablet instruments had been relocated from Nantyronen. The total cost was £255 7s 10d.

A level crossing at Plascrug, Aberystwyth, had been criticised by the borough surveyor, who remained unsatisfied even after it had been raised more than 18in. In August 1904, Sir James Szlumper said that he had agreed to raise the track to match the level of the adjacent Cambrian line when men were working in the locality. This seems to have been one of several locations where the railway interrupted the area's natural drainage. On 18 October 1904, the *Manchester Guardian* reported that the track had been washed away at Llanbadarn, delaying the 10am from Aberystwyth for several hours. Although the afternoon train was cancelled it had been possible to run the 'evening trains', presumably the 6pm from Aberystwyth and return.

C. D. Szlumper's request for 600 new sleepers implies that some of those installed by the contractors had not been of very good quality. He was given permission to buy the six wrought-iron platform seats that he had obtained on approval.

Several carriages required repainting, Szlumper reported in September. Green *(see* Bibliography) said that the paint had been affected by the resin in the pitch pine of their bodies. However, as the Capel Bangor carriage shed only held four vehicles, it can be no surprise that paintwork of those left outside soon weathered. In 1920 the shed was to be described as the 'carriage painting shed'. Approval for two carriages to be painted with one coat of paint and two coats of varnish for £6 each was given in November. The ledger reveals that three carriages and two vans had already been painted at a cost of £31 in June. A further £13 13s was to be paid for painting two more carriages on 9 October 1905.

During the year, locomotives spare parts had been bought, costing £79 4s 6d, together with a screwing machine for the workshop. Three wagons had centre couplings attached as an experiment. In November, the secretary reported that *Rheidol* was 'being overhauled in order that the engineers might prepare a specification of the repairs necessary.' Presumably he meant that it was being dismantled, although why the loco should require any repairs when it had been overhauled the year before is not clear; Green said that the loco required boiler and firebox repairs. Tenders were obtained from the Yorkshire Engine Company (£105), W. G. Bagnall Ltd (£48 10s), and Davies & Metcalfe (£44 15s), the latter being accepted.

No 2 bound for Devil's Bridge. The absence of passengers in the first carriage suggests that the train was run for the benefit of the photographer. *Pictorial Stationery Ltd/Paul Ingham Collection*

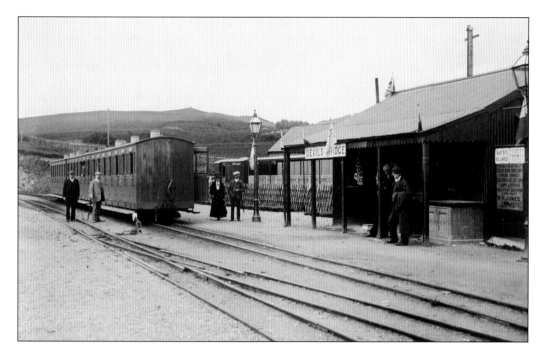

Expenditure on *Rheidol* recorded in the ledger in 1904 was £2 5s 1d for two new wheels from the Hadfield Steel Foundry Company, and £2 17s 7d to the Cambrian for transporting the boiler on 31 December 1904; it costing £3 3s 5d when it was returned in February 1905. Perhaps it was tyres rather than wheels that were replaced. Davies & Metcalfe's bill of £41 10s 10d was paid on 27 June 1905. B. Loveday, who had painted the carriages, was paid £7 6s 3d for painting the loco, for labour only.

Traffic issues that came to the directors' attention during 1904 were mainly to do with special tickets. The rates for annual season tickets from Aberystwyth to intermediate stations were set at: Llanbadarn, £2; Capel Bangor, £6; Nantyronen, £9 and Aberffrwd, £10. Rees was also authorised to issue market tickets at reduced rates from 25 March and half-fare season tickets could be issued to pupils of Aberystwyth County School. Groups of more than five passengers were allowed to reserve a compartment providing everyone in the party held a ticket. Through bookings from the Cambrian were approved when the larger company agreed to take only 5% commission.

In April 1904, the directors were concerned that the passenger traffic for the year to date was lower than in 1903. Rees was instructed to bear this in mind and 'do all he possibly could to bring the passenger traffic to what is considered it ought to be.' His earlier request for his post to be designated general manager had been rejected out of hand.

When Rees reported, on 27 August, that coach operators had been spreading rumours that the railway was unsafe, the directors took the pragmatic view 'that these matters should be allowed to take their course' whilst agreeing to consult the solicitor when convenient.

In October, the directors took a dim view of Rees's proposal to upgrade the harbour branch for passenger services, asking if he had considered the costs. After reviewing his response they decided that the time was not right and that he was to do everything possible to promote the Devil's Bridge line to visitors.

Postal traffic was reviewed in November 1904, Rees having negotiated to carry the mail for £120 per annum, including the operation of one train a day at the company's convenience.

The county council had extended its deadline for contributing to the Aberayron extension by three months in May 1904. A broker employed to raise the remaining capital, at 2½%

commission, explored the possibility of the Cambrian taking on the line's operation, Denniss saying that it would do so if the railway was extended to New Quay and made as standard gauge. On 2 August 1904, Pethick reported that he had informed the council that the company was unable to raise the necessary capital, bringing the extension scheme to an end. It was to be 1911 before Aberayron got its light railway, a standard gauge link to Lampeter.

After allowing for debenture interest, a loss of £226 16s 9d had been made during the first half-year of 1904, revenue being slightly down and expenses increased because track and locomotive maintenance had become the company's responsibility. The situation for the second half-year was much improved, with £1,176 2s available for distribution after payment of debenture interest. Traffic revenue had increased not only because the number of passengers had tripled over the first half, but because the return fare had been raised. Compared with the same period in 1903, some 5,000 fewer passengers had been carried, doubtless reflecting a desire to try something new in 1903. A dividend of 3% was declared.

The directors met less often during 1905, their primary interest being outstanding conveyances for the land taken by the railway. One claim was for loss of crops during construction; starting at £8 19s it was eventually settled for £7 10s. Infrastructure matters dealt with included installing a weighbridge at Devil's Bridge to attract coal traffic, and enlarging the Devil's Bridge booking office. Also at Devil's Bridge, Pethick Brothers acquired the lease on a disused smelting factory there, to secure a water supply for the railway, the company not being allowed to buy the property although it did pay the rent of £6 annually. To improve facilities at the Cambrian transhipment siding, the directors decided to ask for a crane to tranship timber and for a financial contribution towards the cost of a shelter, Rees having claimed that some goods traffic was lost for want of a shelter in bad weather.

Traffic results were varied. The conversion of two compartments in each of two carriages to 1st class in the spring showed sufficient benefit in terms of increased revenue, so that a third carriage was ordered to be converted at the end of the season. Rees reported that Sunday trains between October and Easter had made a loss and was told not to run them from the end of October 1905. In August he was called upon to explain the loss of passenger traffic since 1 July, nearly 5,000 by the end of the year. The directors appeared to be less concerned about their passengers' comfort, leaving Rees's suggestion to install lavatories at Devil's Bridge in abeyance.

Responding to the directors' question about increased locomotive running costs, Rees explained that wear and tear made them less economical, which the directors accepted. Inadequate maintenance probably also played a part.

The only additions to rolling stock during 1905 were six box wagons ordered from the Midland Railway Carriage & Wagon Company in June, for which £252 was paid on 14 November.

One of the reasons for the lack of directorial activity might have been because Pethick Brothers was trying to offload its investment in the VRLR to the Cambrian Railways, a process that was to take eight years to bring to fruition. Discussions started following a letter to Denniss on 2 June 1905, suggesting a meeting 'on a matter which we think would be to our mutual interest.' The meeting and an exchange of correspondence, took place before Pethick Brothers withdrew, 'the scheme … cannot be carried out at the present moment …'

In January 1906 the directors discussed the reduction in goods traffic being carried, Rees explaining that it was due 'in some degree' to decreased output. He had, however, made arrangements to tranship timber with the Cambrian and that traffic was about to start. By 5 May, revenue from this source had reached £88 11s 11d. In 1944, Rees was to tell enthusiast W. E. Hayward that wagons were used as bolsters to carry timber up to 60ft long, the trains travelling at a crawl.

Rees also told Hayward that at its peak the ore traffic was enough for the wagons to have to make two return trips in a day. Most was destined for smelting works at Padeswood via the Cambrian, and Swansea via the MMR. Some ore was exported

via the harbour to Antwerp and iron or sulphur pyrites to Nobels' works at Arklow, Ireland. Back traffic was usually coal, lime and merchandise.

Thanks to a little bit of horse-trading, it was in 1906 that Rheidol Falls and Rhiwfron got their waiting shelters. The Rheidol Mining Company agreed to let the company have the land it needed for a shelter at Rheidol Falls, providing the company erected a shelter at Rhiwfron. The directors agreed to this on 31 January.

The GPO had made some unilateral changes to the fee payable for the carriage of mails early in 1906, eventually offering £40 annually to be paid via the Railway Clearing House. The company held out for more, settling for £60 for a minimum of two years in June 1906.

C. D. Szlumper was given a two-year contract from 30 June 1906. During the year he reported on a rock fall of some 300 tons half a mile from Devil's Bridge, which cost £1 18s 3d to tidy up, and proposed improvements to the culvert at Aberffrwd. He had also gained approval to buy 5 tons of new rail.

Three years after the lack of refreshments was first mentioned, a confectionary stall was set up at Devil's Bridge, earning the company £2 rental for the 1906 season. 'Sweetmeat machines' installed there and at Aberystwyth earned £3 per annum. The establishment of a W. H. Smith & Son bookstall at Devil's Bridge was reported in August 1906, the company receiving 5% of its revenue. When the Hafod estate objected to the stall in March 1907, it was told that the usage was not in contravention of the land's conveyance.

The possibility of selling the VRLR to the Cambrian arose again on 6 July 1906, with a letter to Denniss from Sir James Szlumper asking for a meeting at which Smith would be present. Following the meeting, Szlumper confirmed the offer on 20 July, the debenture interest to be guaranteed and the line worked for 55% of the gross receipts with a minimum rent of 3% on the £51,000 ordinary stock.

At another meeting on 16 October, Denniss rejected the proposal as absurd. The guarantee was £2,206 yet the net revenue in 1904 had only been £1,739, and in 1905, £1,495, an

Looking in to the Devil's Bridge station, Nos 3 and 2 are ready to depart for Aberystwyth. There is evidence of timber traffic at the rear of the station building and of mineral traffic in a wagon stabled behind the spare carriage. The weighbridge building can be seen to the right of the station building. *Ian Allan Library*

evaluation that seemed to catch the VRLR party unawares, Denniss wrote to a Cambrian director. After 'considerable' discussion the meeting broke up with the VRLR contingent going away to consider Denniss's best offer, to guarantee the debenture interest and to work the VRLR for 65% of the receipts. On 2 November, Pethick Brothers countered with 60% 'on the understanding that the gross earnings do not fall below the average of the three years ending 31 December 1906.' Denniss rejected this and Pethick Brothers again withdrew.

Despite this, the Cambrian continued to work on the proposal, getting reports on the rolling stock and permanent way in December 1906. The locomotive superintendent said that he did not think that the locomotives had been maintained as they should have been. The 'larger engines' had not had any boiler or firebox work done on them since they were built, they were run down, dirty and neglected. The one he saw working was knocking badly. *Rheidol,* in better condition, was used on ballast trains and 'very light' passenger trains.

The carriages seemed in fair condition but he could not see the bogies to assess them, the paint was deteriorating. The loco shed was in poor condition with holes in its roof. There were few spares and few tools but one of the drivers had been a fitter and occasionally did shed repairs. A joiner did what he could for the carriages and wagons and also undertook repairs to the station buildings. More serious locomotive repairs, he said, had been carried out at the former Davies & Metcalfe foundry; this had been bought by the MMR and taken over by the GWR, which leased the MMR from 1 July 1906. This facility was being closed on 12 December, the day of the visit, and he did not know where the loco repairs would be carried out in future.

The engineer said that 'the general condition of the road is good and it has been well maintained.' The rail was in excellent condition, very little worn, and was apparently about 52lb/yard. There were different sections by different makers, with 1885 and 1895 dates noted. A short distance had much lighter rail, probably not more than 40lb or 45lb. There was ample siding space at Aberystwyth, Capel Bangor and Devil's bridge, single short sidings at Nantyronen and Rhiwfron and the exchange siding at Plascrug.

Sleepers of larch and other native timber were uncreosoted and sawn roughly out of small trees. They were in good condition with the rails fastened with dog spikes, iron clips and coach screws. The ballast was fairly good, and there was plenty of it.

Denniss had submitted a detailed report to the traffic and works committee on 5 December 1906. He liked the idea of taking on the VRLR, if only to stop the GWR getting it and diverting the exchange traffic to the MMR route. The Cambrian could save on management costs and on the VRLR's winter mileage, he explained. Working the Welshpool & Llanfair Light Railway cost 59% of receipts and he saw no reason why the VRLR should not be comparable. The railway needed developing though, and its shareholders would have to provide the capital.

On 21 December he wrote to Pethick Brothers again, stating at the outset that he could not accept their proposal. The track was not satisfactory, some rail was more than 20 years old, sleepers were of inferior quality, the rolling stock was far from satisfactory, the locomotives were run down, and the carriages were of slight construction and required expenditure. The cost of putting the railway into good order must be considered when calculating the VRLR's worth.

The Cambrian would work it for 70% of receipts for the five years, followed by 65%, the difference paying for the refurbishment. It would undertake to develop the VRLR 'reasonably'. Capital expenditure would only be incurred with the owning company's consent; if the Cambrian found such capital because the owners could not, it would be recouped from any balance of gross receipts above working expenses and attract interest at 4%. The Cambrian could use any surplus VRLR land. Any rights attaching to the Aberayron LRO would be transferred to the Cambrian. The agreement would be for 99 years or in perpetuity, subject to review on a decennial basis. Denniss applied pressure by stating he wanted to put the proposals to the Cambrian directors when they met early in January, that the matter could not be left in abeyance, and that if the proposal was not accepted by the end of December it must be considered withdrawn. Perhaps not surprisingly, Pethick Brothers rejected the offer on 2 January 1907.

There was another meeting that found little common ground. Denniss made a further report to the traffic and works committee on 13 February 1907, urging that a way should be found to reach an agreement, otherwise the GWR might make an agreement to take the VRLR's exchange traffic, which was worth about £1,000 a year to the Cambrian. A final meeting took place on 20 February, when Denniss offered to guarantee the debenture interest; 'after further conversation it was understood that the negotiations were at an end.'

			Transhipment at Plascrug	
Year	Lead ore	Blende ore	Revenue to Cambrian
1903	13t 10c		£5 3s 5s
1904	16t	1,321t 13c	£362 10s 9d
1905	260t 11c	2,684t 11c	£717 8s 6d
1906 (six months)	150t 19c	977t	£261 15s 4d

Pethick Brothers must have tried to dispose of their VRLR interest elsewhere, for on 14 May 1907, Denniss received a letter from an intermediary, 'a friend of mine has the option', offering 42,750 shares at 6s and the debentures at £4 10s. Offering the debentures at this price must have been an error. The offer seems to have been ignored.

William Hughes had issued a summons against the company in September 1906, alleging damage to his cattle due to defective fencing. Such claims were usually settled by Rees out of petty cash, in the previous three years ranging from 10s and £1 5s for lambs to 10s for one sheep, £1 5s 6d for two sheep, and £8 for a bullock. Other claims dealt with included 9s for a lost sack of oatmeal, 12s 6d for lost corn, and £5 19s for damage to a horse. The only claim by passengers was in September 1906 when 9s was paid after a connection with the Cambrian had been missed.

Some of the land purchase claims dragged on for a long time, that of Ann Morgan over land near the river at Llanbadarn being particularly troublesome. At Aberystwyth, only half of the £800 purchase price of corporation land there was paid, the remainder being placed in a deposit account in the names of the council's treasurer and the VRLR's chairman. In 1907, the company agreed to pay interest on the outstanding balance at 3¼% less tax from the date of possession until 31 March 1907, and then at 4%.

When he was asked to account for a decline in receipts March 1907 Rees explained that it was due to the withdrawal of the 10am from Aberystwyth, cancelled as an economy measure, on board instructions the previous November. Having chosen the cancelled train Rees was presumably aware of the likely outcome.

It is difficult to form an opinion on the relationship between Rees and the directors. They refused to allow him to take the title of general manager when that was the function he

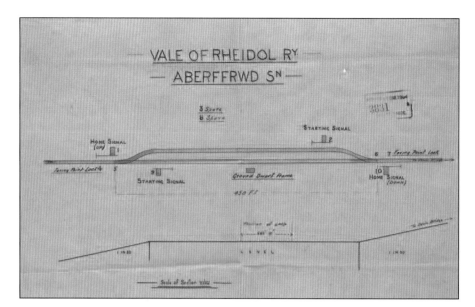

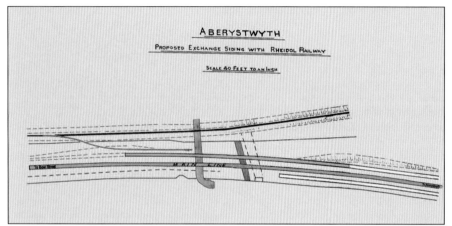

Right: **The diagram submitted to the Board of Trade in support of the application to make Aberffrwd a passing place in March 1904.** *National Archives*

Below: **A sketch of the Plascrug exchange siding, produced by the Cambrian Railways in 1904. South is at the top.** *National Archives*

performed, his request for a pay rise was refused, he was rarely invited to attended their meetings, and they were quick to jump if they thought he was acting beyond his status. On the other hand, he appeared to have a free hand on staffing levels and pay, subjects that were never mentioned in the minutes. It may be just the secretary's intervention in recording his, Rees's, reports that sometimes give the impression that he took advantage of their remoteness from the railway, to give the directors less-than-helpful information.

Consideration of Rees's May 1907 proposal to acquire two open carriages was 'adjourned' on 28 January 1908. Also on that date, Szlumper's report on couplings was adjourned until Rees could attend a London meeting. Considering a letter from him on 14 February, the directors agreed to a trial on a short train at £1 15s per carriage. How these couplings differed from those already in use is not known.

Six years after the railway had been opened the financial position was becoming critical. The capital account was £2,267 3s 6d overspent, that amount being a liability on the revenue account, and although the debenture interest had been paid, dividends had never reached 2%. The revenue and construction reserves, nearly £1,000 together, were to be transferred to the capital account during 1908.

Due for redemption on 1 January 1908, Pethick Brothers refused to accept new debentures, accepting a two-year extension instead. Their subsequent transfer to the Eagle Insurance Company went unrecorded.

On 28 January 1908, the secretary reported that an overdraft of £750–£1,000 would be required to cover the

debenture interest in July; the bank had agreed, if the directors gave personal guarantees. Cottier resigned as a director on 2 April, possibly as a consequence of being asked to give a guarantee; he had not attended a meeting since 25 February 1904.

In March 1908, the Aberystwyth town clerk complained about the harbour branch, asking the company to have the area between the rails paved with granite setts. On learning that this would cost £35, the directors asked the council to do the work and offered to pay half towards it. The council refused.

When a nine-hole golf course was opened behind the Hafod Arms Hotel, within a few hundred yards of Devil's Bridge station, in June 1908, its owner asked for cheap weekend tickets. Rees could not see any benefit for the company, especially as it was a private venture and especially not in August, and the directors agreed with him. However, Rees returned with a proposal to issue combined rail and golf day tickets for 2s 6d, of which the railway would take 1s 6d. This was accepted.

Another joint venture that came to fruition at the same time was a combined rail and coach tour from Aberystwyth to Hafod via Devil's Bridge. The fare was 3s, the company receiving 1s 6d plus 10% of the balance.

A combined board meeting and inspection took place on 6 July 1908. Having inspected the harbour branch the directors thought that it would be pointless trying to make a satisfactory roadway unless the quay wall was raised to the same height. A copy of Szlumper's report was sent to the town clerk who passed it on to the public works committee. Ultimately, no action was taken despite the council's insistence that the company was liable.

The locomotive water supply at Aberffrwd was obtained from an adjoining landowner at a cost of £3 a year. Szlumper suggested that installing a hydraulic ram would be cheaper and arrangements were made with another landowner to install such a ram to supply the water, at a cost of 5s a year.

Rees returned to the subject of open carriages, suggesting that two goods wagons could be converted for seasonal use. Szlumper was to enquire of the Board of Trade if such vehicles could be run without vacuum brakes. Two wagons were equipped and put into service during August. Rees was to tell Hayward that they were so popular that he charged 3d extra to travel in them.

More attempts were made to interest the Cambrian in the VRLR in June and July 1908. By now, the debentures and 40,000, or 42,250, ordinary shares were on offer for £27,000. To one Denniss replied that the Cambrian had already considered the VRLR and he would not care to put it before the directors again. The other offer had been made to David Davies MP, a Cambrian director and son of the famous Welsh contractor, who asked Denniss about it. Sending the correspondence and reports, Denniss explained that Pethick Brothers had been rebuffed by the GWR and doubted that it would ever be possible to agree on a valuation.

Passenger traffic and revenue in 1908 was reduced compared with 1907, although mineral traffic was slightly increased. On 26 August, the directors called upon Rees to attend the next board meeting and in the meantime to report on Sunday trains, winter traffic, opening the sides in some of the existing carriages, and running circular tours.

Discussing the report on 6 October, the directors immediately ruled against the circular tours. Two carriages were to be converted and the Sunday and winter services were to be continued as previously. Work on converting the carriages was to be started straightaway; the estimated cost was £34 18s each but it turned out to be £43 18s.

D. C. Szlumper submitted a detailed report on 23 November 1908, saying that although the track was in good condition (another) 5 tons of new rail was required 'without delay'. Unspecified precautionary measures were needed to protect the railway at the river bridge. Authority was given to purchase the rail whilst the river bridge was to be dealt with in the most economical manner.

The drop in traffic in 1908 was followed by a slight improvement in 1909, and then there were three years of very good figures, the best in the railway's independent existence. Costs were contained, too, so the improvement translated to the bottom line, if not to the dividends. From an operating perspective the VRLR appeared to be a successful undertaking,

with its ratio of expenditure to receipts always less than 80%, but this was at the expense of carrying around £1,000 of unpaid bills on the balance sheet for several years.

Even Rees tried to find a buyer for the railway, writing to David Davies on 6 March 1909. If a scheme to electrify the railway that he had been investigating was put into effect, the return could be as much as 6% he thought. If Davies replied his response was not retained.

The bank manager was becoming concerned about the railway's financial health, for on 23 July 1909 the secretary reported that 'he had interviewed the manager of the National Provincial Bank at Aberystwyth and had made satisfactory arrangements in connection with the company's account for the current half year.' Considering that he had to travel from London to Aberystwyth for the 'interview' that sounds more as if he had responded to a summons to attend.

The successful prosecution of a passenger for travelling with an out-of-date ticket was recorded on 5 May 1909. J. A. Jenkins was fined a nominal 6d and the costs were £1 4s. This did not act as a warning to H. W. Morgan who was caught travelling from Aberystwyth to Capel Bangor without a ticket in November. When Rees reported that this was the third time Morgan had travelled with an invalid ticket in two years, the directors resolved to start proceedings against him. Morgan's apology was sufficient to prevent action from being taken.

There was personal success for Rees on two fronts on 5 May 1909, for the directors not only agreed to giving him an increase in salary of £20, his first since appointment, but they also agreed to his position being that of general manager, with duties and powers remaining unchanged.

Expenditure during 1909/10 included £13 19s 7d on boiler tubes in two batches, £58 3s 9d on rail also in two batches, £23 14s 6d for vacuum brake fittings, £4 13s 9d for wheels from Hadfield & Company, and £15 8s to the Expanded Metal

From 1912, the hire of the Festiniog Railway's 0-4-0STT *Palmerston* became a common occurrence in the summer. With three carriages and a brake van in tow it sets off from Aberystwyth in 1913. *K. A. C. R. Nunn/Paul Ingham Collection*

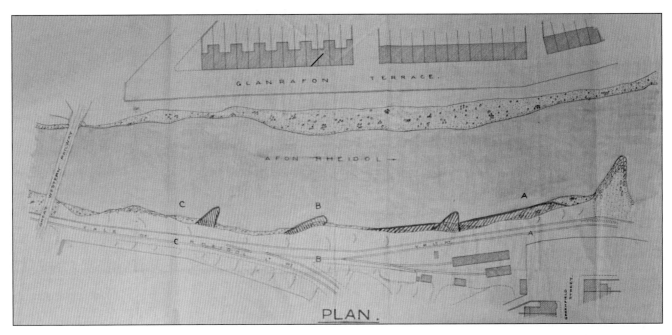

PLAN.

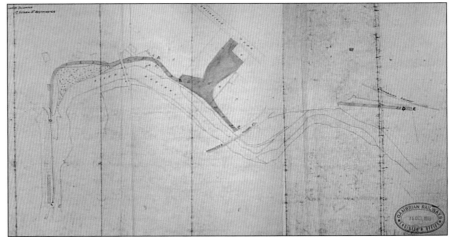

Above: **The plan produced to show how scouring on the river bank might undermine the railway also showed the track layout and the buildings in the locality** *(see p77). National Archives*

Right: **Szlumper's plan of the council-owned land at Aberystwyth that had not been paid for** *(see p67). National Archives*

Below: **No 1 in Cambrian Railways livery at Aberystwyth in 1921.** *S. F. Wesson/Author's collection*

Company for the open cars. Lightfoot, the painter, appeared several times in the lists of payments made. Not explained were payments totalling £24 16s to the Midland Railway Carriage & Wagon Company with the description 'wagons' attached.

When the directors visited Aberystwyth on 30 August 1909 they inspected the converted carriage; it had retained its original sides and doors. Satisfied, they told Rees to have two more ready for the 1910 season. They also considered the desirability of extending the railway up to the main line station at Aberystwyth, shared with the GWR and the Cambrian. Szlumper produced a plan and estimate, but it was necessary to determine that the GWR's compulsory purchase powers over the land required had expired. The VRLR could not obtain powers to use it if the GWR still had powers to use it for its own purposes.

Asked to devise means of reducing the expense of winter operating, Rees suggested obtaining a 'petrol car', saying that it would not only save money but would increase revenue. Such a vehicle would cost up to £700 and would not cope with the VRLR's gradients, Szlumper reported the Rheidol Foundry's owner telling him, on 3 November 1909. This was the right judgement for the time and Rees was probably in advance of the market in making the suggestion. A quote of £600 for a petrol locomotive was obtained from an unidentified manufacturer in 1910. The directors offered to pay £300 after a six-month trial and the remainder after a further three months, but in May decided that an experiment was not justified.

One of the reasons for this 'enthusiasm' for a petrol loco might have been a problem with *Rheidol*. This loco had been mentioned in one of Szlumper's reports and discussed by the directors without any explanation being recorded. Having refused to proceed with a petrol loco, consideration was given to 'a small steam locomotive' on offer from Bagnall, until Szlumper reported, on 6 June, that the summer traffic could be worked by the existing fleet. When Szlumper obtained quotations for *Rheidol's* repair in October 'the matter was referred to the chairman.'

When the debentures matured again in 1910, the Eagle Insurance Company refused to convert them to debenture stock, agreeing instead to them being extended for five years. The most likely explanation for the insurance company's interest in the debentures is that it was holding them as security for advances made to Pethick Brothers.

In July 1910, the VRLR removed the MMR exchange siding, much to the consternation of the local GWR manager who pressed for its reinstatement. Establishing that there was no contractual obligation to maintain it the directors refused. Whether the siding's removal was a deliberate act on the part of the directors in the knowledge that the Cambrian might take over the line, or was just a coincidence, there is no way of telling.

Now that he had his general manager title, Rees wanted the same conditions as his fellow officers, to have the security of a three-year contract. On 6 July 1910, he was given one that expired in June 1912, the same as the others.

A Territorial Army (TA) training camp was based at Lovesgrove, near Capel Bangor, in July–August 1910 and Rees had arranged trains in connection with it, installing a loop using unused track from Aberystwyth, according to Green, and earning £375 14s 11d against expenditure of £103 10s 1d. Telling the directors that the camp's commanding officer had told him how satisfied he had been with the railway's service, Rees said that as he had taken on extra work and responsibilities he should be paid an honorarium. He was granted £12 12s. One exercise had involved, incidentally, the concept of a revolt in Ireland being followed by a landing of forces north of Aberystwyth, the defending troops fighting a rear-guard action and using the VRLR as cover.

The harbour branch came back on the agenda in August 1910, after the council submitted a bill for £9 9s for nine years' rental of the right of way, saying that there was an agreement that the borough accountant had overlooked. The secretary being unable to find any evidence of such an agreement, the council was asked to supply a copy. It was not mentioned again.

Amongst the papers is an undated and unsigned briefing note passed to Conacher by Davies's office in June 1910, although almost certainly not written by him. Referring to Rees's electrification proposal it states that Siemens had estimated £4,800 for six motor coaches and £4,750 for 'overhead equipment and material', to which a hand-written comment 'can be done cheaper' had been appended. At 1d per unit the maximum annual cost of working an 'efficient' service would be less than £500. Assuming savings in locomotive operation and maintenance, maintaining previous business and carrying 'lost' passengers, a rather crude calculation showed the balance available for distribution to shareholders and servicing debt would be more than doubled.

The anticipated 15,000 participants in the TA camp and 11,000 attending a forthcoming National Union of Teachers' conference made the future look even rosier. Apart from the comment referred to in the next paragraph, nothing more was to be said about electrifying the VRLR.

Of the railway, the report states that with only three locomotives there were long intervals between trains, the engines were old and only capable of light loads, it had always been impossible to cope with heavy traffic at peak times, 'compulsory sacrifice of passengers affected the revenue … while uncomfortable crowding in stuffy compartments diverted a considerable number of passengers to the road brakes.' Other factors were the Aberystwyth station's location, a mile from the Marine Parade, and the irregular running of trains. This last was undoubtedly a consequence of trying to accommodate both local and tourist demands. A note on the report suggested bidding £29,000 for the Pethick shares and debentures, and allowing £10,000 for electrification.

Following some investigations carried out during June, Conacher had submitted a report to the Cambrian directors on 11 July 1910. The offer of all the debenture stock and £42,000 ordinary stock had been made to one of the Cambrian directors, Alfred Herbert, initially for £29,500, but now reduced to £23,250. A few days previously, £3,350 ordinary shares, the syndicate's, had been offered at 25% by a Swansea broker. The syndicate had entered voluntary liquidation in January 1910, unable to continue its business 'by reason of its liabilities'.

Conacher had been presented with two scenarios supporting the concept of the Cambrian taking over the VRLR, protecting the company against a competitor using it to develop a competing route into Aberystwyth, and as a means of strengthening the Cambrian's position in relation to the competitive Vale of Rheidol traffic. The topography made the former unlikely, he thought, such competition was more likely to arise if the East & West Wales Railway's 1898/9 schemes for a railway from Kington through Rhyader, to connect with the MMR, was revived.

In his opinion, if the offer was to be pursued it should be on the basis of whether the stock could be bought to make a return. He thought that an average profit of £1,250 could be assumed and on that basis forecast a return of 4¾% on the £23,250 offer price. A further benefit would be the guaranteed retention of the VRLR's exchange traffic, most of which was routed via the Cambrian. 'One of our colleagues' he wrote 'is willing to contribute in a substantial degree if others … will join in …' on the basis that the VRLR would be merged into the Cambrian as soon as it was convenient.

The directors moved quickly, with Davies, Thomas Craven, Herbert, Charles Bridger Orme Clarke and Conacher participating in the purchase, the first taking the largest share. Only one of them, Herbert Stern, Baron Michelham, objected, saying that the valuation was too high and that the figure given for average profits misrepresented them as they had declined every year from 1903. Herbert's company, Herbert Brothers, subsequently bought the syndicate's shares. The news of the takeover was first published in the *South Wales Daily News* on 5 August 1910, and on 10 August Conacher reported to the Cambrian board that 'certain directors of and other friends interested in the Cambrian company had acquired a controlling interest in the Vale of Rheidol Light Railway Company.' The VRLR directors dealt with the transfers of shares and debentures on 26 August without comment.

When they next met on 5 October 1910, Pethick announced that owing to the transfer of certain ordinary stock, Fowler and N. J. Pethick were no longer eligible to be directors. He therefore proposed the election of Craven and Conacher in their stead. Herbert was elected to replace Cottier at the same time. Herbert was to be elected chairman on 14 March 1911.

Pethick submitted his own resignation on 6 October, to be replaced by Clarke. Just Szlumper remained of the old regime,

so the Cambrian had de facto control of the VRLR, and not only through the Pethick assets but also the Works Syndicate shares. Some shares remained in private hands, including former directors.

During the autumn, in a reversal of what might have been expected, Williamson conducted what is now called 'due diligence', enquiring further about the VRLR, its assets and its liabilities. It had 30 employees, as shown in the table.

Employees – 1910

Number of men	Trade	Rate per day	Per week (six days)
3	Gangers	1 @ 5s 5d; 1 @ 3s 6d; 1 @ 3s 4d	£3 13s 6d
8	Platelayers	All @ 2s 10d	£6 16s
1	Carpenter	4s 1d	£1 4s 6d
2	Drivers	1 @ 5s 4d; 1 @ 4s 2d	£2 17s
2	Firemen	1 @ 3s 4d; 1 @ 3s	£1 18s
1	Cleaner	3s	18s
1	Fitter	5s 8d	£1 14s
1	Painter	3s 9d	£1 2s 6d
3	Station masters	1 @ 4s 5d; 1 @ 3s 9d; 1 @ 2s 9d	£3 5s 6d
2	Clerks in charge	1s	12s
1	Porter	1s 8d	10s
3	Guards	1 @ 3s 6d; 1 @ 2s 11d; 1 @ 1s 8d	£2 8s 6d
1	Transhipper	3s 2d	19s
1	Clerk	1s 5d	12s 6d
30			£28 11s

The land bought from the council at Aberystwyth in 1902 and only half paid for (*see p67, 70*) was one of the liabilities. No conveyance had been prepared, Williamson understood, because the VRLR's solicitor had been the town clerk. In 1914, the council was to try to make completion conditional on the harbour branch being paved. The sale had still not been completed in 1916 because the council was unable to prove that it owned the land in the first place, and the Cambrian could, if it wanted, claim possessory title because it could demonstrate occupation since 1902. It still dragged on.

For the time being there were no alterations to the railway's administration although notice to quit the London office by 25 March 1911 was received from Pethick Brothers in December; the registered office was moved to Oswestry on that date.

Notified that the TA was returning to Lovesgrove with 5,000 men at Whitsun, 4/5 June 1911, Rees sought permission to reinstate the previous year's arrangements. On receiving his assurance that the arrangements were not in contravention of Board of Trade regulations, permission was given. Perhaps the directors were right to be cautious. There had been no consultation with the Board of Trade and no expenditure on the tablet machines necessary for a loop to be properly managed.

Both rail and sleepers were replaced during 1911. Because Rees had been unable to obtain any second-hand sleepers he was given permission to buy new. He was also authorised to sell the stock of old rail, valued at £30, and to use the money to buy

new rail. On the locomotive front, he was given permission for Williams & Sons, Aberystwyth, to repair *Prince of Wales* against an estimate of £50.

The link with the Cambrian had become even closer by 5 April 1911, with that company's secretary, Samuel Williamson, acting as VRLR secretary. The accountant was given notice that his appointment would be terminated on 31 December and that he was relieved of his duties immediately. The Cambrian's audit office clerks subsequently received £5 between them for their services in preparing the half-yearly accounts. Williamson's involvement was recognised formally on 19 September, with his appointment as acting secretary.

Fresh arrangements were made for the combined rail and coach tours in 1911, with the company arranging to hire a charabanc from Commercial Car Hirers Ltd. The 20-seat vehicle cost £17 per week and was hired in August and part of September.

Traffic, locomotive and permanent way personnel were given a day off with pay to celebrate the coronation of King George V on 22 June 1911. Those who had to work could take a day's leave in lieu, still with pay.

Conacher died on 18 October 1911, prompting the inclusion of a fulsome tribute in the minutes. Davies, the largest shareholder, was elected a director to replace him on 10 January 1912. Later in the year, Charles David Szlumper, the engineer, was to die on 27 October, aged 41, and Smith, the first chairman, on 10 November.

Further steps to bring about the full integration of the VRLR with the Cambrian were taken in 1911, when on 6 December, the VRLR directors resolved that the locomotive and permanent way departments be placed in the charge of the Cambrian's equivalents, with effect from 1 January 1912 for the former, and at a date to be arranged for the latter.

On 14 February 1912 the directors approved the fitting of central couplings to 15 wagons, costing £6 14s, unspecified expenditure on the harbour branch, £50 on signalling apparatus, and £20 on repairs to the loco shed. The engineer was to produce an estimate for providing a carriage inspection pit. Without comment, this was the last time they met.

The demands of the tourist traffic and the TA camps put pressures on the VRLR locomotive fleet that could not easily be met. In 1912, the Festiniog Railway was asked if it had a locomotive to spare, its directors agreeing on 20 July, adding that the daily charge should be £1 5s for the loco and driver. With modifications to its coupling gear, the England 0-4-0STT *Palmerston* spent several weeks at Aberystwyth, an arrangement that was repeated for several years.

The Cambrian directors formally resolved to take over the VRLR on 6 November 1912 with £15,022 'A' 4% debenture stock being issued in exchange for £16,900 VRLR debentures, and £12,715 for £51,000 ordinary stock. The amounts were calculated on the basis that the 'A' stock would reimburse the 'friends' their £23,000 investment, allowing for the stock being

Top: **The GWR renewed most of the VRLR's rolling stock and this photograph is said to be one of a series sent to Paddington to justify its replacement. It was certainly not a typical train formation. No 2 has been renumbered No 1213.** *Ian Allan Library*

Left: **Three new locomotives were built in 1923, Nos 7 and 8, and in 1924, No 1213. No 7 arrives at Devil's Bridge.** *G. F. Parker/Author's collection*

worth 94% of its par value, and producing, at 4%, at least, the same interest as the VRLR debentures and shares. The calculations also took into account the VRLR debentures not being worth face value, a move that had the effect of slightly increasing the value of the shares.

Two days later, Herbert wrote briefly to the shareholders informing them of the proposed takeover, writing again in more detail on 17 December 1912, explaining that the debentures became redeemable at par on 31 December 1914, and it was considered impossible to raise this amount except on onerous terms. The railway needed additional locomotives and rolling stock and 'a considerable amount' spending on the track. The Cambrian would take over the whole of the debentures and assume all of the VRLR's liabilities, including £1,354 12s 5d overspent on the capital account, and pay all expenses of the amalgamation. He observed, too, that £24 of 4% stock would produce 27¾% more than £100 VRLR had in 1910 and 1911. It was pretty much a paper exercise as the Cambrian's nominees already controlled the debentures and most of the ordinary stock.

Amongst the shareholders were four members of the Pethick family, four of the Szlumper family, Bruner, Mond & Company, owners of the Cwmystwyth mine and later a part of ICI, Cottier, Madge, Mellowes and Francis, the latter one of the original promoters. Thirteen shareholders held sufficient shares, £250 or more, to entitle them to be elected directors, not just the current or former directors. The Cambrian's intention to deposit a bill for permission to take over the VRLR and for other purposes had been advertised in the *London Gazette* on 19 November 1912.

Evan James Evans, a chemist, was one of only two shareholders with an Aberystwyth address. Objecting to the proposals, on 26 December 1912 he wrote to Herbert saying that he spoke for 250 shares and would get his friends and others to object unless he received face value for the shares. In his report to the Cambrian directors on 7 January 1913, Williamson noted

that Evans had bought 250 shares for £150 in 1906 and had sold 70 of them for £43 10s. Evans persisted with his objections into 1913, even getting Herbert to meet him in Aberystwyth.

Another objector was Denniss, the former Cambrian general manager, who complained that issuing more 'A' debentures to acquire the VRLR would reduce the 'alarmingly low' value of those already issued even more. Writing on 26 February 1913, he thought the proposal was a mistake and 'cannot be any great advantage to the Cambrian', apologising for having to 'express these divergent views.'

Williamson wrote to VRLR shareholders and debenture holders on 1 August that under the terms of the act that had received the royal assent on 4 July, the VRLR had been amalgamated into the Cambrian as from 1 July 1913. He now asked for VRLR certificates to be sent to him to be exchanged for the Cambrian 'A' debenture stock. The surrendered debentures were in the names of Davies and his two daughters, Craven, Clarke and Herbert; they also controlled £46,400 of the ordinary stock.

Wrapping up the administration of the amalgamation, the Inland Revenue required conveyance duty to be paid at 1% of the liabilities (£1,706 15s 4d) and on 87% of the debenture stock issued to the VRLR shareholders, £12,693, and debenture holders, £15,018; total £258 10s. Loan capital duty of £34 15s was also payable. The only time the effect on personnel was considered had been on 4 June 1913, when Williamson told the Cambrian board that they must be prepared for the VRLR staff asking for parity of pay and conditions with their new colleagues. It had not been the Cambrian's practice to make any distinction between personnel working on the main line and the branches and light railways, but in this case he thought that any attempt to change VRLR pay and conditions should be resisted.

The question that must be asked is, why after rejecting Pethick Brothers' overtures since 1906, did the Cambrian finally agree to take on the VRLR? Was it simply that the vendors had become so keen to sell, being prepared to accept a lower price that made sense in terms of investment potential? A mistaken belief that it was a bargain perhaps, despite the engineer forecasting a substantial sleeper renewal programme at an early date, and replacement of the loco and carriage sheds. The onset of the Great War prevented the Cambrian from having to spend too much money on it.

The GWR's plan of Aberystwyth station produced in support of the application for the Ministry of Transport order to extend the VRLR to a new site alongside the standard gauge station.
Parliamentary Archives

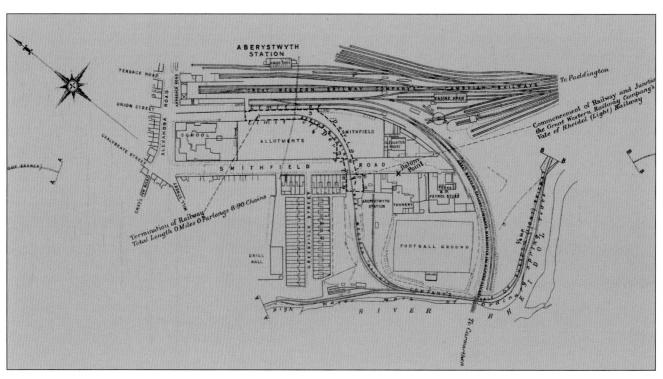

Top: **A view of the newly installed level crossing with the incomplete road surface looking towards the original station. The building next to the vehicular entrance was used by the traffic superintendent. The goods shed is to the left of the station building. Examination under a glass reveals an amazing amount of clutter lying about. Amongst it is a 'booking office' sign behind the station building and a carriage or wagon wheel set beyond it. Judging by its vintage, the home signal had been previously used elsewhere. The old station site and goods yard were to become a Crosville bus depot.** *Adrian Gray collection*

Middle: **The view towards the new station shows the crossing keeper's hut and the starting signal. The hut was to be moved closer to the road.** *Adrian Gray collection*

Below: **Only two years old, No 8 heads over the incomplete crossing with what appears to be a test train.** *Adrian Gray collection*

The most notable change to the VRLR under Cambrian control was to the locomotives. They had their names removed and were repainted. Nos 1 and 2 had their bunkers enlarged, increasing the locos' width by 12in, and the handbrake layout altered at Oswestry. It was decreed that a jack should be carried on the front running plate during this era.

A report on the state of the VRLR to determine where savings could be made was submitted by the Cambrian's senior officers, W. H. Williams (traffic), A. Craig (loco department) and James Williamson (permanent way), on 3 November 1913. Rees had been consulted.

Since 1 October, one engine worked the service except on Wednesdays and Saturdays when an extra train required a second loco. From 1 November, the entire service could be worked by one loco but the hours of duty required two crews. By re-arranging the duties and running the last return trip with a Cambrian driver and fitter's assistant Millman, a passed fireman, the services of a fireman, £1 4s per week, could be saved. The loco crews did not sign on or off duty. The service was to be worked by *Rheidol* as it used less coal, although it was under repair. Trains comprised one carriage only except on market days and early-closing days.

Joiner W. J. Jones was shared between the loco and permanent way departments. He was no longer required by the former but retaining his services on carriage and wagon repairs on both the VRLR and the 'Cambrian proper', would save the expense of sending someone from Oswestry.

Traffic personnel were stationmasters at Aberystwyth, Capel Bangor, Aberffrwd and Devil's Bridge. At Aberystwyth there was a guard and a 'transhipper'. A 'summer hand' was covering for holidays until 6 November. None of the others could be spared. The decrease in ore output meant that the transhipper, B. Goulding, would not be fully occupied but the transhipping charge of 3d per ton on coal, lime and merchandise covered his wages; casual labour would be difficult to provide and would cost as much. Goulding could clean carriages or help with station duties if not engaged on tranship work. Guards cleaned the carriages, when time allowed, at the terminals.

Rees could take on the position of Aberystwyth canvasser as well as having oversight of the VRLR. As canvasser he would look after the area from Carmarthen to Glandyfi, which entailed trying to poach GWR traffic from the former MMR. He could also look after the Cambrian's interests in Aberystwyth, which the joint-station staff could not do.

Switching out the loops at Capel Bangor and Aberffrwd during the winter, or working the railway by staff-and-ticket was considered. For the latter, the 'boy's' wages would be saved but the cost of disconnecting the loop and providing a new set of instruments would exceed the saving. Notice that the traffic department's stationmaster is now a boy. Capel Bangor could be switched out but the volume of goods traffic would still require the 'man in charge' and ticket issues by the guard would delay the trains. Staff-and-ticket working received little consideration in view of the heavy summer traffic. New locking equipment would be required at the exchange sidings, Nantyronen, Rhiwfron and Capel Bangor, and there would only be a benefit if station personnel could be withdrawn.

The Cambrian's 1913 working instructions give an insight into train operating.
- Sounding three long whistles at milepost 9½ warned the Rheidol Mining Company that the train had goods to be unloaded at Rhiwfron.
- Tickets were checked and collected at Aberffrwd (up trains) and Llanbadarn. Carriage doors were locked on the station side after tickets had been collected at Llanbadarn. Ticket checking on up trains had been transferred to Capel Bangor by 1919.

Photographs of VRLR No 1 running as overhauled by the GWR as No 1212 are rare. Here it was seen at Devil's Bridge in company with the van numbered 137 in the GWR fleet.
N. Shepherd/Author's collection

No 1213 on shed on 23 July 1934. The steam heating pipe is mounted on the left. The shed looks as though its roof has required additional support to keep it in place.
J. S. Hancock

- Timber and other traffic carried on two or more wagons was not attached to passenger or mixed trains.

- Any traffic on the harbour branch had to be accompanied by a guard who warned 'trespassers' of the movement; loco crews were to exercise the greatest vigilance and caution.

To deal with the anticipated extra traffic accompanying the annual TA camp, on 26 February 1914, the traffic department was given permission to arrange for the hire of a loco from the Festiniog Railway on the basis of paying £25 for two weeks in August, plus £2 per day over 14 days.

As the Rheidol river bank at Aberystwyth was suffering from scour and the nearest property was the VRLR, the corporation thought, on 28 April 1914, that the Cambrian should make a substantial contribution towards the £800 estimated cost of repairing it. The Cambrian's engineer objected, pointing out that the wall between the railway and the river pre-dated the railway and belonged to the council; if the damage continued, the wall, which acted as a flood defence and protected a large area of the lower part of the town, would be damaged before the railway. It was to protect the town that the remedial works were required, not just the railway. With the Cambrian probably the largest rate payer in the area affected, he could not recommend a making a contribution unless all the landowners contributed.

The council was persistent, putting pressure on Davies, now the Cambrian's chairman, and a site meeting took place. Of all the property likely to be affected by flooding only the railway was not council owned. If the Cambrian did not contribute to the repairs the council would do nothing, expecting that the Cambrian's works to protect its own property would also benefit the community. This was undoubtedly a bluff, stated the engineer in December, but if the council did allow the wall to be damaged the railway would have to tip stone along the river bank. In lieu of a cash contribution, 144 tons of stone from Devil's Bridge was donated to the council (see70).

After an inspection another unsigned report was submitted on 18 October 1914. No tail lamps were carried on the trains.

Rule books and appendices were to be sent to each member of staff. At Devil's Bridge the record keeping of parcels arriving was poor, and Hafod Arms Hotel staff took parcels while the stationmaster was busy, avoiding the administration. Calves were carried but there was no rate for them. There was no list of cloakroom charges and the stationmaster did not realise that bicycles and packages left on the station should be charged for. The stationmaster said that he should not be blamed as he had not been properly instructed.

At Aberffrwd and Capel Bangor the waiting sheds would be improved by a cement floor, there were no parcels rate books, and the tablet registers were not fully kept up. At the time of the inspection there were only two vehicles in the Capel Bangor carriage shed. A common complaint for all stations was the delivery of parcels without a signature being obtained.

This report leaves the impression that the Cambrian made little effort to integrate the VRLR and then wondered why its procedures were not being observed. Rees had been transferred to the traffic department at Oswestry and there appears to have been no one individual with responsibility for the VRLR. Rees, incidentally, was to retire from railway service in 1932 and was aged 80 when he died in Bow Street in 1953.

The VRLR was not directly affected by the First World War until March 1917, when the Cambrian wanted to release the stationmaster at Capel Bangor. It decided to suspend tablet working and to work with 'one engine in steam' instead, providing the Board of Trade with a sealed undertaking dated 4 April. Tablet working was to be resumed in April 1919 although the sealed undertaking was not made until 5 May. In October 1920, the Cambrian was to suspend VRLR tablet working for the winter months as an economy measure. Realising that this would be a regular feature of VRLR operating in the future, the newly created Ministry of Transport suggested modifying the undertaking to avoid it being renewed twice a year.

The Cwm Rheidol mines changed hands in 1918, the new owner asking for the Rhiwfron siding to be replaced. He offered to pay £20 for the work and to complete the standard agreement for its use.

During the last quarter of 1918, traffic was interrupted on several occasions because of the activities of timber merchants cutting trees near the railway between Rheidol Falls and Rhiwfron, cut timber and its debris falling on to the railway with no effort being made to prevent it or to remove it. Despite several letters and promises to protect the railway, the Cambrian was eventually compelled to seek an injunction on 24 January 1919. Judgment was given to the railway for £125 damages and costs, £100 of the damages not to be claimed if the contractors replaced and repaired damaged fences to the company's satisfaction.

The Cambrian Railways' return to the light railways investigation committee in 1921 gave an understanding of the VRLR's operation just before the Cambrian lost its independence to the GWR. The railway still had control of the goods traffic at Devil's Bridge because road competition existed only between Aberystwyth and Aberffrwd.

Goods traffic 1919	Tons
Grain	345
Groceries	101
Pitwood	4,560
Ale and porter	26
Manure	20
Basic slag	93
Bricks	31
Coal and coke	747
Lime	148
Spelter	244
Lead ore	42

	1913	1919
Engine mileage		
Coaching, loaded	25,210	12,840
Coaching, empty	91	-
Freight	13,421	13,252
Shunting		2,600
Total	38,722	28,693
Passengers	144,593	118,569
Goods (tons)	475	4,908
Minerals (tons)	1,853	497
Revenue		
Goods etc.	£701 4s 11d	£2,779 1s 5d
Passengers	£4,887	£7,092

The 1919 figures for goods and minerals do not correlate with the figures in the previous table

Other items from the return include:

- The shed at Capel Bangor was described as a 'carriage painting shed'.
- The harbour branch was unused.
- Maximum passenger train length was seven carriages, the average was two in winter, five in summer.
- Mixed trains comprised two carriages, a brake van and four wagons.

When it discovered that the river bank at Aberystwyth was still at risk of scour in December 1921 the council returned to the railway for a contribution towards the repairs. The engineer was in favour of providing support, but suitable stone was no longer available from Devil's Bridge and it would be cheaper for the council to buy it than the company. The outcome was not recorded.

From 27 March 1922 the Cambrian, and with it the VRLR, was amalgamated with the Great Western Railway in accordance with the requirements of the 1921 Railways Act. This was a consequence of the government's management, some would say mismanagement, of the railways during the First World War, when they had been effectively nationalised. During the period of government control the railways had not only been run down but there was no mechanism set in place for the companies to be compensated adequately. The grouping of railways into four regional companies enabled the larger companies to absorb and, in effect, cross-subsidise the smaller companies and protect them from bankruptcy. Compulsory fare increases in 1917, intended to discourage discretionary travelling to make rolling stock available for use on the Continent, opened up the market for military-surplus motor vehicles to be put into use to carry both goods and passengers.

Any records of VRLR traffic under GWR ownership have not survived. Although the minutes of the locomotive and traffic committees record the major decisions taken, the whereabouts of the briefing notes that would have been produced in support of the decisions are unknown.

As a part of the GWR, however, the VRLR was to benefit from more investment than at any time since it had been built, and not just on a one-off basis, either. As early as 11 January 1923, the locomotive committee resolved that 'under circumstances represented by the chief mechanical engineer it was agreed to recommend an expenditure of £5,000 in the construction of two locomotives, 2-6-2T types, weighing 25 tons each for use on the Vale of Rheidol branch.' On 12 April 1923 approved the construction of four additional 32ft open passenger cars at a cost of £2,400.

The original locomotives had been renumbered by the GWR, Nos 1212 and 1213 for the Davies & Metcalfe engines and No 1198 for the Bagnall. The last probably never carried its

Train staff	Summer months	1 guard, 4 drivers, 4 firemen, 2 cleaners
	Winter months	1 guard, 2 drivers, 2 firemen, 1 cleaner
Station staff		3 stationmasters, 4 porters, 1 goods porter at exchange siding
Maintenance staff		1 fitter and assistant, 1 joiner, 8 platelayers in two gangs and supervised by one of the main line inspectors
Part-time staff	Summer months	1 driver, 1 fireman

Accommodation at stations

Aberystwyth	3 sidings and loop, accommodation for 25 wagons, goods yard accommodation
Exchange	accommodation for 12 wagons
Capel Bangor	2 sidings and loop, accommodation for 30 wagons, 1 siding into carriage shed
Devil's Bridge	2 sidings and loop, accommodation for 18 wagons, goods yard accommodation
No accommodation for dealing with livestock, van or carriage traffic.	

new number and was to be condemned and cut up at Swindon on 26 July 1924. It did, however, incur repairs that cost £97 12s 4d before withdrawal.

The new locomotives, Nos 7 and 8, were delivered in October 1923, in effect GWR versions of the Davies & Metcalfe machines adapted to suit Swindon practices. They had Walschaerts valve gear, copper-capped chimneys and brass safety valve bonnets. They were three tons heavier and Green (see Bibliography) states that they could haul trains of nine carriages and a brake van without losing time. This compared with five or six carriages previously.

Now it appears that the locomotive committee practiced a measure of deception on the accountants. In November 1923, No 1213 was sent to Swindon for an overhaul. Its record card shows that the work was completed on 24 July 1924. Including a new boiler, wheelsets and cylinders, the work had cost £2,589 18s 5d, almost the same as Nos 7 and 8 cost to build from

scratch. It was returned to Aberystwyth identical to Nos 7 and 8 in every significant respect, including the valve gear and cylinders; it was a new loco.

Engineers familiar with these locos have told the author that No 1213 (No 9 since March 1949) is the same as Nos 7 and 8 and could not have been rebuilt from No 1213. Green gives more details about the way the new locomotive was built without approval but it has not been possible to track down all of his sources.

No 1212 was twice sent to Swindon, first in December 1922, for repairs that cost £847 2s 8d, including £260 19s 3d for boiler work. It had only done 1,959 miles since its previous repair at Oswestry. Then in November 1924, having worked 15,298 miles, it was sent again for repairs that cost £334 6s 3d and which took until 25 May 1925 to complete. On this occasion the boiler work only cost £2 5s 4d. It kept its original cylinders and valve gear and received new tanks and a brass

No 8 runs along the riverbank as it leaves Aberystwyth with the morning train on 17 May 1937. The back of the train obscures the loco shed. The loco's train heating flexible connecting pipe has been removed.
J. G. Dewing/Author's collection

safety valve bonnet. Back at Aberystwyth it was, it is said, retained as spare engine until it was condemned in December 1932. There are few photographs of it in this condition on the VRLR, but several exist of it at Swindon where it was stored pending a possible sale before being scrapped on 9 March 1935.

The GWR called the four new carriages summer cars; they were open above the waistline and could seat 48 passengers. Two cattle vans were supplied to the VRLR in 1923. There had been no need for such vehicles previously and there is no evidence of these finding much use; in 1937 they were regauged and sent to the Welshpool & Llanfair Light Railway.

Along the line, the engineers' department approved the expenditure of £2,000 for ballasting and making up cesses on 24 February 1924. Locomotive water supplies were the responsibility of the locomotive committee which, on 27 March 1924, authorised the erection of a second-hand water tank and stand pipe in place of the existing water tanks, 'in bad condition', at Devil's Bridge, the work to cost the locomotive department £255 and the signal department, £10. Two water cranes with swing jibs, costing £125, were approved for Aberffrwd on 18 December 1924, and the installation of a larger water tank at Aberystwyth on 26 February 1925, for £292.

In 1923, the GWR had started a three-year project to rebuild the standard gauge Aberystwyth station. As the works approached completion, on 25 June 1925 the traffic committee sanctioned an extension of the VRLR 'from present terminus to a site adjoining the general station now in course of construction.' The budget was £850 from the engineering department and £100 from the signal engineer.

A notice dated 16 July 1925 advised of the application to the Ministry of Transport for an order to be made under the terms of article 16 of the 1921 Railways Act. This little-used device allowed railway companies to make minor alterations, extensions or improvements to existing facilities, provided the cost did not exceed £100,000. In the case of the VRLR, the extension could have been achieved by means of a Light Railway Order. Copies of the plan that accompanied the application are kept at the National Archives and the Parliamentary Archives, with draft copies of the order held at the latter.

The GWR announced that the order had been made on 20 October 1925. It authorised both the extension '… commencing by a junction with the Vale of Rheidol (Light) Railway of the company at its termination and terminating at a point in the road abutting on the western side of the Aberystwyth station of the company's Cambrian Railways, six chains or thereabouts south east of the junction of that road with Alexandra Road' and the acquisition of the necessary land from the corporation. The capital works ledgers contain details of the expenditure.

Aberystwyth: extension of Vale of Rheidol line to general station 1925-6

	Capital	Engineering	Signals	Telegraphs
Provision of loop to hold 7 coaches and van and necessary connection; crossover in station; fencing at each end of ramp; cattle guards at Smithfield Road	£753			
Substituted permanent way		£77		
Removal and refix buffer stops		£15		
Removal and refix shelter and station nameboards		£5		
Original cost of wall displaced in providing opening for platform gate		£18		
Signals			£75	
Telegraphs				£25
Raising level of land by tipping		£750		
Contract with Jones Bros for filling gardens	£300			
Additional expenditure due to extension of departure line and provision of gates at Smithfield Road	£130			

Traffic department staff	Expenditure		Receipts					
	1924	1925	1924	1925	Passengers	Parcels	Goods	Total
Aberystwyth	£434	£886	£4,745		£4,114	£39	£992	
Devil's Bridge	£210	£362	£955		£308	£10		£5,463
Summer staff	£282	–						
	£926	£1,248						
Loco department, engine and train running expenses – passenger		£3,757						
freight		£766						
Engineering department, maintenance and renewal		£2,215						
Signal department		£187						
Clothing		£14						
Fuel, lighting, water and general stores		£5						
Rates		£226						
		£8,414						

Opened without comment in 1926, the extension appears to have been overlooked when the remainder of the works at Aberystwyth were inspected.

The money spent on these capital projects indicates that the GWR thought that the VRLR was worth supporting although there must have been some concerns about costs, for it was one of 53 branch lines subject to a review completed in March 1926. The results for 1924 and 1925 were tabulated (above) although a full comparison was not provided. In 1925, 3,959 tons of minerals, 540 tons of merchandise and 32 trucks of livestock had been carried. The last item gives the lie to the claim that there was no livestock traffic to be had on the VRLR.

No explanation was given for the increase in staffing costs over the two years, but had they remained at the 1924 level then in 1925 the railway would have made a profit. The report recommended making economies of £1,527 annually by dispensing with the stationmaster at Devil's Bridge, reducing services to a single-shift, eight-hour operation and reducing winter services to Mondays and Saturdays only. The timetables show that the last was not put into effect. Comments on a meeting held to discuss the report on 30 June 1926 cast some doubts on its methodology so probably little notice was taken of it. The report, however, did recommend the abolition of 1st class travel from all branch lines and that measure was adopted from September 1926.

On 27 November 1930, though, the traffic committee took action about the VRLR's costs, resolving to withdraw the goods service from 1 January 1931. It also decided to suspend VRLR passenger services during the winter months, using road motor services in lieu of both.

More expenditure was approved by the locomotive committee on 28 October 1937. The VRLR carriage stock had been condemned, prompting a decision to spend £7,995 to replace it. The estimates were produced in such a way to produce an element of betterment, the difference between what the vehicles 'should' cost and what they 'would' cost. The traffic committee agreed to pay the £681 difference, the remainder being allocated to the renewals account. The new stock was itemised as follows:

An article in the July 1938 issue of the *Great Western Railway Magazine* explained that the 56-seat thirds and 48-seat brake thirds were bogie carriages built on steel underframes with oak and teak body framing and internal cladding of birch. Like the 1923 stock, it was 32ft long, 6ft wide with steel clad exteriors. The brake vans were four-wheeled, 13ft long and 6ft wide. They were also on steel underframes with steel cladding on oak body frames. Three of the thirds turned out to be summer cars. The old stock was scrapped, and according to Green, some parts were reused. It would be interesting to know the logic behind the ordering of the brake thirds and the brake vans.

On the outbreak of war in September 1939, VRLR services were withdrawn without comment. With the return of peace a service of two trains daily was operated from 23 July 1945 according to the *Welsh Gazette* on 26 July, but the 'restoration of passenger services on the Vale of Rheidol branch' was not formally approved until the traffic committee met on 28 March 1946. John Edward Davies, the driver on 23 July, had joined the VRLR as a fireman on 21 December 1902, at the age of 15. The locos in traffic, Nos 7 and 8, were painted plain green.

Along with the remainder of the GWR, the VRLR became a part of the nationalised British Railways' Western Region on 1 January 1948, placed under the command of the divisional traffic manager at Cardiff.

According to Green, No 7 was repainted in GWR livery in 1948, ensuring that the initials of its former owner plied the Rheidol Valley until the end of the 1953 season. It would make more sense if such a perverse act had been carried out in 1947. Following an overhaul, No 1213 was painted black and renumbered No 9 in March 1949.

The earliest item surviving in the BR-era files is dated 8 April 1953 and dealt with what became a common theme of the VRLR's post-war years – will it be re-opened and is it available for sale or lease? In this case the enquirer was a G. C. W. Beazley, a farmer of Pavenham near Bedford. The answer was that there were no plans to close the line and arrangements were being made 'for the usual operation of passenger trains this summer.' On 31 August, Beazley wrote again that he had heard

Description	No of vehicles	Estimated replacement cost	Description	No of vehicles	Estimated cost
Thirds	10	£5,659	Thirds	10	£5,900
Brake thirds	2	£1,142	Brake thirds	2	£1,240
Brake vans	3	£513	Brake vans	3	£855
	15	£7,314		15	£7,995

rumours that the line was to be closed and expressing his willingness to take it over; again he was told that there were no plans to sell it.

The date that LMS-style numberplates were fixed to the VRLR smokebox doors is unknown, the earliest dated photographs being taken in 1953. The existence of photographs showing the mounting brackets and no numberplate in 1957 or later, may be a record of a driver expressing a personal preference.

Over the three years from 1955 the locos ran in three different liveries. In 1955, Nos 7 and 8 were plain green whilst No 9 was black, all having the first BR logos affixed centrally to the tank sides. In 1956 they were all plain green and were named (No 7 *Owain Glyndŵr*, No 8 *Llywelyn*, No 9 *Prince of Wales*), with the crests moved downwards to accommodate GWR-style brass nameplates. In 1957 they were re-painted green and lined out in full GWR fashion with transfers of the second BR logo mounted under the nameplates. The carriages were painted GWR chocolate-and-cream from post-war lake and cream at the same time. The decision to turn out the trains in GWR style may not be unrelated to the visit made to the railway by BR's Western Area Board in the spring of 1956.

Publicity, with the operation of evening excursions and the resumption of Sunday services in 1955, attracted increased numbers to the VRLR. Another boost occurred on 24-26 July 1957, when the Royal Welsh Show was held at Llanbadarn. With echoes of the TA camps, the VRLR ran eight-car shuttles to the showground at, according to a local newspaper, 12 minute intervals. A total of 25,260 return tickets at 6d were issued, many more travelled only one way and the railway maintained its normal service to Devil's Bridge. Green records that the Aberystwyth tablet machine was moved to Llanbadarn and it became part of Aberystwyth station limits for the duration. Might this aspect of the operation have repeated what Rees did to accommodate the TA?

Great changes occurred during the 1960s, socially and on the railways. The advent of budget holidays at exotic destinations where the sun could be guaranteed to shine and the increased use of cars had an effect on both the traditional British seaside holiday and the railways. The development of preserved railways that had started in Wales in 1951 had shown that there was a market for steam railways, even in the face of modernisation that was to see steam removed the national network. Preservation had demonstrated that with the input of enthusiasm and volunteers steam railways could attract passengers and pay their way, but they needed to be regarded as entertainment rather than as a pure means of transport.

With regard to the VRLR, BR was always going to struggle to find a balance. On the one hand, the unions would always insist that the driver of a train to Devil's Bridge was paid the same as the driver of an express to King's Cross. On the other, it had all the resources one could ask for to ensure that maintenance and repairs were carried out quickly and effectively and, with it a bit of imagination, at marginal cost. It must be emphasised that many of the managers involved with the VRLR over the years were either enthusiasts, or enthusiasts of the VRLR, who wanted it to be successful and to be a part of the national network.

Mounting losses incurred by the railways under the management of the British Transport Commission (BTC) increasingly concerned the government. The situation was partly self-inflicted; costs, particularly wages, were rising but the government would not allow fares to be increased. Dr Richard Beeching was appointed chairman of the British Railways Board (BRB) from 1 June 1961 with the objective of reducing costs. BRB was to take over from the BTC on 1 January 1963.

With services restricted to the summer, the VRLR would not have figured in the network-wide traffic survey conducted for Beeching in April 1962. However, when the divisional managers were consulted about lines that might be closed it was not overlooked. At a divisional conference held on 21 August 1962 it was agreed to sell the VRLR as a going concern.

The managers were probably informed by a correspondence between the divisional traffic manager and traffic headquarters at Paddington under the heading of 'unremunerative railway services – Aberystwyth–Devil's Bridge' that had been started in January 1962. The cause was the 'estimated deficiency of revenue' of £2,340 in 1961 and the overdue decision on whether the VRLR should be run during the forthcoming summer. In 1961, 28,387 passengers had earned £6,818; the adult return fare for the full journey had been 6s. This compared with 31,395 passengers earning £4,570 in 1960 when the adult fare had been 3s 6d. No explanation was given for the large increase; the size of it implies that the results for 1960 had been marginal.

The traffic costing officer produced a report dated 24 January. The costs for 1961 are shown in the table. While trains were running, a ganger, sub ganger and two lengthmen were employed full time on the VRLR. It had not been possible to determine where the costs of three ballast trains run during 1961 had been allocated. Although additional summer season signalling posts had been authorised, in 1961 the district reliefmen were used.

Estimate of operating costs 1961

Train movement costs			
Provision, renewal, interest and maintenance of engines and coaches	£3,634		
Running costs – engines and coaches	£1,348		
Trainmen	£1,426	£6,408	
Station costs			
Staff – no basis of apportionment available			
Building maintenance – branch stations only	£8	£8	
Track and signalling			
Permanent way gang wages and materials	£953		
Track relaying proportion	£154		
Bridge, fences, cabins etc. maintenance and renewal (proportion)	£213		
	£1,320		
Signalling staff costs	£723		
Maintenance and renewal (proportion) of facilities	£121		
Rental of GPO telephone line	£184	£1,028	£2,348
Publicity		£394	
			£9,158

Closing the VRLR would not result in immediate savings. The costs included provision for interest and renewal of locos and rolling stock. Labour costs related to men employed elsewhere and who would not be laid off if it closed. Costs would be affected, increased by the introduction of a 42-hour week.

Sending the report on to London, the divisional traffic manager asked for approval to operate the VRLR in 1962 and said that he would review the position in the autumn, analysing train loadings and the use of personnel. Permission to operate was given on 5 February 1962, with a rider that the 6s fare was the maximum allowed by statute, 3d per mile, and could not be increased.

On 5 September 1962, the Western Region's accountant wrote that although working expenses for 1961 had actually been £12,590, increasing the deficit to £5,770, they included interest and depreciation on the rolling stock (£4,149), and non-variable overheads of £1,241, which should be disregarded. As a result, the deficit was only £380 'which is not significant'. He pointed out that deficit was almost equal to the cost of publicity.

R. F. Hanks, the chairman of the BTC's Western Area Board, had written to the region's general manager on 28 August 1962: 'I fear the days of the … very attractive little railway are numbered.' Observing that societies had been formed to purchase 'old and outmoded' railways', citing the Talyllyn and Festiniog Railways, and saying 'neither of these had anything like the attractive assets we can offer in the case of the Vale of Rheidol Railway … by dint of a good deal of enthusiasm and hard work by volunteers they are running again', he suggested that the VRLR should be valued and advertised for sale. 'We might get much more this way than by merely closing it, pulling up the track and having left on our hands the locomotives, rolling stock etc.'

Approval to sell the VRLR was given by the BTC on 6 September 1962, with a rider that the commission's operating powers could only be transferred to a new owner by means of a Light Railway Order.

The decision to sell the VRLR was addressed on 19 October and the various departments were asked to submit valuations of the line and its equipment on 6 November 1962. Receipts for the year were £6,368 from 26,849 passengers; 147 passengers per train generating £34 8s 9d in 1962 compared with 137 passengers and receipts of £32 13s 2d the year before, because the number of operating days had been less. Costs, reduced to £10,950 largely because of a reduction in civil engineering expenses, produced a deficit of £4,580.

The valuation was produced on 14 December 1962, in time for a meeting with members of Aberystwyth Corporation on 17 December. The rolling stock valuation was scrap value, its gross replacement value being £63,990.

British Railways took a while to identify VRLR stock as its own, with No 8 retaining its GWR livery until 1953 and Nos 7 and 9 running without any indication of ownership at all. No 9, painted black when it was renumbered from No 1213 in 1948, was photographed at Devil's Bridge on 14 June 1950.
R. E. Tustin/Author's collection

Valuation of Vale of Rheidol Light Railway, December 1962

Land	£36,000
Permanent way, buildings, bridges, fences, level crossings, culverts, drains etc. (in situ)	£32,750
Signalling and telecommunications equipment	£390
Rolling stock	£3,660
	£72,800

Valuation of rolling stock, 30 November 1962

	Type	Quantity	Year built	Book life	Original cost	Gross replacement cost	Residual value
Locomotives							
No 9	2-6-2T	1	1902	50 years	£1,750	£10,750	£390
No 7	2-6-2T	1	1923	50 years	£2,737	£10,750	£390
No 8	2-6-2T	1	1923	50 years	£2,737	£10,750	£390
Coaching stock							
	Non-gangwayed corridor 2nd	4	1923	40 years	£2,604	£8,050	£520
	Non-gangwayed corridor 2nd	10	1938	40 years	£4,790	£15,700	£1,300
	Non-gangwayed open 2nd brake	2	1938	40 years	£990	£3,250	£260
	Luggage and brake	3	1938	40 years	£678	£2,340	£260
Freight vehicles							
	Mineral wagons	4	1904	25 years	£168	£1,120	£60
Service vehicles							
	Ballast wagons	4	1904	35 years	£108	£720	£60
	Rail wagons	2	1904	40 years	£84	£560	£30
					£16,646	£63,990	£3,660
Conversions							
	Flats (stores and material)	2					£30

The meeting took place at Paddington. The railway made a small profit without taking renewals into account, but when major capital expenditure was required it was inevitable that it would be recommended for closure. No case could be made for hardship that the Transport Users' Consultative Committee could use to recommend retention. The line had been valued at £140,000, an amount that was too high to be considered, therefore, on the basis that by reducing wages and staffing levels the railway could make a profit of £1,500 to £2,000, the council could buy it for £20,000. Or, to put it another way, an investment of £20,000 might earn up to 10%. These figures were pure guesswork, for the railway team had no idea what wages the council would have to pay or how many employees it would need.

When the council team tried to negotiate on the price they were told that it was not negotiable. It was subject to survey, however, and the council had three months to respond. From 1 January 1963 it would have to negotiate with the London Midland Region (LMR) which would then be taking over responsibility for the former GWR lines in mid Wales. The details were confirmed by the town clerk the next day, when he concluded by stating that the council's preference was for the VRLR to be continued under BTC control.

On 7 January 1963, the LMR informed the town clerk that the survey had revealed minimal liabilities over the next five years – permanent way, £770; bridges, £400, fencing, £20 and painting, £90.

News of the offer to sell the VRLR started to leak out. The National Trust declared an interest and Beazley renewed his interest from 1953, after a story about the possible sale had been published in the *Cambrian News*. The council failed to respond to a letter seeking information about its intentions on 3 April, leading to the LMR writing: 'I presume that your council is no longer interested ...' on 26 April 1963.

The town clerk replied straight away. Yes, the council was still interested, but as it had heard that arrangements were being made for trains to be run it had assumed that it had been withdrawn from sale. This was a rather fatuous response. Arrangements had been made to run the line because the council had been quiet on the subject since the meeting the previous December, and it had ignored the letter of 3 April.

The 26 April letter was mistimed, for unknown to Euston, a meeting with council representatives and the divisional manager at Chester had taken place at Aberystwyth on 25 April 1963. The outcome was that the LMR decided make an effort to promote the VRLR during 1963 with a target of attracting 5,000 more passengers and turning the loss into a profit. If it did not succeed then the railway would be closed. The council played its part by accepting that it had a responsibility to create fresh business for the VRLR if it was to continue in BR management.

The effort was worthwhile. By 25 August, 27,122 passengers had earned £6,135 compared with 21,913 earning £5,159 over the same 12-week period in 1962. At the end of the season a profit of £610 was declared. This had been aided by the unremarked-upon removal of the loops at Capel Bangor and Aberffrwd; the VRLR was now a much more basic railway. In 1961 a standard gauge Wickham trolley was regauged to aid

permanent way maintenance; it ran until 1984. The Capel Bangor carriage shed was probably demolished when the loop was removed; it had survived into BR days only with the aid of poles supporting its walls.

An irregularity concerning the VRLR's goods service was uncovered in March 1964, for although it had been withdrawn by the GWR in 1931, the stations were still listed as freight depots. After due processing, the stations were listed as only handling passenger and parcel traffic from 1 June 1964.

The LMR made its mark by painting the carriages dark green in 1964, intended to represent Cambrian bronze green, lettered VofR on the sides in gold. It did not wear well and apparently some were repainted, without the lettering, within three years.

Another would-be purchaser surfaced in August 1965, when Roland F. White of Cromar White Developments Ltd, miniature railway engineers, declared an interest. He was told that, whilst

Above: **The first style of BR emblem had been applied to No 9 when it was photographed at Devil's Bridge on 8 September 1954. The carriage livery was maroon and cream; a 1938 brake third is coupled next to the loco.** *Adrian Gray collection*

Below: **1956 was the first time that the GWR-built locomotives carried the same livery, green with the first BR logo on the tanksides, seen here on 29 June 1956.** *H. C. Casserley/Author's collection*

it was true that the VRLR's circumstances were reviewed occasionally, no firm decision as to its future had been taken.

The review of 1965 reported income of £10,820, including £900 attributed to non-VRLR stations and £300 of miscellaneous income from Devil's Bridge. There were no through bookings, the £900 was an estimate of re-bookings. Costs of £9,040 comprised £5,990 for movements (operating),

Top: **Aberystwyth main line station as rebuilt by the GWR in 1935. The VRLR station is to its right; a poster board advertising services is just visible. A banner above the main entrance also promotes VRLR services.** *C. B. Swallow/ Author's collection*

Below: **No 8 heads a short train out of Aberystwyth c1964. It had been named** *Llywelyn* **in 1956 and painted in lined-green livery in 1957.The faux Cambrian carriage livery was replaced in 1968.** *Ian Allan Library*

Bottom: **Two trains are prepared to leave the 1925 station in 1953. The vantage point might have been the home signal post.** *C. L. Fry/Author's collection*

Seen from a point closer to the ground, No 8 crosses Smithfield Road with a good load on 5 August 1966. The crossing box has been moved next to the road since 1925. *R. E. Toop*

£400 terminal and £2,650 for track and signalling. There had been two drivers, two firemen, a guard and two signalmen, one each at Aberystwyth and Devil's Bridge, all posts for the summer only. There was no allocation of personnel for permanent way or other maintenance. The ordinary return was still 6s but there were also cheap day returns of 4s in the off-season and 5s in the peak-season. These compared with the 6s 1d return bus fare, a situation that attracted the suggestion that they should be increased.

In 1966, the VRLR made a loss of £2,128. The Stoke-on-Trent divisional manager, George Dow, who now had responsibility for it, was asked to report on the situation and did so on 11 April 1967. The principal reason for the loss, he explained, was the limited use that could be made of train crews outside the holiday season. At the present time they were used to relieve staff undergoing diesel training, but that was not a permanent solution. He would like to investigate the possibility of employing medically-fit retired railwaymen on a seasonal basis; doing so would save £3,217 a year although he realised that the unions might not agree to it.

Savings might also be achieved by straightening the line at Aberystwyth, a move that would eliminate a level crossing and produce a plot of land that could be sold to offset the cost. It would also allow the standard gauge locomotive shed to be used as 'much improved garaging accommodation' for the VRLR locomotives and coaching stock.

These changes would make the line viable in the short term but expenses were still likely to increase and the time would come when no more economies could be made. Dow proposed a two-stage programme. First, to make the line profitable and, if possible, to divorce its operation from BR by using seasonal

staff then to seek a council guarantee to cover any future revenue shortfall. If the council would not agree then the possibility of a sale would have to be investigated.

The report did not refer to a meeting that had been held on 3 March 1967, where it had been agreed to develop a scheme to divert the VRLR into the main line station and to make the standard gauge locomotive shed, closed in April 1965, available to the VRLR.

Responding to the report, the LMR's general manager told Dow not to open negotiations with the unions over staffing, doing so might only give short-term relief and could be abortive, but that the time was right for a sale to be pursued, especially as the locomotives and rolling stock would not incur heavy maintenance costs for 'a year or two'. As it would take time to conclude a sale and it was desired to sell the railway as a going concern he should proceed with plans to operate the 1967 season.

Writing to the LMR's assistant general manager on 19 May, Dow thought that his recommendations had been dismissed in a cavalier manner. Surely, the land requirements should be clarified before the line was offered for sale. He had written after attending a priorities meeting the same date, where the general manager had given verbal approval to realign the track. Its £2,800 notional cost would release land valued at £7,000–£8,000.

By the time that a response was sent to Dow on 1 June 1967, the British Railways Board had approved the line being put up for sale. The question of the realignment and the disposal of the surplus land could be dealt with as a part of the disposal as the

The VRLR's original station site seen from the crossing on 14 June 1950. Carriages are stabled on a siding made out of the former loop, the end of the rake obscuring the loco shed. *R. E. Tustin/ Author's collection*

purchaser might want to buy the land as well. The assistant general manager agreed with Dow that BR's staffing agreements were inappropriate to the VRLR, saying that the effort involved in changing them was out of proportion to any possible gain.

A letter from Dow to the general manager dated 26 June 1967 explained that the seasonal signalling post at Devil's Bridge was normally covered by an Aberystwyth-based relief signalman, but in 1966 it was covered by a redundant guard. Dealing with a maximum of four trains a day at that time, this would not have been the busiest post on BR. In another letter on the same date he mentioned that one of the reasons the line did not cover its costs was because it paid the trainmen for 52 weeks whilst it only needed them for 16 weeks. He was instructed to inform the staff and the council that consideration was being given to selling the line.

The VRLR's profile was raised considerably by a visit from the minister of transport, Barbara Castle MP, on 1 July. En route to a Welsh Labour rally at Aberystwyth, she joined a train at Devil's Bridge. Asked about the line's future, she said that the BR board had made no proposal to close it. Whilst this was true it paid no regard to the situation or the fact of a sale not being a precursor to closure. The ministry had been briefed in advance of the journey and Dow had briefed the minister during it. Following newspaper reports about the proposed sale and a display of anger by the council, the minister's Parliamentary secretary demanded an explanation.

The key to what was called a 'misunderstanding' was that the ministry failed to understand the subtlety of the statement: 'there is no proposal to close the line, but the position is reviewed at the end of each season.' BR admitted that whilst the LMR had not informed the ministry of its intention to sell the railway, the final decision on a sale would be the minister's, who would have to decide whether or not to make a Light Railway Order.

BR officers met at Aberystwyth to consider the VRLR on 13 July 1967. The standard gauge level crossing at Llanbadarn, 80 yards from the VRLR's crossing on the same road, was due to be automated. A suggestion that the VRLR be realigned to run parallel with and adjacent to the main line to eliminate its crossing was rejected because of the amount of agricultural land that would be required and the peak summer service was only three return trains a day.

At Aberystwyth, two options were considered for realigning the VRLR. Retaining the existing station site was considered impracticable owing to the existence of the cattle market on some of the land that would be required for the altered route. The alternative was to use the MMR bay on the south side of the station. This would have the advantage of bringing the VRLR close to the standard gauge locomotive shed, which it could use, and save BR the expense of demolishing it.

Dow was informed on 19 July 1967 that the area board had agreed to the sale of the VRLR as an alternative to closure. He was still expecting the council to buy it, although he thought the Western Region's price of £20,000 was far too low. Within a few days political pressure had both changed and clarified BR's position. On 24 July 1967, Elystan Morgan, the MP for Cardigan, posted a written Parliamentary question calling upon the minister to use her powers to prevent a sale. Three days later, he too was told that the minister would be the final arbiter.

It will come as no surprise that by 2 August 1967 the BR board had decided to 'disengage' from negotiations with the council on the basis that it intended to continue running the VRLR itself, 'a bit longer'. Despite all the publicity and talk of closure at the height of the season, the VRLR still made a loss of £954.

During the summer, arrangements had been made to relocate the VRLR terminus into the former MMR platform, disused since 1964. Before it could take place the Shell Mex & BP oil depot, served by a private siding on the stub of the Carmarthen line, required removing to the goods yard. As BR's programme left the oil company with insufficient time to relocate its installation a temporary pipeline was required. The works order for the alterations was issued on 21 February 1968.

Work on the re-alignment was well under way but arrangements for using the loco shed still had not been finalised. On 25 April 1968, the general manager wrote that he was prepared to agree to its use providing that it was only used for storage, that any servicing and repairs were carried out outside, otherwise the building would be regulated by the Factories Act. As no-one would be working in it for more than 21 hours per week the Offices, Shops & Railway Premises Act would not apply either. The existing inspection pit in the shed must be filled in too; he was emphatic about that.

Estimated outlay for re-routing Vale of Rheidol line into main station

	Original	Revised
Track alterations, loco facilities, platforms	£2,950	£5,020
Signalling	£948	£2,378
Shell Mex & BP pipe line	£1,650	£1,831
	£5,540	£9,229

Explanation of overspending on re-location works 1968

Signalling and telegraphs		
Amount underestimated for original work	£357	
Additional signalling not originally taken into account Down refuge siding	£1,081	£1,438
Civil engineering		
New sleepers and track not originally allowed for	£200	
Tarmac road surface, under estimated	£25	
Additional labour costs	£127	
Widening internal pit (estimate)	£200	
Repair to transfer siding for passenger train operation during first week, £75 plus overheads, cost over recovering 846 yards of plain line and 110 yards of crossing work. Only 400 yards allowed for in original estimate.	£583	
Consequent loss of credit	£275	£1,410
Shell Mex & BP		
Original amount authorised	£1,650	
First account	£1,275	
Final account	£556	
	£1,831	
Overspending		£181
Additional work		
Civil engineering		
Internal pit to be deepened from 2ft to 3ft	£50	
Internal pit rail support wall to be replaced by piers with 4ft centres (£390) and external ashpit to be lengthened to 10ft between rails and on the side (£140)	£530	
Track alterations inside shed to permit stabling of coach sets and coaling of locos beyond the shed. Will allow VRLR coal wagons to be recovered.	£80	
		£660
Total		£3,689

As the tables show, the works were not carried out to budget and they were not finished on time. The additional work was carried out in December 1969/January 1970 after experience had revealed shortcomings in the original scheme. There was no complaint about the overspend, perhaps because the 7½ acres of land released by the realignment was valued at £26,625. When the works order was closed in December 1970 the total expenditure was given as £7,489 including the pipeline, an underspend of £1,740. The cost of removing the MMR platform canopy in 1968/9 was probably absorbed in the station maintenance budget.

At Easter, 13-16 April 1968, the last trains ran over the old line and on Monday, 20 May the first train over the new line, the 14.15, was waved off by the mayor-elect of Aberystwyth, Ceri Jones. Intriguingly, there was, as shown above, a cost of £75 to accommodate passenger trains at the former Cambrian exchange siding 'during first week', probably the Easter operation; the significance of this has not been uncovered.

Approval for the internal pit was given of 18 June 1968, after the chief mechanical and electrical engineer had complained. A 'fairly extensive' overhaul of locomotives and carriages had been carried out during the mild winter of 1967/8 with great difficulty; there was a considerable back-log of essential maintenance required on the locomotives due to neglect over a long period. The nature of the work justified main workshop repairs, but with conscientious and co-operative staff and experienced supervision it could be carried out at Aberystwyth, provided facilities were reasonable. The heavy maintenance had to be done during the winter and covered accommodation was essential to avoid delay due to weather and lack of light.

To comply with the Factories Act, expenditure in the order of £1,655 was required. Before approval was given, Dow was told: 'An amount of £3,740 has already been invested in this unprofitable line ... I would like to know what adaptation of the pit is likely to cost.' The estimate was £150, but it actually cost £350.

Services in 1968 were accompanied by the introduction of mechanised ticket issuing. At Aberystwyth the five most common tickets were issued using an Ultimatic machine whilst other issues were made from a Setright machine. Guards were also issued with one of these machines for issues at intermediate stations and Devil's Bridge. Accompanying this modernisation the signalling at Devil's Bridge was removed, permitting the signalman's post to be abolished, and the distinction between the arrival and

The parapets of the Manchester & Milford Railway bridge that No 8 and its train have just passed under may just be discerned to the right of the loco's chimney in this 26 August 1948 view. *H. C. Casserley*

departure lines ceased. Train control by staff and ticket was introduced, minimal signalling at Aberystwyth protecting any local movements when a train was on the main line.

At Devil's Bridge, train crews would use the telephone to obtain permission from Aberystwyth signalbox to depart. The ticket machines cost £251 and the staff savings were £450. The guards were paid an extra £44, in total, to compensate them for the extra work entailed in issuing tickets at Devil's Bridge as well as the intermediate stations. An estimated £100 car park revenue would be lost at Devil's Bridge, the implication being that the signalman had supervised the car park, issued tickets and looked after the trains. Why the changes to train operating were linked to the ticket issue mechanisation is not clear.

It was also in 1968 that the standard BR Rail blue livery was adopted for the VRLR locomotives and carriages. The double-arrow symbol was applied in white. The work was carried out at Aberystwyth and was seen for the first time at Easter, 13-16 April. Along the line, all the stations and halts received new signs in the standard format, white with black lettering. So, with its new station, new livery, new tickets and new signs, the VRLR of 1968 looked very different from that of 1967. Dow retired on 29 June 1968 – he should have been well satisfied with what he had achieved.

An undated and unsigned consultant's report on the VRLR appears to have been compiled during 1968. Correspondence in another file suggests that it was compiled by John Crawley, an enthusiast better known for his interest in road steam vehicles, and submitted, with an apology for delay, in July 1969. It stated the adoption of the Rail blue livery deprived the railway of its character and was an error of judgment. The new layout at

Aberystwyth was an operational improvement, but hid the railway from public view; previously the terminus was alongside the largest car park and coach park in the town. At Devil's Bridge the station was tucked away and signing was poor. The timetable left a lot to be desired and was sparse. Recommendations included painting the locomotives and carriages in GWR livery, erecting 'steam railway' signs at the termini, establishing a shop in a portable building at Devil's Bridge to replace the existing outlet in the old weighbridge office, locating two Pullman cars at Devil's Bridge as a catering facility, retaining card tickets, introducing a railway letter service and running inclusive DMU excursions to the VRLR complete with refreshments, and improving the timetable and reinstating Aberffrwd loop.

The report concluded that the railway was ripe for exploitation, efforts had been made, having a manager who could run the line and exploit it would be better. 'I would also imagine that the railway suffers at the hands of the BR accountants in arriving at charges for work done by the different departments. Given a fair chance the railway could be made profitable, the extent of which will depend upon … the funds … put aside … for future maintenance.' Some of the recommendations were acted upon; the timetable was improved, without a loop, Devil's Bridge got catering, but not in Pullmans, a shop was set up in the station building, a railway letter service was started in 1970, and signage was improved.

After 11 August 1968, the VRLR was the only steam service operated by BR. During the year, 48,532 passengers were carried, earning £12,873. The deficit was £15,000.

The future of the railway between Aberystwyth and Machynlleth was threatened by the possible sale of the VRLR to a 'London-based syndicate', the Aberystwyth Trades Council and the Association of Locomotive Engineers & Firemen declared in February 1969. In 1967, only 31,000 passengers had left the town by train compared with 47,000 who had travelled on the VRLR. A two-year grant to support the line to

No 8 leaves Aberystwyth on the original alignment on 13 August 1956. The standard gauge carriages mark the alignment adopted by the VRLR in 1968. The railway's new workshop and loco shed was being built on the site of the former water tower, to the left of the stabled carriages, as this book was being prepared for publication. *H. N. James/Author's collection*

Shrewsbury, which had been under threat of closure, had been announced a few days before, but they felt that its future was still insecure and would be weakened if the VRLR traffic was lost. They also objected to the round-trip fare being increased from 7s 6d to 10s.

The syndicate had first approached BR to enquire about the possibility of buying the VRLR in February 1968. Despite the uproar after the minister's visit the year before, BR was still a willing vendor and notwithstanding the minister's antipathy

towards the idea, had engaged with the ministry to establish a strategy for the VRLR's disposal. It was considered that rather than formally closing the line before disposing of it, it should be sold as a going concern to the highest bidder who was able to obtain a light railway order. The price had been reviewed and bids in the range of £20,000 to £27,000 would be sought. On 11 July 1968, John Bernard Snell, the syndicate's spokesman, told BR that he wanted to complete the sale by around 1 January 1969.

The minister was moved to a new post in April 1968, removing one possible obstacle to a sale, although her successor, Richard Marsh's, approval to it had not been obtained. The political pressure was continued, though, in the form of a letter from John Morris, MP for Aberavon, who had holidayed at Aberystwyth and had found himself bombarded, probably an overstatement, about the VRLR's future.

Staff employed on VRLR 1968

Position	Wages	Overtime	Sunday duty	Bonus	Consequence of sale
Drivers (2)	£1,096	£140	£74	£74	Redundant – difficult to place for 38 weeks per annum
Secondmen (2)	£806	£110	£60		Ditto
Shedman	£175	£49	£63		Ditto
Fitter	£195	£137	£84		Ditto
Guards (2)	£474	£65	£69	£30	Deployed elsewhere, would lose VRLR overtime
Carriage & wagon examiner			£36		Deployed elsewhere, would lose VRLR overtime
Signalman			£78		Would lose VRLR Sunday overtime
Station foreman			£68		Would lose VRLR Sunday overtime
Porter			£61		Would lose VRLR Sunday overtime
Clerk			£84		Would lose VRLR Sunday overtime
Carriage serviceman and porter *	£336			£42	Would not be re-engaged

Wages under these heads totalled £4,401.

Employment costs totalling £1,270 were incurred by the civil and signalling engineers for VRLR maintenance.

* Temporary summer staff

Right: **Explosive exhaust from No 7 as it passes the Plascrug exchange siding on 18 July 1968.** *M. Dunnett/Ian Allan Library*

Below: **Even in the 1960s the little-used intermediate stations were kept in good order, as illustrated by this view of No 7 at Llanbadarn in August 1968.** *J. Reeves/Ian Allan Library*

Bottom: **Llanbardarn's busiest moment came with the Royal Welsh Show on 24-26 July 1957, when 25,260 6d returns were issued. Two locos worked eight carriages on a push-pull basis at 12-minute intervals.** *Author's collection*

Correspondence with Snell continued throughout 1968. Nothing could be done until the minister sanctioned a sale, he was told. He asked for the surplus turnouts from the old terminus to be retained for sale with the railway, and was concerned to see the entire redundant track listed for sale by the stores department in October. He was told that although the sale could be deferred for a short time, deterioration caused by much delay would reduce its value – perhaps he should make an offer for it. The invitation was declined: 'we are not interested in becoming small-scale scrap merchants'. With the sale of the land to the council proceeding, the track was lifted and put into store alongside the loco shed before the year's end.

Although the correspondence was ultimately fruitless, Snell was treated seriously by the LMR's assistant general manager, I. M. Campbell. In November 1968, he submitted a copy of a business plan and the draft of a letter to be sent to the council for comment. On 25 November, he pointed out that the VRLR's omission from the list of unremunerative lines to be subsidised or likely to be subsidised, made it difficult to avoid speculation about its future. He had asked the enthusiast press to avoid commenting on the VRLR, but could do so no longer. Campbell, however, did not take kindly to Snell's proposal that a notice should be issued about the negotiations, saying that the correspondence had been conducted on a personal basis and that Snell had not been negotiating with BR.

Eventually, the minister was persuaded to take a position on the VRLR's future. On 7 May 1969, the LMR's general manager was informed that he had decided 'not to proceed with the sale of this line in the near future.' 'In the near future' he was told, was code for 'not before the next general election.' Would-be purchasers and others concerned should be told that this was the board's decision and that it would be better to say:

'during the next two years' in preference for 'in the near future'. Snell was informed of the decision by letter dated 12 May.

His response must have been unexpected. So far as he was concerned the situation was unchanged. The decision was obviously politically induced, the Shrewsbury–Aberystwyth line's subsidy expired at the end of 1970, so therefore BR intended to operate the VRLR during 1970. The syndicate's involvement was founded on the basis that it was correct for BR to dispose of the railway and that BR agreed that it was a policy to be adopted when circumstances allowed. A company would be formed and would be in touch.

Vale of Rheidol Railway Limited was registered on 12 August 1969. Its objectives were to purchase or otherwise acquire 'the railway now existing between Aberystwyth and Devil's Bridge … and to carry on the business of running a railway.' The founding shareholders were Geoffrey Stuart Drury, John Bernard Snell, John Brian Hollingsworth, Patrick Bruce Whitehouse, Patrick John Garland, Peter Christopher Allen, and Richard Hugh Dunn. They were railway enthusiasts of the first magnitude.

Drury and Hollingsworth owned standard gauge steam locomotives. Snell, Garland and Whitehouse had been involved in the revival of the Talyllyn Railway, and Garland and Whitehouse had strong links with what is now called the Tyseley Locomotive Works, Birmingham, and the Dart Valley Railway (now the South Devon Railway). Allen was the chairman of ICI, the major chemical company, and of the Transport Trust. Dunn was a solicitor with strong links to the Severn Valley Railway.

The historic church at Llanbadarn is visible on the left of this view of No 7 on the Rheidol river bridge, c1968. *G. D. King*

Above: **No 8 approaching Glanrafon on 18 August 1965. A brake van is coupled next to the loco. The area is now an industrial estate.** *P. F. Plowman*

Right: **Facilities at Glanrafon were always minimal, but it did retain its sign.** *P. J. Sharpe*

Snell informed BR and the council that the company had been formed, but only told the latter the company's name. On 27 August 1969, the council's town clerk wrote to BR that he was concerned, 'the use of this name ... must assist in giving the impression ... that the company has a proprietary interest in the railway ...' Was BR aware of the intention for form the company and did it object to, or propose to object to, the use of the name?

Apologising for not having told BR about the name, Snell said that it was an oversight. Internally, BR's solicitor wrote that he doubted that the company's name was 'so misleading as to be likely to cause harm to the public', the only cause for objection after a company has been registered, but he was willing to make representations if required.

Letters of complaint about the company were sent to BR by the rail unions, resulting in BR having to defend its position to the local MP, and Campbell formally terminating his correspondence with Snell. Campbell informed the council that

little would be gained by objecting to the company name. However, the council's response and the other letters prompted a change of view, 'that it might be politic' to make a formal protest to the registrar of companies.

Before making a protest, BR's solicitor decided to see if the company could be persuaded to change its name voluntarily. As a gesture of support, the name Vale of Rheidol Equipment Limited was chosen, BR being informed on 10 November 1969.

In 1969, the VRLR made a profit of £229 on a turnover of £20,073. Takings at the new Devil's Bridge shop, which had not been open for the full season, were £1,580 from stock purchased for £1,370. A longer season and operation of more trains to be operated in 1970 were anticipated to improve results.

Dialogue between Snell and BR was resumed in 1970, apparently at the latter's instigation, the copy of the letter concerned is missing, although the relationship soured in November when Snell revealed that the company's name had not been changed. He argued that as the company was inactive there did not seem to be much point. There is nothing more in the BR files relating to the company.

No 99.3461, an 0-8-0T, was bought from the recently closed Mecklenberg–Pommersche Spurbahn in the former East Germany, for possible use in December, and was stored at Carnforth. Another locomotive, 0-8-0T No 99.3462, was obtained from the same source in 1972. BR engineers did inspect the latter while it was in store at the Festiniog Railway, but failed to see how it could be usefully adapted for the VRLR. Both locomotives were to be sold in 1978 and the company was to be struck off the register of companies in 1984.

Initiatives in 1970 were the establishment of the Vale of Rheidol Railway Supporters' Association and a railway letter service. Set up with the objective of promoting the VRLR under BR ownership, the association was run from the district manager's office at Stoke-on-Trent. Members received a quarterly duplicated newsletter and a discount voucher for travel on the VRLR.

There had been changes in BR management and the government elected in June 1970 might have brought with it a change in policy regarding the VRLR. At the end of the year the LMR asked the divisional manager at Stoke to make a financial case for sale or retention. The results for 1970 were much better, turnover of £29,233 producing a profit of £4,951, including £800 from the shop. The divisional manager reported on 24 March 1971, that if the line was to be sold he recommended starting at £150,000 and being prepared to settle for £100,000. The realisable assets, locomotives, carriages and track were worth much more than the £30,000-£40,000 previously proposed as an asking price.

Whilst the headquarters' files concentrate on the VRLR's financial position, there were developments on the ground that escaped attention. In December 1970, No 7 was sent to Chester wagon repair shops for a light overhaul; No 9 was sent for a general overhaul 12 months later. A full-colour guidebook was published in 1971.

An extension of track was put in place for the 1972 season. In order to run more trains it was necessary to accommodate three trains simultaneously at Devil's Bridge by lengthening the siding by 38 yards at a cost of £345. The extra trains were expected to increase revenue by £800.

Reorganisation within BR in 1974 saw responsibility of VRLR maintenance taken over by the area maintenance engineer at Wolverhampton. Operating responsibility was transferred from Machynlleth to Shrewsbury.

Also in 1974, No 7 was sent away again, this time to Swindon, where it received a new boiler, returning to traffic in June 1976. Its blue livery had been enhanced by being lined out in black and white, with brass BR logos being applied to its cabsides. In September 1975, three carriages and the brake van were sent to Shrewsbury station where Wolverhampton-based personnel carried out repairs in a workshop established on an unused platform. They too were repainted with the BR blue livery lined out in black and white. One carriage was repainted in this form at Aberystwyth. All were in traffic by June 1976. Further carriage overhauls were carried out at Chester. No 9 was overhauled at Swindon in 1976/7.

Facilities at Devil's Bridge had also received attention in 1974. A portable building accommodated ladies' facilities and a connection was made to the mains water supply. The space previously occupied by the ladies' was incorporated into the shop. The budget was £1,900.

The hot summer of 1976 and a number of lineside fires prompted a review of locomotive policy and the conversion of

the fleet to oil firing. No 7 was converted and trialled in February 1978; the system was the same as that used by the Festiniog Railway and the equipment required was made at the FR's Boston Lodge Works. In September 1977 No 8 had been sent to Swindon and two carriages to Shrewsbury. The locomotive work had cost a total of £75,000.

A landslip near the Erwtomau mine, when a part of the embankment slipped into an old mineshaft, closed the line for four days from 6 July 1979.

Changes to liveries were started in April 1981, when No 8 appeared in GWR green, complete with shirt-button logo. The repainting had been carried out at Aberystwyth. The divisional manager explained that the new livery was part of an effort to revitalise the VRLR. It started a trend, and sponsorship was obtained for more repaints. When No 9 was turned out in 1902-style VRLR livery in 1982, the work was sponsored by Richard Metcalfe, a descendent of James Metcalfe, not knowing that the locomotive had been built by the GWR in 1924. Shell (UK) sponsored the repainting of No 7 in BR Western Region livery in 1983. In 1986, No 8 was repainted again, being turned out in Cambrian Railways' black livery, with its nameplates removed.

The carriages were not ignored either. From 1982 VRLR crest transfers were affixed to the bodysides, then from 1983 the passenger stock was repainted in GWR livery, a paint company sponsoring the work. Also in 1983, the Wales Tourist Board and the Development Board for Rural Wales sponsored the conversion of one of the carriages into a vista car, travel in the vehicle attracting a supplement. In 1983 and 1984, the Westinghouse Brake & Signal Company Limited sponsored the conversion of the brake thirds to brake firsts. In 1986, two of the carriages were named *Myfanwy*, after Myfanwy Talog, a TV announcer, and *Lowri*, for Laura Ashley, the Carno-based designer.

A series of special trains and events through the 1970s and '80s helped to keep the VRLR in the public eye. The highlight of these was the visit of the Festiniog Railway's Alco 2-6-2T *Mountaineer* on 13/14 September 1986, an occasion that attracted large crowds. Despite this effort, the traffic figures inexorably declined, and by 1987 they were less than they had been in 1969. Notwithstanding the declining revenue, a Permaquip personnel carrier had been supplied to the line in 1985, replacing the Wickham trolley, in 1986 a glassfibre liner was fitted in the GWR water tank at Aberystwyth, and in 1988, Mid Wales Development made a grant of £15,000 towards the £45,000 cost of a 140hp diesel locomotive obtained from the Brecon Mountain Railway.

Whatever profits were made by the VRLR they were insufficient to cover the costs of renewals. A serious derailment at Nantyronen on 26 May 1986 demonstrated that underneath the fresh paint the railway was not as sound as it should have been (see104). The loss in 1986 had been £108,000 and with a Conservative government in power since 1979, thoughts were turning to privatisation of the railways. More than ever, there was no reason for BR to be involved in the operation of a tourist steam railway.

Operating costs 1986

8 footplate/guards, 2 seasonal staff, 50% one clerk		£67,000
Locomotive costs		
5 staff	£43,000	
Materials	£10,000	
Fuel	£25,000	£78,000
Civil engineering costs		£85,000
Publicity		£10,000
Total		£240,000

The area manager at Shrewsbury thought that he could eliminate a traffic manager's post without the VRLR. Costs could be reduced by increasing staff productivity and eliminating restrictive practices.

Work on evaluating the VRLR's future started early in July 1987 and a report was submitted on the 27th. The options were: to retain the line in BR ownership and restore it to profitability, to make an agreement with Ceredigion District Council whereby BR would operate the line, the council promoting it and covering losses, or an outright sale. If the line was retained a loop would be reinstated to increase train frequency and operating flexibility. If it was sold, a price of at least £250,000, the current valuation, should be sought.

On 27 August 1987, a group of BR employees informed board members that it wished to buy and operate the line, pointing out that if it did so, it would recruit from the existing pool at Aberystwyth, avoiding transfer/redundancy costs 'or legislative difficulties', would promote share ownership amongst staff and increase through traffic from BR.

On 14 September 1987, the steps to be taken to sell the VRLR were agreed. In summary, the sale would comprise these elements:

● Register a company

● Make a scheme under Section 7 of the 1968 Transport Act to transfer the assets to the company

● Issue tender documents inviting bidders to tender to buy 100% of the company's share capital

● Initiate closure procedure once a successful bidder had been chosen and paid 10% deposit

● When consent for closure had been given, the vesting day for the asset transfer would be set, the successful bidder paying the balance of the purchase price within a specified period of time

Top: **Capel Bangor could still attract local passenger traffic when this photograph was taken on 19 September 1953, the last day of the season. The station building and carriage shed are still in situ. The loco is No 7.** *G. F. Bannister/ Author's collection*

Right: **No 8 stops for passengers at Nantyronen in the 1960s. On the ground near the back of the train lies a permanent way trolley.** *P. B. Whitehouse*

Installed by BR in 1982, the new water tank at Nantyronen
was seen in use on 4 December that year. Using No 7, the Vale of
Rheidol Railway Supporters' Association operated a special train
to mark the railway's 80th anniversary.
Andrew Bannister/Author's collection

BR's legal advice was that it could not sell the railway without formally withdrawing the service so it was necessary to withdraw the service only when a buyer had been identified. Lazard Brothers & Company was appointed to handle the sale, being paid a retainer of £20,000 per month from October 1987, plus a success fee of £60,000, plus expenses. A press release announcing the intention to offer the line for sale was issued on 18 November 1987.

Earlier, on 7 October 1987, the staff consortium, eight employees, had reaffirmed its interest in taking over the VRLR. By cancelling the bidding process and selling to the consortium for a nominal sum BR would save on the fees charged by the bank appointed to handle the sale. The sale would not take place within the present parliament without 'our active blessing and co-operation', the closure procedure and the weight of public opinion ensured that.

An off-the-shelf company named Crodall Limited and incorporated on 4 November 1987 was obtained and renamed Vale of Rheidol Railway Limited on 24 December 1987. A £100 share capital was created and on 5 August 1988 £1 was issued to Britravel Nominees Ltd and £1 to the British Railways Board.

The BRB's chief accountant had unexpected difficulty producing figures relevant to the VRLR, writing to colleagues on 7 January 1988 that he had discovered that the VRLR cost centre had been used as a 'dumping pot' for miscellaneous headquarters expenditure. He instructed that more care should be taken to ensure that figures were accurate.

From BR's perspective, the Department of Transport upset the applecart in a letter sent to its solicitor on 24 February 1988. Although the 1968 Transport Act could be used to transfer property rights and liabilities it could not be used to transfer operating rights. Therefore a light railway transfer order would be required. There was considerable debate about the rights and wrongs about this approach, but in the end both procedures were followed.

It was determined that whatever happened, 1988 would be the last year BR would operate the VRLR – the timetable leaflet even bore a black flash with the legend 'last year in British Rail ownership'. Following the publication of advertisements soliciting interest in the VRLR in January 1988, the invitation to tender, a 44pp brochure, was issued on 6 June and the advance notice of BR's intention to close the line was published on 29 June. As shown in the table, four bids were received.

Bidder	Bid	Net value of bid
Brecon Mountain Railway Limited	£306,500	£141,500
C. H. Eaves	£165,000	–
Oval (414) Limited (staff consortium)	£95,000 + £66,000	-£4,000
R. J. Harris	£10,500	-£154,500

The consortium had agreed to forego any redundancy benefits, valued by BR at £66,000. The net value of the bids was calculated by taking into account redundancy payments to the 18 persons likely to be affected by the sale, £150,000, £84,000 in the case of Oval (414) Limited, and site separation (fencing, gas and water supplies, re-siting a location cabinet) costs estimated at £15,000.

The Brecon Mountain Railway was then two miles long, established on a part of the Brecon & Merthyr Railway trackbed in 1980. A financier and stockbroker, Eaves was also the owner of Bury Football Club and a director of the Festiniog Railway Company; any documents that might have accompanied his bid were not retained. Nothing is known about Harris; his bank reference said that he owned substantial assets and could provide the £400,000 working capital he said the VRLR would need. The Brecon Mountain Railway (BMR) was selected as the preferred bidder on 4 August 1988 and notified on 8 August.

Above: **No 8 takes water at Aberffrwd in the early 1950s. The water tank, at Nantyronen until 1910, and groundframe, are on the left.** *P. B. Whitehouse*

Right: **Aberffrwd station buildings, starting signal and water column on 16 August 1952.** *F. W. Shuttleworth/ Author's collection*

Below: **When Aberffrwd loop was removed in 1963 the standpipe was moved to a position more convenient for the single line. No 9 takes water in the 1970s.** *Michael Whitehouse collection*

No 8 close to Devil's Bridge on 2 June 1977, its last season in unlined BR blue livery. Rails for stabling the permanent way trolley are to the left of the loco.
Graham B. Wise

On hearing that it had not been successful, the staff consortium wrote to BR on 10 August, complaining that its bid had not been properly evaluated, that it had not been given an opportunity to improve its bid and saying that it should have been given preference. On 23 August, it also wrote to the local MP and to the corporation: 'From our enquiries we know that our bid has not been read or fully understood by the BRB ...' and appealing for help to achieve preferred bidder status.

At a meeting with BR on 5 September, the consortium re-stated its case for preference to no avail and followed it up with a letter summarising its position the next day. It still wanted to acquire the VRLR, it was saddened that BR's decision was highly detrimental to its [BR's] public image, irrespective of the bid value the consortium's bid had many unique advantages – it did not identify them. If it had been allowed to meet the officer handling the disposal it could have established a rapport with him and the consortium would have saved money on professional advice. If BMR personnel visited the VRLR before the sale was complete they should be escorted by a senior BR manager 'to avoid embarrassment'.

This was followed up with another letter on 9 September 1988, alleging that the BMR had taken advantage of prior information about the consortium's bid. Around July 1987, the consortium had consulted the Great Little Trains of Wales Joint Marketing Panel (GLTW) and had been put in touch with the panel's treasurer, A. J. Hills, manager of the BMR. Claiming that it had obtained assurances that the BMR was not interested in the VRLR, the consortium had given details of its proposals to Hills and now claimed that he had used the information to make BMR's bid.

When Lazard Brothers interviewed Hills and his business partner, Peter Rampton, about the allegations on 19 September, a different picture emerged. On being told of the approach to the GLTW, Hills had suggested issuing a general statement to the effect that the VRLR should be kept open and jobs preserved. After the GLTW had sent him, unsolicited, several pages of figures produced by the consortium his response was that the organisation was not in a position to act as professional advisers, and did not know much about the VRLR. Looking at the figures, however, he saw errors, including a fundamental mistake regarding VAT. He told GLTW that he did not think much of the proposals and that it should adopt his proposal about a statement.

A consortium member telephoned him later to complain about the lack of support, when he explained his reservations about the figures, recommending professional advice be obtained.

Hills and Rampton had first become interested in the VRLR in September 1987, when it appeared that scrap merchants were interested in it and that it might be broken up. They were interested in the locomotives and other items – Rampton had a large collection of narrow gauge locomotives. They walked along part of the line and found it in better condition than expected.

Lazard Brothers and BR accepted that there had been no impropriety during the bidding process and that there was no agreement over the part the GLTW involvement might have played in the BMR formulating its bid. Both agreed that the BMR should continue as the preferred bidder. In letters to BR and in statements to the press the consortium continued making disparaging remarks about the BMR. *Private Eye*, published on 14 October 1988, had been told that if a VRLR train was derailed passengers faced a 400ft drop to their deaths and the only persons with sufficient skills to operate the line was the consortium or employees of the Festiniog or Snowdon Mountain railways. The consortium had valued the redundancy payments of its members at £205,000.

A problem had arisen with the sale, BR's solicitor informed the bid team on 3 October 1988. The BMR was concerned about the condition of the piles of the Rheidol river bridge and a retaining wall uphill from Rhiwfron. Either the purchase price should be renegotiated or BR should agree to carry out the works. The civil engineer had surveyed the bridge in 1987, when it required repairs estimated to cost £30,000, and the retaining wall would cost £5,000. The solicitor recommended asking BMR for a contribution towards the cost of the repairs if they were undertaken by BR.

The BMR refused to countenance the works being carried out by BR and when the purchase agreement was signed on 7 October, and the deposit of £30,650 paid, BR agreed to pay up to £30,000 towards the bridge repairs subject to them being carried out within five years. BR also undertook to carry out closed-season maintenance as if it were not selling the railway while the BMR undertook to run a minimum service of two trains a day, six days a week on five consecutive months for at least five years. Reciprocal travel facilities for employees were to

Devil's Bridge in September 1953. The goods sidings were to be removed in 1963 and the signal in 1967. The centre siding was realigned to the goods shed site and extended to store carriages in 1978.

be provided for five years and the shares could not be sold within five years without approval being obtained from BR.

Solicitors acting for the consortium had tried to delay proceedings with a fax to Lazard Brothers on 6 October, saying that they had been appointed and that the exchange should be deferred until they had had time to be fully briefed about their clients' claims the following week. No comment on the request has been found; it appears to have been ignored. The consortium then tried to get BR to meet its expenses, treating an offer that BR would 'consider' contributing to them as a firm commitment. Peat Marwick McLintock, the accountants, claimed £10,000 on 28 November 1988 and the solicitors claimed £3,890 on 25 January 1989. On 16 March 1989, BR offered to make an ex gratia payment of £10,000 towards the expenses. Cheques for £3,000 and £7,000 were sent to the solicitors and Peat Marwick McLintock respectively on 25 April.

The sale was completed with a flurry of legal activity on 28-31 March 1989. The ministerial decision on the application to close the VRLR prior to its sale was published on 28 March, when consent was given to the closure. The scheme to transfer the assets to the company was made on 28 March with the vesting date set as 29 March and £98 of the company's share capital was issued to BRB on 29 March, when the minister gave his approval to the sale. The company's £34,900 non-interest bearing unsecured loan stock was issued to BRB on 30 March.

The British Railways Board (Vale of Rheidol) Light Railway (Amendment) Order 1989 was made on 29 March, effective from 30 March. The crucial point of the order was that it defined Railway No 1, the 1968 diversion and its associated land, as a light railway. The officers who dealt with the order thought that

the 1925 extension had been constructed without powers, not realising that it was actually the 1968 works that had no legal sanction. Finally, A. J. Hills and P. J. Rampton were appointed directors of Vale of Rheidol Railway Limited on 31 March. The BMR elected to pay 45% of the sale price immediately, deferring the remainder, and paying interest on it, until 31 July.

The end of the BR era had been marked on 5 November, with a bonfire night special that was met by fireworks at the stations. The last train had been a Santa special on 18 December. With 31 March 1989 being a Friday, the BMR took over the VRLR from April 3; Aberystwyth booking office staff handed over the keys in silence. Considering the fees due to Lazard Brothers, at least £120,000, and the money due to the BMR for outstanding work (£53,000), BR did not do too well out of the sale. Train services under the new management started on 21 May.

BR had done well to keep the VRLR going for so long, although had it not been for the unwitting intervention of

Tickets sold 1958-87

1958	25,894	1968	48,532	1978	84,842
1959	29,559	1969	52,090	1979	72,481
1960	31,384	1970	62,241	1980	60,752
1961	26,667	1971	69,317	1981	59,412
1962	26,420	1972	76,680	1982	55,700
1963	34,560	1973	89,131	1983	55,100
1964	40,365	1974	92,369	1984	58.400
1965	42,808	1975	96,334	1985	52,700
1966	46,471	1976	85,668	1986	50,300
1967	46,301	1977	86,559	1987	51,000

Barbara Castle in 1966 the line would have been closed or sold much earlier. The VRLR's purpose as a general carrier had long gone but it still had, and has, a future as a tourist

Devil's Bridge water tank is outside the station. In BR days the loco would be left here while the crews took refreshments at one of the lineside houses. Since the line changed hands in 1989, the loco is stabled in the headshunt while the crews take refreshments in the station.
G. D. King

attraction. BR's management was hampered by its inability to treat it differently to the rest of the network and by the unwillingness of the unions to accept different conditions for personnel running it. Despite the difficulties, a number of innovations were introduced that ensured that the railway was not forgotten.

BR did not complete the 1988/9 winter maintenance on the VRLR rolling stock as agreed, probably because of the fuss that would have followed when it was discovered that it was doing work from which it would not benefit. On 31 March 1989, the BMR offered to release BR from the obligation provided it agreed to pay the BMR for doing the work.

Later, one of the invoices was passed for payment but rejected by BR's accounts department. On 29 August 1989, Hills informed BR that the final payment for the sale due on 31 July

had been deposited with the BMR's solicitors pending settlement of the outstanding invoices. The impasse was soon resolved.

In one sense, the new owners continued to operate the VRLR in the same way that BR had attempted, as a commercial line without volunteer input. In another, it was very different, in that their priority has been to concentrate on the line's infrastructure, rather than marketing.

Most of the track has been replaced with new rail, the first ever used on the railway, and the loops at Aberffrwd and Capel Bangor were reinstated in 1990 and 2004 respectively. Renewal of the Rheidol river bridge was carried out over the winter of 1991/2 at a cost of £105,077, the cheque for £30,000 due to the BMR being issued on 7 April 1992. A storage shed was erected at Capel Bangor in 2004.

No 9 was sent to the BMR's workshop at Pant, Merthyr Tydfil, to be overhauled on 19 May 1989, returning to service in

Work carried out by the BMR at BR expense 1989

Coaching stock

2	Carriages to have repairs and repainting completed	
12	Carriages to be fettled up and repaired as needed	
12	Wheelsets to be fitted after reprofiling and brake gear to be reassembled	
4	Bogies to be exchanged	
All remaining wheelsets to be examined and changed as needed		
Labour and materials		£10,900

Locomotives

No 8 to have repairs completed including rebushing and remetalling of motion, re-riveting of front frame and pony truck stretchers, repairs to bunkers and tanks, adjustments to axle centres running out of true, attention to pipework and fuel leaks, fitting refractory material to firebox and completion of boiler inspection. Labour and materials	£3,200
No 9 to have repairs completed including re-fitting tube plate, stays, tubes and smokebox, re-fitting and repairs to tanks and bunkers, re-bushing and re-metalling of motion. Repairs to pony trucks. Strip and repair boiler fittings, re-metalling of axle boxes, fitting re-tyred wheelsets and re-erection of locomotive and boiler inspection. Labour and materials	£8,900
	£23,000

maroon livery and with air brakes in July 1991. It was returned to the BMR in November and used on that railway's Santa trains during December. No 8 was overhauled at Pant between May 1993 and July 1996. By the time it was returned to service all the stock had been converted to air brakes. During the intervening years most of the railway's carriages have been rebuilt.

The sale agreement clause covering the sale of the company's shares was put into effect in 1990, when the BMR sought and obtained approval to sell them to the Phyllis Rampton Narrow Gauge Railway Trust, a charity founded by Rampton in 1985. The transfer was completed on 11 December 1990. The commercial relationship with the BMR was ended in November 1996. To validate its relationship with the trust, the railway company was registered as a charity on 16 June 1999. By the end of 2009 the company had received loans of more than £2.1 million from the trust.

The idea of developing a museum to house Rampton's locomotive collection at Aberystwyth was floated quiet soon after the purchase, and most additions since 1998 were sent to Aberystwyth or Capel Bangor for storage. Ownership of the remainder of the collection was transferred to the company in 2003. In 2004, the Heritage Lottery Fund rejected the first of several applications for financial support, but in June 2010 the Welsh Assembly Government announced that it would make a £300,000 contribution towards a £1.1 million project to develop a restoration/training workshop at Aberystwyth, the first stage of a 10-year development that will include a new station and enhanced passenger facilities. Construction of the workshop was well advanced at the time of publication.

With the continued support of the trust, the VRLR has a sound future. It is already in much better condition than at any time in its past and there is every reason to expect that situation to endure.

Right: **The 1925 station at Aberystwyth was used for the last time at Easter 1978, seeing blue-liveried trains for just a few days. No 9 waits to leave on Easter Monday, 15 April.** *J. A. M. Vaughan*

Below: **No 8 was photographed in the 'new' station on 11 April 1971, Easter day, as it waited to take an extra train to Devil's Bridge. The left-hand platform was to be demolished in 2011.** *A. G. Banton*

Above: **New alignment, new livery, new home. No 9 passes the standard gauge shed in August 1968. The signal gantry for Carmarthen-line trains is just visible in the loco's exhaust. The railway's new workshop is being built in the area to the left of this picture.** *J. Reeves*

Middle: **On 24 June 1968, No 7 was photographed passing the point of diversion between the original line and the diversion into the standard gauge station.** *D. L. Percival*

Bottom: **Locomotive maintenance in progress on No 9 in the 'new' shed on 8 December 1969.** *P. J. Lambeth*

Top: **In April 1977, No 9 returned from being overhauled at Swindon in lined-blue livery and with brass BR symbols. Its first train was photographed near Devil's Bridge on Good Friday, 8 April. The carriages had been repainted and lined out to match; the fleet numbers had not been reapplied.** *David Eatwell*

Middle: **The lack of attention given to the VRLR under BR management was highlighted on 26 May 1986, when two carriages tipped over on the curve at Nantyronen, fortunately without causing any major injuries.** *Alan C. Butcher*

Below: **During the VRLR's last years in BR ownership the locos were turned out in different liveries, represented by this view of No 9 in VRLR company livery approaching Devil's Bridge on 2 May 1983. The first carriage illustrates the programme to replace the standard BR blue livery with GWR chocolate and cream.** *Author*

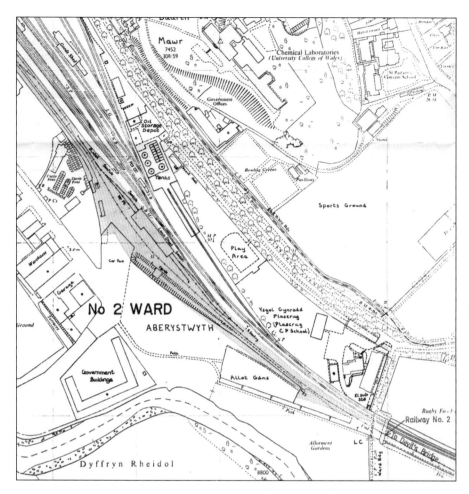

Left: **An extract from the plan deposited with the 1989 Light Railway Order application to validate the 1968 VRLR diversion at Aberystwyth. The diversion and station area were designated Railway No 2.** *Author's collection*

Below: **Representing the VRLR under private ownership is this view of No 9 at Aberffrwd on 20 August 1992. The loco had been overhauled at the Brecon Mountain Railway's Pant works and returned to service with air brakes. The loop here had been reinstated.** *Author*

3

Welshpool & Llanfait Light Railway

Nine miles from the market town of Welshpool, Llanfair Caereinion is a village at the centre of a rural community that grew around the junctions of the local road network and a crossing of the Afon Banwy, which by a somewhat circuitous route is a tributary of the River Severn. It is around 400ft above sea level, surrounded by hills rising to 1,141ft at Rhos Fawr to the south east, but more usually around 600ft. Agriculture was the mainstay of economic activity in the locality yet, despite maintaining a static population in 1841 and 1851, labourers leaving in search of work thereafter saw the parish decline to 1,839 by 1901. A hundred years later, the population was 200 fewer. Life was obviously hard for some of those who stayed behind. In December 1900, the *Border Counties Advertiser* reported that Mrs Howell of Craigydon, Aberdovey, had sent parcels of winter clothing for distribution amongst the parish's poor.

Originally known simply as Pool, Welshpool developed from the 13th century at a point around 300ft above sea level, close to the western bank of the navigable River Severn and some four miles from the English border. The General Post Office instigated the town's change of name in 1835, to distinguish it from Poole in Dorset. The economy was typical of that required to sustain the town and its surrounding locality. The only manufactory was flannel, with six makers listed in an 1858 directory. To the west of the town the Powis estate was the largest and most influential landowner. To the southeast, the broad Severn Valley is ideally suited to agriculture, elsewhere farming life is harder, with ground reaching around 600ft above sea level to the northwest with Y Golfa dominant at 1,118ft two miles to the west. Until 1881, Welshpool parish was expanding, with its population peaking at 4,988. Decline into the 20th century was eventually countered by revival and expansion, the population reaching 6,269 by 2001.

Welshpool, too, developed around a road network, with two routes from England meeting others from the west and the hinterland. Transportation was improved with the arrival of the Montgomery Canal in 1797 and the Oswestry & Newtown Railway in 1860. By 1864 it was possible to take a train from Welshpool eastwards to Shrewsbury and westwards to Aberystwyth.

In the 19th century, the road between the town and village was a poorly maintained turnpike, imposing additional costs for transporting goods and livestock to market. The way to obtaining a railway to unite them turned out to be as rocky as the road.

The first proposal came in 1864, with the advertisement of the appropriately named Llanfair Railway in November. This line started from a junction with the Cambrian Railways, three furlongs southwest of the Welshpool station, and followed a route close to the unclassified road passing Powis Castle and turning towards Castle Caereinion near Trefnant Hall. Passing to the east and north of Castle Caereinion it picked up the route of the later railway at Dolarddyn but instead of crossing the Banwy it kept to the south of the river to terminate near the Llanfair bridge, 10¼ miles distance. The engineer was George Owen, encountered in Chapter 1, working with Messrs Mickleburgh. The gauge was not mentioned in the Parliamentary papers, Cartwright (*see* Bibliography) states that it was to be narrow gauge, with mixed gauge on the Cambrian section. The alignment was almost on a continuous gradient towards Llanfair Caereinion, the easiest gradients where it diverged from the Cambrian, 1 in 256, and two short level sections. The prospect of trains pounding up the 1-in-40 gradient past the front of Powis Castle can have done nothing to endear the scheme to the earl. The proposal was abandoned.

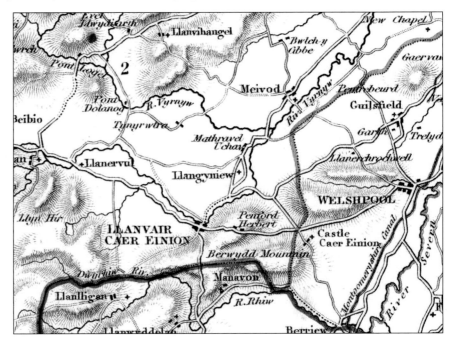

Montgomeryshire location map, 1840; extract showing the area around Welshpool and Llanfair Caereinion.
R. Creighton, Lewis's Topographical Dictionary, extract/Author's collection

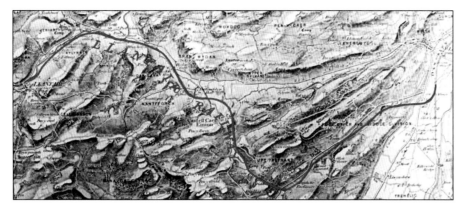

Left: **The Llanfair Railway, 1865.**
Parliamentary Archives

Below: **The Shrewsbury & North Wales Railway's proposed route to Llanfair Caereinion from Llanymynech, 1866 (see p109).** *Parliamentary Archives*

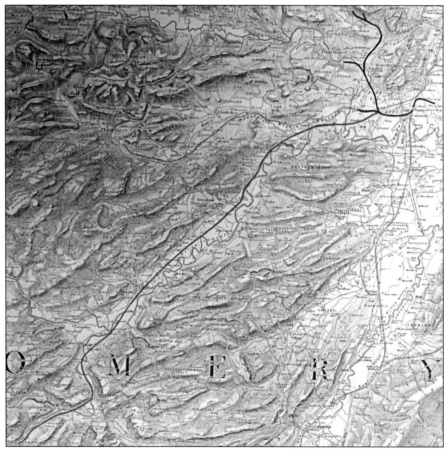

Promotion of the first Welshpool & Llanfair Railway bill, with Powell, Bell & Swettenham as engineers, was advertised in November 1876. The route was quite similar to the 1864 proposal but with a separate line parallel to the Cambrian, as well as a junction, and its own terminus at Welshpool, at Castle Caereinion passing to the west, and on the approach to Llanfair Caereinion crossing the river to terminate in the field to be used by the light railway for that purpose, 400 yards from Llanfair bridge. The road by the Llanfair Caereinion terminus was intended to be diverted in what appears to be a quite unnecessary manner. The total length was just short of 10½ miles. The gradients were easier than on the 1864 scheme, with several level sections, but the steepest was still 1 in 41 near Powis Castle.

When the royal assent was given on 10 August 1877, the separate line into Welshpool had been removed, making the railway just over 9½ miles long. The capital was £39,000 with power to borrow an additional £13,000. The promoters were Ralph Dickinson Gough, Owen Jones, Richard Owen and Frederick Bromley Jones; they and one other to be nominated would be the first directors. An unusual mitigating measure, although not described as such, was an obligation to contribute not more that £2,000 for a carriage road from the road at Pont Sychcoed, near Cyfronydd, to Mathyrafal Castle, no money to be paid over until responsibility for maintaining the road had been accepted by the Llanfyllin highway board *(see illustration on p108)*.

The next stage in the advancement of this scheme was rather bizarre. Notices announcing the intention to deposit two bills were issued dated 14 November 1881 and published a few days apart. The first was an application to abandon the undertaking, dissolve the company and release the deposit, while the second was to revive and extend the time for the compulsory purchase of land, the completion of works and other purposes! The other purposes included reinstating the independent line to Welshpool, deviating from the authorised route at Dolrhyd y David Mill and authorising the use of a gauge narrower than standard. The plans were signed by W. N. Swettenham. The purpose of the deviation is unknown, the plans merely showing an increase to the permitted limit of deviation that would have required crossing the river twice if it had been used.

Cartwright states that the revival attempt arose when the promoters became enthused by the results of the 2ft gauge North Wales Narrow Gauge Railways, opened partially in 1877, and they thought that they could be emulated in Montgomeryshire. As the NWNGR only made £4 profit in its first five years of operation, and rarely did better, it was a poor example for emulation. Perhaps the promoters were covering their bets by publishing both notices whilst they made a last-ditch attempt to raise more capital. Only the abandonment bill became law, assent being given on 19 June 1882. The company's inability to raise capital was cited as the reason for its failure.

Another Welshpool & Llanfair Railway bill was deposited in December 1886. Engineers Simpson, Davies & Hurst produced a route similar to the earlier schemes, with an independent line into Welshpool and no junction with the Cambrian, passing to the east of Castle Caereinion before picking up an alignment close to that later adopted by the light railway, crossing the river at Heniarth and terminating at the later station site, 340 yards from the Llanfair bridge, a distance of 10 miles 2 furlongs 8 chains. This time the gradient near

Powis Castle was slightly easier, at 1 in 68 and 1 in 58, but it then steepened to 1 in 40 for nearly a mile. There was a summit for nearly a mile near Dolarddyn before the line fell to the terminus. Gaining assent on 23 August 1887, the act authorised a 3ft gauge railway. The promoters were William Page, John Greenbank and John Wilmer Ransome; with two others to be nominated, they were the first directors. The capital requirements were the same as for the 1877 railway.

Just as the 1877 and 1887 schemes used the same name, the outcome was the same. As the powers expired, an abandonment act was obtained, receiving assent on 20 May 1892. Once again, the inability to raise capital was given as the cause.

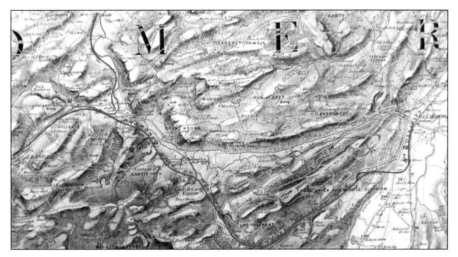

Above: **The Welshpool & Llanfair Railway, 1877.**
Parliamentary Archives

Below: **The Welshpool & Llanfair Railway, 1887.**
Parliamentary Archives

Above right: **The Welshpool & Llanfair Railway, 1882.**
Parliamentary Archives

Bottom: **The Welshpool & Llanfair Light Railway, 1896.**
National Archives

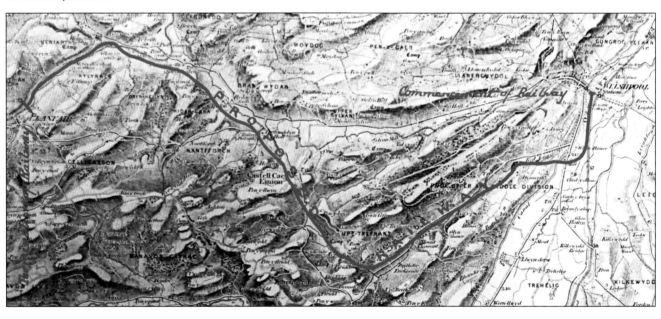

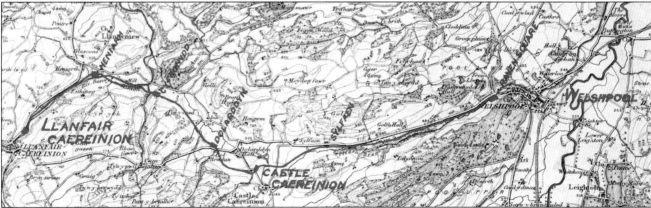

The Llanfair & Meifod Valley Light
Railway, 1896. *National Archives*

The 1896 Light Railways Act provided the impetus that
finally gave Llanfair Caereinion its railway to Welshpool, but
before it was settled there were competing routes to contend
with. The first application, submitted in December 1896, was
for the Llanfair & Meifod Valley Light Railway, a standard
gauge line 14 miles long from a junction with the Cambrian's
Welshpool–Oswestry route at Arddleen that put Llanfair
Caereinion 20 miles from either Oswestry or Welshpool by rail.
The steepest gradient was 1 in 66, its sharpest curve 600ft and
it was expected to cost £41,000. The engineer was John E.
Thomas. It was not the first time that a railway to Llanfair
Caereinion via the Meifod Valley had been mooted, for the
Shrewsbury & North Wales Railway's application for a branch
from Llanymynech had been rejected in 1866 (*see* 107).

The second application arose from the efforts of the
Welshpool Corporation, led by the mayor, William Forrester
Addie, who circulated landowners on 15 December 1896, asking
them to attend a meeting on 21 December to examine the plans
and discuss a scheme for a Welshpool and Llanfair light railway.
Including Addie, 13 people attended the meeting and an engineer
named Moorsom addressed it. This was most likely Lewis Henry
Moorsom, engineer of the LNWR/GWR joint lines around
Shrewsbury since 1866. After some discussion, the meeting
decided to support the scheme. The council was to contribute
£438 towards the costs of obtaining the order.

A committee, comprising 87 persons, councillors, landowners
and others, was formed on 28 January 1897, a more manageable
executive committee of 20 being appointed a week later. The
route was considered on 18 February 1897. There are no plans
surviving from this period although the committee's minutes
contain clues. On 11 February, a sub-committee was appointed
to go over the route with the engineers to determine if a way of
avoiding 'the line being carried along the roads' could be found,
to avoid the 'the probable hostility that may be expected from the
county council should the railway be carried here and there along
the turnpike road.' On the same occasion, 'the Golfa route' was
adopted which might suggest that in parts alternative routes had
been suggested.

Moorsom & Ward had been appointed the railway's
engineers on 8 February 1897. Frederick Derwent Ward was
the architect and surveyor of the Powis estate and appears to
have been the partner most closely involved with the railway
project during the planning stages.

The recommendation that the route should 'be kept off the
road after passing Raven Square' was accepted. The further

recommendation that the route shown on the plans be adopted
'until the Independent chapel at Cyfronydd is reached … that
the route be diverted to the south side of the Banwy river and
kept as near to the river as possible until the mill opposite
Eithinog is neared. There … the line should cross the river on
the westerly side, but close to the mill, and that thence it should
be kept as close to the northern side of the river up to Llanfair.
We further suggest that the railway should terminate in the field
adjoining the last cottage on the left-hand side of the road
before getting into Llanfair and that there the terminal depot
should be located', was countered by the suggestion that the
river crossing should be 'about 15 chains below Heniarth mill',
the amendment being accepted.

In the town, the sub-committee's recommendation that the
line be diverted around the back of the Montgomery Militia's
armoury, re-joining the proposed route to Smithfield at Severn
Stars was also accepted. This amendment probably reduced the
number of houses requiring demolition.

Considering the engineers' comparative estimates on the
cost of standard gauge and 2ft 6in gauge lines, the latter was
adopted with a proviso that a statement be issued explaining the
reasoning behind the decision.

The county council and the corporation were to be asked to
subscribe to the capital on 25 February. The former was to be
asked to contribute £6,000 and the latter £8,000, half as a loan
and half in shares. On 17 April, Forden Rural District Council
was to be asked for £2,500.

Addie announced, on 25 March, that he had arranged for E.
R. Calthrop to assist the engineers in presenting the case to the
light railway commissioners. Calthrop had put his theory that 2ft
6in was the ideal gauge to accommodate maximum tonnage at
minimum cost into practice with the Barsi Light Railway in India
from 1896 and was to do the same again with the Leek &
Manifold Light Railway in Staffordshire in 1904. Expenses of £4
2s 11d were incurred in accommodating a 'lecture' by Calthrop.

The light railway order application and £50 deposit were
submitted to the Board of Trade in the names of Addie, John
Morris and others after 6 May 1897, the notice being dated 17
April. Calthrop & Ward's estimate was for £21,309 8s.

A single sheet from what must have been Calthrop's
specification survives in RAIL1057/613 at the National
Archives. Under the heading 'rolling stock', it states that it was
intended to order two six-coupled tank locomotives capable of
hauling 40 tons up a gradient of 1 in 30 initially, then, if traffic
required it, a locomotive 'of the Barsi type', capable of taking 80

tons up the 1-in-30 gradients would be used on market days and when traffic was heavier. One carriage 40ft long by 7ft 6in would be provided, capable of carrying 60 passengers. It would have end doors, a central gangway and be 'of the tramway type'. 'A similar car of shorter length will also be provided.' The wagon stock would comprise two low-sided wagons 24ft long by 7ft wide fitted with loose ends and bolsters, capable of carrying goods or timber; two cattle wagons 30ft long, capacity 12 to 16 beasts; two transportation cars 22ft long to carry standard gauge wagons without transhipment of contents, and four small high-sided four-wheel goods wagons. A five-ton travelling crane would also be required.

The promoters wanted to capitalise the railway at £26,000 and had obtained agreement in principle for Montgomeryshire County Council and Welshpool Corporation to make the advances proposed on 25 February. If an application for a £6,000 Treasury grant was successful the promoters were left with £6,000 to be found from other sources. Making arrangements for the inquiry, the committee appointed Calthrop, the Corris Railway's Dix and others as witnesses. Calthrop was to be paid £30 1s 8d in fees and expenses, Dix £11 9s.

The county council told the Board of Trade that it was prepared to back either scheme but not both, and required the light railway commissioners to adjudicate on their merits. The commissioners held a public inquiry in Llanfair Caereinion on 3/4 August 1897 and extensive reports were published in three newspapers.

There was support for the Meifod railway but some landowners, whose backing would be required if the Treasury grant application was to be successful, opposed it. The Cambrian had agreed to construct and work it on terms to be agreed, but Owen, its engineer, had not inspected the route. The sparseness of Arddleen's population was illustrated by drawing attention to its meagre train service, two trains on one day a week, and the Cambrian was only considering running through trains to Oswestry on market days. For the Cambrian, its general manager C. S. Denniss explained that annually, the Meifod area produced 2,400 tons of traffic via Llansantffraid while Llanfair Caereinion generated 3,500 tons via Welshpool. In summary, the witnesses demonstrated that only the area around Meifod would generate railway traffic and it was clear that the railway would only be worthwhile if it abstracted traffic from Llanfair Caereinion presently routed via Welshpool.

Addie was not only the chairman of the promoters, he was the Earl of Powis's

The wheelbarrow and spade used by Lord Clive when he cut the first sod on 30 May 1901. The items are on display at the Powysland Museum in Welshpool (see p114).
Author

agent. He put the case for the Welshpool line with ten points of advantage. Llanfair's fairs brought livestock in from the surrounding areas. Welshpool was the natural outlet for the area's produce. Welshpool had better railway facilities and the benefit of competition from three railway companies, the LNWR, the GWR and the Cambrian. Oswestry was not so good an outlet. The Powis estate would benefit from the railway's timber-hauling capability. Narrow gauge was suited to the district, would cost less to construct, was more likely to be a success, and was therefore less likely to be a burden on the ratepayers. Taking that into consideration there was no benefit to be gained from the Meifod line. A narrow gauge line could cheaply and easily be extended to Llanerfyl, 5½ miles, or Garthbeibio, 9 miles. The essential commodities of life would be cheaper with the railway. In addition to Llanfair, Welshpool market was the one used mainly by residents located between the two; it was the best for the area and Powis's tenants were in favour of the proposal.

Powis had instructed Addie to say that whilst he, Powis, would be glad to see the Meifod line constructed, both lines could not be a financial success and he had to decide which would most benefit his properties and the locality generally, supporting the Welshpool line on that basis.

Calthrop explained that he supported standard gauge railways if there was sufficient traffic. Narrow gauge construction and operating costs were about half those of standard gauge. The Welshpool line would start with two six-coupled locomotives; engines and stock would have automatic brakes and the carriages would have centre gangways. There would be two cattle wagons capable of carrying 16 cattle each. Narrow gauge transporter wagons could carry standard gauge wagons. He thought that the Meifod line was under-estimated.

Dix said that a line to Welshpool could be made to pay, but not one to Arddleen, which was nowhere. Traffic was insufficient for a standard gauge line. There was no trouble on the Corris Railway with regard to transhipment. He had not been over the Meifod route but he had been to Arddleen.

The commissioners reserved their decision and subsequently inspected both of the proposed routes before deciding that the public interest would be best served by the Welshpool line. Progress was slow. An offer of a £7,500 Treasury loan made in February 1898 was rejected because the promoters could not comply with the terms under which it was made, section 4 of the Light Railways Act, probably the requirement that half of the capital required was to be share capital and that half of that should be subscribed by persons other than local authorities. If that is so, it demonstrates unwillingness on the part of the promoters to contribute to the capital in any substantial amount themselves.

Section 5 of the Light Railways Act allowed for a free Treasury grant to be made if, inter alia, the railway was constructed and operated by an existing railway company (see p58-9). In October 1897, a fruitless approach to the GWR and LNWR as operators of the Shrewsbury–Welshpool joint line had been made. After rejecting the section 4 grant the promoters turned to the Cambrian. In the meantime, the Board of Agriculture certified that the railway would benefit agriculture in the district on 26 August 1898, meeting another requirement of section 5.

On 4 September 1898, Denniss wrote that the Cambrian was prepared to enter into an agreement to construct and operate the railway provided the necessary capital was subscribed. Realising that the Cambrian's involvement would have some effect on the status quo, on 10 January 1899 the committee resolved to approach the Cambrian's engineer and

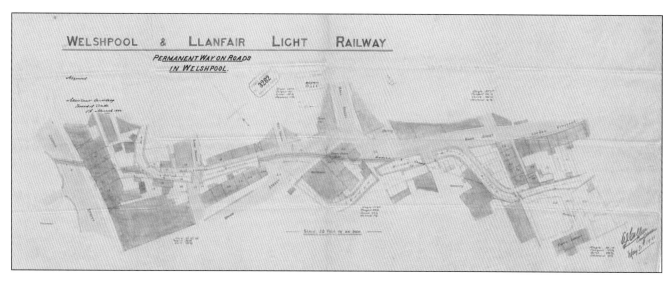

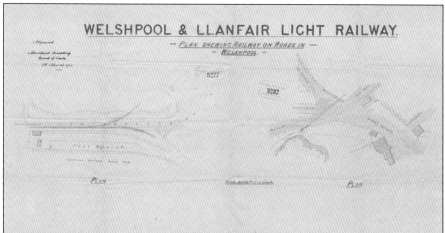

Above: **Collin's plan showing the road crossings of Church Street, Union Street and Brook Street.** *National Archives*

Middle: **Collin's plan of the crossings of Smithfield Road and the Raven Square junction. Both of these plans were dated 31 May 1901 and were approved on 5 March 1902.** *National Archives*

Below: **Collin's proposed method of constructing the Welshpool road crossings when he was intending to use grooved tram rails.** *National Archives*

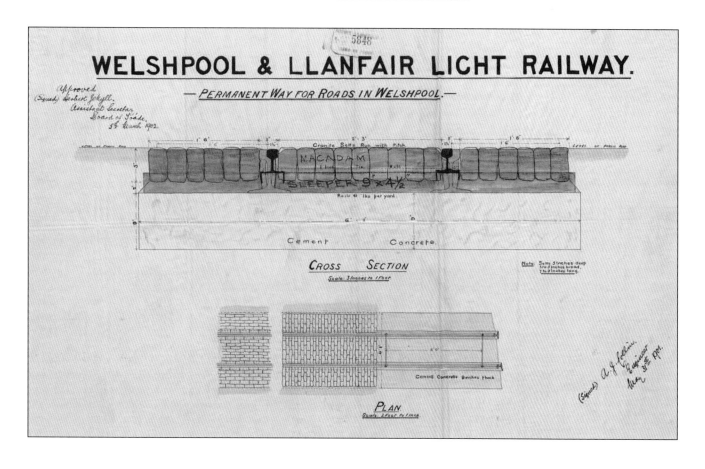

Right: **Strachan's men and one of his locomotives on the Banwy bridge.**
Author's collection

Below: **Some of the assembled multitude at Llanfair on 4 April 1903, the day the railway was opened.**
Author's collection

find out what his charges would be to oversee the construction, and to ask Calthrop if he would act as consulting engineer. Moorsom & Ward's involvement would terminate when the order was made.

On 19 December 1898, the Treasury offered to make a free grant of £7,000. Here, though, the condition that caused difficulty was easily overcome. The Treasury required that no more than £3,000 should be paid for the land. The agents explained that the Earl of Powis and other landowners had offered land for about five miles of the route free of charge. However, in Welshpool urban property was required from owners who would gain no direct benefit from the railway and who could not be expected to treat it favourably. Further, until the company was in a position to know precisely what land it needed and to treat for it, the cost could not be estimated. The matter was settled with an undertaking by the promoters, communicated on 10 March 1899, that if the land cost more than £3,000 they would raise additional capital to meet the excess. In addition to the money already promised by the county and corporation, Llanfyllin Rural District Council had agreed to contribute £1,600 and Forden RDC £500.

Before committing to the WLLR, Denniss decided that he, Collin, Addie and Winnall, the WLLR's solicitor, should visit the Lynton & Barnstaple Railway in Devon. He had read about it in *The Railway Magazine* and thought that a visit would be

worthwhile before any decisions were taken about equipping the WLLR. On 4 January 1899, he asked the LBR for facilities, including a special train. The LBR offered accommodation by timetabled train from Barnstaple to Lynton and back to Blackmoor, then a trolley down the gradient to Chelfham where a train would meet the party to return it to Barnstaple. All stations except Wooda [sic] Bay could be visited with this schedule. The visit was proposed for 13 February, travelling from Welshpool the previous day, and back the day after. Denniss also requested free passes from the GWR for the journey.

Just as the committee thought that it had done all that was required for the order to be made, in April 1899 the Cambrian produced a shock. Its solicitor had noticed that the draft order included clauses obliging the company to make a siding to the Shropshire Union Railways & Canal Company (SURC) wharf at Welshpool. The position was not serious, the solicitor told his directors, and the connection was at Welshpool so traffic arising on the light railway would be carried the maximum distance before it was transferred to the canal, but the Cambrian would still suffer. It would not enter into an agreement unless the clauses were removed.

The committee was embarrassed. It had agreed to the clauses to secure the withdrawal of the canal company's objections to the order. They had been included in the draft orders that had been approved by the Cambrian and it could not be expected to ask the canal company to agree to their withdrawal. Meeting the promoters at Oswestry on 2 May, Denniss implied that they were at fault for not drawing attention to the clauses. The Cambrian still wanted to make an agreement and would 'assist the promoters in inducing the Board of Trade to strike out these clauses.'

Two days later, the committee resolved that before asking for the clauses to be removed it would ask the SURC if it was prepared to construct and work the line. Maybe the committee was unaware that the SURC was leased by the LNWR, which had already indicated its lack of interest in their railway. Despite a three-page impassioned appeal from the promoters' solicitors sent on 2 June, the Cambrian stood its ground. The light railway commissioners called all parties to a meeting in London on 11 July and the Cambrian got its way, the 'objectionable clauses' being removed. The SURC was given an opportunity to appeal against the decision but took no further action. Strangely, in November 1901, the Cambrian was to approve a siding being located near the canal for the benefit of the Powis estate. 'It is not intended to give the canal company facilities for traffic, in violation of the agreement already arrived at' Addie wrote to Denniss on 20 June.

The Welshpool & Llanfair Light Railway Order was made on 8 September 1899. The authorised railway was 9 miles 1 furlong 1.50 chains long, and 2ft 6in gauge. Instead of taking a route to the southwest of the main line station like the earlier schemes, the WLLR started from a point in Smithfield Road, opposite the station, taking a sinuous route through the town with some street running and partially astride the Lledan brook before passing the Standard quarry and reaching open countryside at Raven Square. Here, it ran to the south of the turnpike, making the best of the contours as only a narrow gauge railway can, passing to the north of Castle Caereinion and then picking up the previously proposed route near Dolarddyn. Three years were allowed for its construction. The company was not required to fence the railway where it ran along the road in Welshpool. There could be up to five directors plus one appointed by the county council, and three by the corporation.

The first directors were the 4th Earl of Powis, Athelstane R. Pryce, Robert C. Anwyl, and John C. Hilton, all landowners. The capital was set at £6,000 in addition to any treasury grants or shares subscribed by the local authorities. In setting the rates that could be charged, the commissioners incorporated those of the Cambrian, except for the carriage of goods and minerals, where they allowed an increase of 25%, saying that the traffic would not be worthwhile at the Cambrian's rates.

The first directors' meeting was held on 30 September 1899, when Powis, Anwyl and Hilton were joined by Addie, David Jones and W. A. Rogers, appointees of the corporation. Little business was conducted. Even with the order, it was going to be more than two years before trains ran to Llanfair Caereinion.

Arthur J. Collin's, the Cambrian's engineer's, offer to work for the company for 5½% of the contract price, was accepted on 14 November 1899. The directors were not so happy with his demand for £500 to be paid if the railway was abandoned after the plans had been made, however, but he refused to move.

A prospectus for £10,000 share capital was issued with a deadline of 19 December 1899. With the £4,000 already agreed to be taken by the corporation, £9,077 had been subscribed by 29 January 1900. Powis headed the list with £1,500, Hilton took £400, and Anwyl £300. There were several subscriptions for £1, but most were for £5 or £10. The agreements with the investing authorities were sealed on 23 April. The Cambrian's agreement of 99 years for 60% of the gross receipts had been sealed on 1 March, the date of the first ordinary shareholders' meeting.

Payments agreed on 3 July 1900 were £250 to Collin for work carried out to date, and £9 17s 4d to Edward Jones, the town clerk. Jones had billed the company for 'perusing' the agreement between it and the corporation and for negotiating the council's £500 loan enabling it to pay the deposit on its shares. There appeared to be no question about the payment, but it does appear to be rather strange.

The Treasury had written on 21 June, seeking assurances that if the cost of the land and property required by the company exceeded £4,100, the company could raise additional capital to cover it. The solicitor was instructed to give the assurance required.

Collin's revised estimate of £32,480 was submitted on 1 October 1900, prompting the directors to ask the Treasury for an additional grant of £7,500 and to make an application to amend the light railway order. Dated 20 November, the notice explained that the company wished to increase its capital, extend the time for land purchase and completion of works, to empower the local authorities to make further advances to the undertaking, and to permit the Cambrian to subscribe to the capital.

Including Collin's estimate, the directors produced a total estimate of expenses totalling £43,204 on 27 November 1900.

Construction including land		£32,480
Rolling stock		
3 engines	£4,500	
2 large bogie passenger coaches	£900	
2 smaller 3rd class coaches	£400	
40 goods wagons @£25	£1,000	
4 covered goods wagons	£150	
12 covered cattle trucks	£1,000	
Travelling crane	£150	
		£8,100
Expenses		
Engineers	£1,624	
Legal and other	£1,000	
		£2,624
Total		£43,204

On 5 December 1900, Collin suggested deferring requesting tenders until February 1901, when prices were likely to be more favourable, and obtaining estimates for rolling stock at the same time, otherwise delay might arise. In Welshpool, the line had to have grooved [tram] rail, so he needed to know the wheel profile to be used in order to complete the specification. Land plans could be completed in two weeks and the contract plans, if required, in about six weeks.

The rolling stock requirement was discussed when a team from Welshpool met Denniss and other Cambrian officers at Oswestry on 10 December 1900, producing a new list. Denniss urged that three locomotives should be purchased to provide cover in the event of a breakdown, but the light railway directors said that no more could be afforded at that time. Herbert E. Jones, the Cambrian's locomotive superintendent, was authorised to obtain designs of suitable locomotives and other rolling stock.

Rolling stock	
2 locomotives @ £1,600 each	£3,200
2 large composite passenger coaches @ £450 each	£900
1 extra 3rd class coach for use on fair days &c	£200
40 goods wagons @ £25 each	£1,000
4 covered goods wagons @ £60 each	£240
2 covered cattle trucks @ £85 each	£170
Travelling crane	£150
10 timber trucks @ £25 each	£250
2 brake vans @ £120 each	£240
	£6,350

Collin had produced plans and specification by 25 January 1901, when a sub-committee of the directors met to consider them. He was asked to make further provision for unloading stock at Smithfield, to straighten the line at Seven Stars, and to locate Cyfronydd station in field No 83. The realignment at Seven Stars required the demolition of the malthouse as well as the public house of that name. Copies of the large-scale plans that identify the field numbers have not come to light. Meeting on 31 January, the directors instructed Collin to obtain tenders as soon as possible. They also agreed to pay Jones 150 guineas for his services in procuring the locomotives and rolling stock. He had recommended ordering the locomotives as soon as possible whilst saying that there was no hurry to order the rolling stock. He also advised against buying a travelling crane.

The six tenders shown in the table were considered on 20 March 1901. Most offered a 2½% discount and an allowance for old materials. Holmes & King had built the Snowdon Mountain Railway in 1895/6. Collin explained that he had kept some items out of the specification because it would be cheaper to let the work locally. Denniss was asked to inquire into the status of the lowest bidder while the sub-committee was to pursue the three lowest bids with a view to reaching agreement with one of them. The solicitor reported that the notices to treat had been served and claims were being made. Addie was appointed to act as the company's valuer.

Tenders for Welshpool & Llanfair Light Railway

A. Braithwaite	£26,353 5s 10d
Holme & King Limited, Liverpool	£26,239
H. & M. Nowell, Leeds	£26,000
Cleveland Bridge Company	£33,212 12s 4d
W. Jones & Company, Manchester	£21,227 3s 10d
J. Strachan, Cardiff	£24,282 13s 2d

Non-tender items

Permanent way materials	£5,790
Station buildings	£535
Engine shed and carriage shed	£310
Water supply at Welshpool and Llanfair	£70
Signalling and telegraph	£240
Sidings in Cambrian company's yard	£260
	£7,205

On 1 April 1901, the status of the lowest bidder was considered to be unsatisfactory leading to consideration of Strachan's bid. A statement was produced showing the company's resources and anticipated liabilities.

The directors resolved that Strachan's tender be recommended to the Cambrian for acceptance, subject to Strachan taking £1,000 in ordinary shares in the company.

The Cambrian accepted the tender on 3 April, saying that Strachan had agreed to take the shares. Passing on the decision, Denniss asked how the capital was going to be raised. When the WLLR directors met on 18 April, the resolution calling on the Cambrian to enter into and complete the contract with Strachan was carried with one director voting against; identity of the dissenter was not revealed.

Still on 18 April, an offer to buy the rails made by William Bailey Hawkins, one of the Cambrian's directors, was considered and accepted. The offer was supported by Collin, who said that it would secure the lowest price. Guest, Keen & Company's bid to supply 800 tons of flat-bottom rail at £5 1s per ton and fishplates at £6 16s per ton was to be accepted for delivery in three monthly instalments from July.

The Treasury had agreed to the additional grant on 11 December 1900. One of the standard conditions for making it was that it would not be paid until the railway had been completed and inspected by the Board of Trade, which would aggravate the poor cash-flow position during construction. Following a resolution to apply for interim payments on 18 April, the Treasury proposed that the first half should be paid when a sum equal to the total grant had been spent, and the remainder on production of the Board of Trade certificate that the railway was complete and open for traffic. With commendable speed the decision was circulated on 28 May 1901.

The directors' attention had turned to cutting the first sod. Viscount Clive, the son of the Earl, was proposed subject to his parents giving approval, and on 10 May 1901 the date was set for 30 May, with 'Colonel Hutchins' field' the location. The company would supply a silver spade while the engineer and contractor were expected to supply a wheelbarrow. The spade cost £15 15s plus the cost of engraving it, £2 5s 9d.

The ceremony was a grand affair and Welshpool took a holiday despite it being a Thursday. There was a grandstand, flags and festoons, several bands, large crowds and speeches. The Powis family arrived in a carriage drawn by a pair of bays and preceded by an outrider. The countess's attire was fully described, as was her son's, it was his first public engagement. Afterwards, the company and guests repaired to the assembly room where 200 sat down for lunch provided by the Earl. If all those listed in the *Border Counties Advertizer*'s extensive report had subscribed £10 to the railway's capital its finances would have been much healthier. Notwithstanding Strachan's

Contract – Strachan		£24,290
Less 2½%	£506 5s	
Old materials	£7 6s 10d	£513 11s 10d
		£23, 776 8s 2d
Works not included in contract, estimate		£7,202 1s 3d
Land, say		£6,000
Rolling stock		£6,500
Expenses		£3,000
Interest on loans during construction		£650
(Nothing allowed for contingencies)		£47,128 9s 5d
Towards which the company has:		
Original capital		£29,100
Additional free grant	£7,500	
Additional loans already promised	£2,250	£9,750
		£38,850
Sum still to be obtained	£8,278 9s 5d	

participation in the event, he erected the grandstand, the agreement for him to build the railway was not to be submitted for sealing until 4 June.

A second prospectus had been issued during May, soliciting subscriptions for the £5,000 unissued share capital. Would-be subscribers were told that although the original £10,000 share capital had been fully subscribed, the high cost of labour and materials had delayed the start of construction. With a degree of prescience untypical in such documents, Denniss's revenue forecast of £3,405 was only slightly in excess of what was to be achieved.

The location and nature of the road crossings in Welshpool had been sent to the Board of Trade by Collin on 31 May. The correspondence was protracted, expanded to include the corporation and the county council, and accompanied within the Board of Trade by doubt as to whether the matter should be dealt with by its railway department or its highways department. The crossings had been intended to be laid with 75lb grooved tram rail. On 21 November 1901, however, the WLLR informed the Board of Trade that rails of the desired profile, with a flangeway 1½in wide, were not made in any British mill. As the track concerned comprised only 300 yards out of nine miles of railway, it asked if the Board of Trade would approve of ordinary rails being used, with the formation between them filled with 'tarred macadam' instead of sets so that the wheel flanges would form their own groove? The approval of the corporation and the county council, as the authorities concerned, was required before permission was given for the change, on 5 March 1902.

Collin recommended that Beyer, Peacock & Company's tender to supply two locomotives at £1,630 each be accepted, on 22 June 1901. If a third locomotive was ordered within six months this would reduce the price to £1,570 each. When the order was submitted to the Cambrian board for ratification on 2 July, Denniss sent a telegram to the WLLR saying that his directors required a third loco to be procured. A streak of rebellion appeared in Welshpool when the telegram was read on 8 July; the matter was not on the agenda so it was deferred until the next meeting. Following a meeting with Denniss, on 26 September the directors were to resolve to delay the matter for the present. Accepting the company's position, the Cambrian said that if the traffic warranted it, a third locomotive must be provided. Jones ordered two locomotives on 10 October.

Construction had progressed during the summer, with the first certificate issued on 29 June. Collin submitted regular reports to the Cambrian directors but not, apparently, to the WLLR directors who were paying him for his involvement. On 2 July, he had reported that some 6,000 yards of spoil had been removed at the Welshpool station site, that Strachan was at work on cuttings and embankments for about 1½ miles of the route, that the bridge over the canal had been started, and the repairs to the walls of the Lledan brook, over which the railway would run, were nearly finished.

On 7 August, he reported that the canal bridge masonry was nearly completed, the retaining wall at Rock Cottage, at the Standard quarry, two cattle creeps and a culvert were well advanced and the rebuilding at the tannery and most of the property alterations were completed. Earthworks for one mile were completed and in hand to two miles. Fencing was being put up as far as four miles and 3,000 sleepers were on site.

The quality of stone being used at the Banwy bridge concerned the WLLR directors meeting on 29 August,

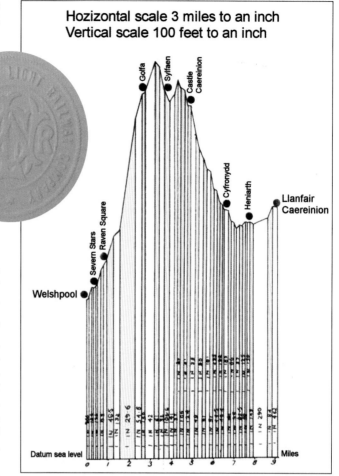

Above: **WLLR gradient profile.**

Inset: **The WLLR company crest.** *National Archives*

however. They had been told that it was 'of a perishable nature' and wanted the Cambrian to check that it was satisfactory. They also wanted to hear from Collin on the subject. He was to report, on 26 September, that he had given instructions for the work to be redone.

With no obvious sense of urgency, the amendment order was made on 22 September 1901. The capital was doubled to £12,000, the amount the investing authorities could subscribe was increased to £19,350 from £16,100, and the company could borrow on mortgage £1,000 per £3,000 of subscribed capital to a maximum of £4,000. No explanation is given in the surviving records for the lack of clauses authorising the extensions of time.

With payments to Strachan and the property owners started, the directors were concerned that those who had promised capital support honoured their commitments. On several occasions the minutes recorded unpaid calls on shares and the apparent tardiness of some of the investing authorities in arranging the loans they needed to meet their obligations. Powis even visited the public loan office to see if the authorities could be bypassed, but to no avail. The bank account was overdrawn by £1,135 19s 10d on 26 September 1901, when £3,000 was received from the county council on account of its loan. £2,000 was received from the corporation by 31 October. Against the outgoings there was a little income – £17 19s from the sale of timber from the former vicarage garden in August 1901.

Of the land required, one small plot, ¾ acre, at Golfa was particularly troublesome, requiring more than two years of

A typical WLLR mixed train en route for Llanfair Caereinion at Raven Square. The entrance to the Standard quarry is behind the end of the train.
Author's collection

negotiations before agreement was reached over its use. It belonged to the Reverend G. R. G. Pughe, vicar of Mellor, Blackburn, who made it clear that he did not want to sell at any price; he had had a clause inserted in the 1899 order preventing access without his prior written approval. Once construction started he changed his attitude and an arrangement was made. The company paid £300 for the land and £59 2s 2d for his solicitor's fees. The minutes contain a note to the effect that the protective clause was repealed, saving £800 in construction costs. As the clause was not mentioned in the amendment order the correct position must be that Pughe had agreed not to enforce it.

Another problem site in September 1901 was the Severn Stars public house in Welshpool, which needed to be demolished. Addie valued it at £1,150 and had offered that amount, but the owner, Ann Dowthwaite, held out for £1,200. The company had already paid £50 as compensation for the tenant; whether the tenant ever saw the money must be open to doubt as it had been paid to the owner. The company solicitor was to reach an agreement with the owner's solicitor for £1,175 but she refused to accept it. On 31 October, the directors resolved that if the offer was not accepted in three days they would put it to arbitration. It was accepted and the building had been demolished by January 1902.

The new vicarage boundary wall had been completed and the Standard quarry weigh house demolished, Collin had reported on 3 October. Several cattle creeps had been started and some of them were ready for arching. The viaduct at Cyfronydd, a culvert at Castle Caereinion station site and the river wall near Llanfair had been started.

Jones submitted a tender from R. Y. Pickering & Company for rolling stock on 31 October. Accepting the recommendation, the directors specified that delivery must be during 1902 or as arranged, and that payment would be made on delivery. Ordering the timber wagons was deferred for the time being.

2 composite cars	£690
1 3rd class	£235
40 goods wagons	£1,020
4 covered goods wagons	£260
2 cattle wagons	£104
2 goods brake vans	£168
	£2,477

When Collin reported on 12 November, bad foundations had been encountered at the viaduct site. It had been necessary to excavate 8ft through soft blue clay before a good foundation of clay was encountered. The excavation had been filled with concrete to ground level. At this time, 70 tons of rail (600 yards), had been delivered.

The corporation expressed its disquiet about the Lledan brook, which had been culverted to accommodate the railway, on 25 November 1901. The councillors thought that the culvert would restrict the flow after heavy rain and subject the locality to flooding. Investigating, Collin agreed that the culvert was too small and suggested that it be removed and replaced by ironwork as on other parts of the brook. He produced a plan and estimated that it would cost £200 to replace. The culvert was actually a modification of Collin's original plans, implemented because it was cheaper. On 20 February 1902 he was to offer to bear the cost of the culvert if it was replaced. He had not mentioned the brook in his 9 December 1901 report although he did say that both it and the canal bridge steelwork were ready for inspection, adding that track laying had been started.

The tripartite agreement between the company, the Cambrian and the Treasury had been made on 7 October 1901, and executed and exchanged on 12 November 1901. The agreement and the county council's financial commitment to the WLLR were the subject of a letter to the Board of Trade from the Manchester & Milford Railway on 20 January 1902. It was signed by J. Rees, principal assistant to the general manager, who would be appointed VRLR general manager a few weeks later. He was told to refer to the treasury concerning the grant and to the LROs for details of the county council's contribution.

Christmas and New Year holidays had contributed to the lack of progress, Collin had reported on 13 January 1902, and 'bad weather had somewhat interfered with the progress of the earthworks.' Considering that the holidays would have accounted for three days at most the first remark does seem rather strange. The canal bridge and some of the Lledan brook steelwork had been erected and track laying was in progress.

The loans from the county council, £7,000, and Llanfyllin RDC, £2,600, had been received by the time the directors met on 23 January 1902. The £3,000 advanced by the county on account in September 1901 was reimbursed, along with interest of £16 11s 5d and costs of £51 12s 6d. Costs of £104 9s 8d claimed by Llanfyllin's solicitor had been paid under protest; the threat of having the bill taxed and adjudicated was enough to have it reduced by £16.

Other matters dealt with included ordering points and crossings from the Isca Foundry Company of Newport (their successors are still trading at the time of writing); £225 14s was to be paid under this heading in March. In January and February a total of £611 0s 5d was paid for dog spikes and fish bolts supplied by Bayliss, Jones & Bayliss of Wolverhampton, a firm that was to become a part of Guest, Keen & Nettlefold in 1922.

The Treasury had been asked to release the first instalment of its grant on 14 January 1902. Seeking evidence from the Board of Trade that money had been properly spent, Major E. Druitt was sent to make an inspection, reporting on 22 February. Accompanied by Collin and Addie, he had walked over part of the route and found half of the formation and half of the fencing were complete. About 1½ miles of track had been laid but not ballasted. The foundations of six of the seven piers of the viaduct had been commenced. The abutments and piers for the bridge over the Banwy had been finished. He provided documentation that supported the company's claims about capital raised and expenditure.

When Collin had reported on progress on 19 February some of his observations duplicated Druitt's. The weather had interfered with progress, stopping all masonry and concrete works, but earthworks had continued. One of the cuttings near Golfa was not quite complete. He expected the contractor to be

in a position to lay three miles of temporary track within a few days. The bridge over the canal was completed except for painting and the Lledan brook steelwork was practically complete. Other work in the town would be nearly complete at the end of the month. Done without mishap and few complaints this section had been difficult to carry out. Consulting with Strachan, he thought that the railway would be ready for inspection in July or August.

The WLLR directors were concerned to learn, when they read Jones's report of 20 March, that not only had Beyer, Peacock not started building the locomotives, but that the drawings had not been finished and delivery could not be expected for another eight or nine months. In his report Jones said that this was because the locomotives were being specially designed. In a letter signed by Powis, Beyer, Peacock was urged to push forward with the locomotives as rapidly as possible. When a delivery date was not forthcoming, the directors decided to enquire of Bagnall & Company if a locomotive could be hired.

The company was £1,445 in credit with £3,000 due from the corporation and £7,250 from the Treasury when the directors met on 26 March. Collin was to give an estimate of the amount required to complete the railway not later than 23 April. The financial position was considered on 22 May, when it

Above: **Everything stops for the photographer in the early days at Llanfair Caereinion. One of the composite carriages is next to the loco.** *Author's collection*

Left: **Market day perhaps? An uncommon picture of a train with all three carriages, seen at Dolrhyd Mill. The locomotive is** ***The Earl.*** *Author's collection*

Right: **Severn Stars was the WLLR's 'town' station at Welshpool.** *Author's collection*

Below: **The timber siding at Tanllan, 1904.** *National Archives*

Bottom: ***The Earl*** **with a timber train on the goods siding at Welshpool. The check-railed track is the main line, with Llanfair Caereinion to the left. The lack of ballasting on the loop line in the right foreground highlights the detail of the flanged fishplates used on rail joints. The location of the loco shed is indicated by the soot above the door; the carriage shed is to its left.** *Author's collection*

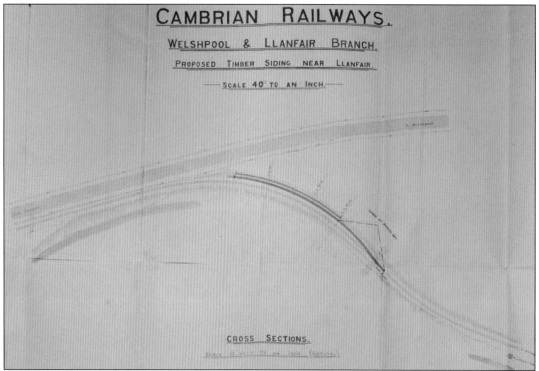

CAMBRIAN RAILWAYS.

WELSHPOOL & LLANFAIR BRANCH.

PROPOSED TIMBER SIDING NEAR LLANFAIR.

SCALE 40' TO AN INCH.

CROSS SECTIONS.

118

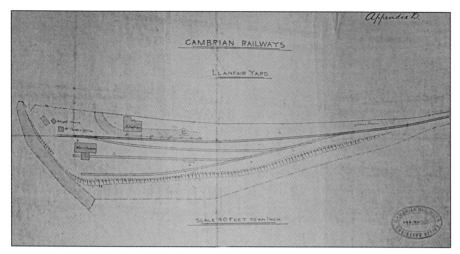

Left: **This 1905 plan of Llanfair Caereinion station shows that in addition to the station building and warehouse, there was a crane, weighbridge, an office for the coal merchant and, on the platform, a urinal. Nothing for the ladies apparently. The plan was produced to support a claim that the yard was inadequate for the traffic, and should be extended.** *National Archives*

Below: ***The Earl*** **with passenger stock at Llanfair Caereinion.** *Ian Allan Library*

became apparent that the company was £6,542 short of the funds it required. Strachan's work was estimated to cost £850 more than his tender, because there had been more rock than anticipated and extra accommodation works had been required. Some savings were identified, the largest being to work the railway with one engine in steam to avoid the cost of signalling. The Treasury would be asked for a larger grant, the Cambrian would be asked to take up the shares authorised by the amendment order and the district would be canvassed to obtain more subscriptions.

Powis wrote to the treasury on the same day, asking for a grant or loan of £3,000. He said that he and other landowners had given land valued at £2,400 and added that fastenings and sleepers had cost more than forecast. Land and property had cost £6, 300, instead of the £2,950 estimated, because of the difficulties in constructing a route through Welshpool and the need to take down several houses including a public house. The solicitor copied the letter to the Board of Trade seeking its support. Powis led a deputation to the Treasury on 11 June and on 21 June received notice that not only had he been successful, but that the limitation on the amount permitted to be paid for land had been withdrawn.

Track laying, most of it ballasted, extended some 2½ miles, Collin reported on 13 May, and more rail had been delivered. The walls of Bryn Heilyn, Brynelin and the viaduct were being proceeded with and 47,000 cubic yards of spoil had been excavated.

Addie had met Denniss on 27 May and the latter had agreed to the line being worked with one engine in steam. The only saving on buildings that he agreed to was the elimination of the loco shed at Llanfair, but it would need to be reinstated if the traffic warranted a loco being stabled there. He was agreeable to a shelter not being provided at Welshpool, saving £40, provided one was located for local traffic at Severn Stars.

By July 10, Collin was able to report that all the cuttings were either finished or 'gulleted', presumably he meant the ground had been cut through, as far as the viaduct. One arch was 'practically turned' and the others were in progress. Between the viaduct and the Banwy bridge earthworks were in an advanced state. Track was laid for 6¼ miles and girders for the bridge delivered.

Without any comment or explanation, on 11 July 1902 the directors resolved to apply to the Board of Trade for an extension of time to complete the railway; six months from the date specified in the 1899 order, 8 September 1902. The application submitted on 14 July 1902 was not considered because it had not been properly advertised. The explanation given to the Board of Trade was that 'owing to the difficulties experienced in raising the capital … the directors were unable to proceed with the work until the spring of 1899.' The contract as let was due to be completed by 1 September and the track was expected to be completed by that date, but the station buildings and other works could not be completed by 8 September. No mention of having no locomotives with which to work a service. The formalities having been completed, the extension was approved on 6 September.

As the works approached completion, in July and August items dealt with by the directors had a tidying up air about them. Collin arranged for Saunders to install the telegraph for £300, reduced from the £427 10s quoted. The £280 tender from the Clyde Structural Iron Company for the loco and carriage shed at Welshpool was accepted. Easements were sought from the Cambrian for a water pipe and the tranship shed. Expenditure of up to £60 for a reserve water supply at Welshpool was deferred. Plots of surplus land were discussed. Plans for waiting sheds at Castle Caereinion, Cyfronydd and Heniarth, the tranship shed and goods sheds at Welshpool and Llanfair were approved. Those for the station buildings at the termini were approved subject to the addition of a verandah. T. F. Evans's offer to construct all the station buildings for £400 was accepted.

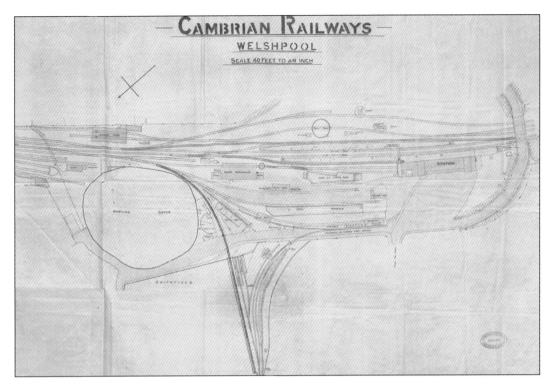

Top: **A 1906 plan of the railways at Welshpool. The corporation's Smithfield siding which borders WLLR property is coloured red.** *National Archives*

Middle: **The 1907 plan of the layout intended at Castle Caereinion when arrangements were made for trains to cross there.** *National Archives*

Bottom: **The Cambrian Railways' 1913 act of Parliament authorised an easement over the corporation's Smithfield siding to enable a WLLR siding to be extended along it. This plan was also deposited, indicating an intention to realign the WLLR across Smithfield Road to make way for a boundary fence.** *Parliamentary Archives*

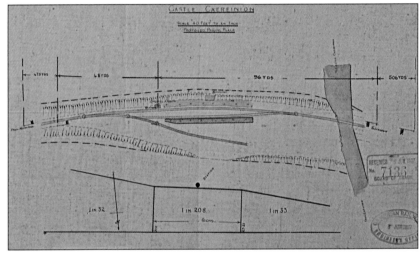

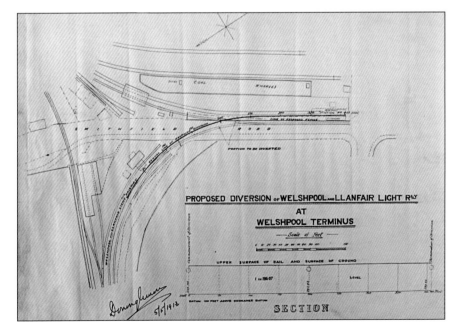

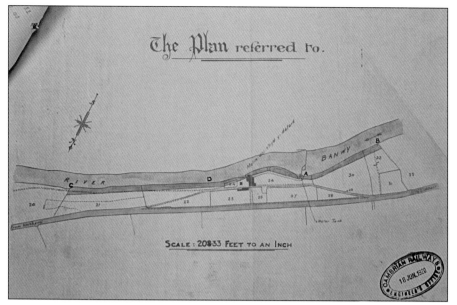

Taken from the 1903 indenture transferring the land at Dolrhyd Mill to the WLLR, this copy plan was produced by the Cambrian Railways to support the discussion about the stopping of trains at Dolrhyd Mill and Eithinog in 1920 (see p140). The mill is in the centre and the railway's land coloured red. The original owners secured a right to found a chain suspension footbridge on river bank land between the points marked A and B as well as the waiting shelter referred to in the text. They also retained the right to make use of the land between the railway and the river between the points A and B, and C and D. The railway's original water tank was at point A, the second one at point B. *National Archives*

The Banwy bridge girders were in position by 7 August, Collin reported. Rails had been laid as far as the bridge and would be continued as soon as the decking had been fixed. The viaduct and fencing were nearly completed.

Jones reported on 28 August, that the first locomotive was finished but he had deferred delivery until there was covered accommodation available for it. The second loco would be finished in September and he expected the carriages and wagons to be available before the end of that month.

Beyer, Peacock was short of space and wanted the loco out of the way. It arrived at Welshpool on 2 September and was stabled on a temporary siding, covered by a tarpaulin. Jones was to hold Beyer, Peacock responsible for the locomotive until it had been accepted.

With the locomotives, rolling stock and other items still to pay for and the remainder of the grant not due until after the final inspection, an £8,000 overdraft from Lloyds Bank was organised in September 1902. The directors had to indemnify the bank against the company defaulting. In October the county council and Forden RDC asked for the first instalments of the repayments due to them; they were asked to wait until the railway had been opened.

Strachan appeared to be experiencing cash-flow difficulties at the same time; he was simultaneously building the Tanat Valley Light Railway. On 1 September 1902 he had asked the company for £1,000 to be paid on account of the retention money. The company was not in a position to oblige, he was told, as his contract was with the Cambrian.

With the exception of forming the slopes on three cuttings, the earthworks were completed, Collin informed the Cambrian directors on 29 September. The track had been laid to Llanfair and most of the sidings in the stations had been laid. Ballasting had been delayed because one of Strachan's locos had broken down and had been out of use for a month.

By 25 October, arrangements had been made to hire the first locomotive, named *The Earl* without any recorded discussion, to Strachan. Collin reported that the second locomotive had been received, that both were in good condition and made according to the drawings and specifications. A trial with the required load was needed before they could be certified as satisfactory. A set of 95 cloth tracings of the drawings supplied by Beyer, Peacock and deposited with the Cambrian had cost £25. Pickering had delivered 11 goods wagons and Collin recommended hiring them and others due shortly, up to

20 in total, to Strachan 'to facilitate completion'. The wagons had been in transit on 1 October, when one of the carriages was awaiting despatch.

The railway would be ready for inspection on 1 November, Collin had forecast at the directors' 25 September meeting. The company gave notice to the Board of Trade on 3 October. Sent separately from the engineer's data that accompanied the notice, were plans of the railway's structures and copies of the deposited plans. Sadly, all that has survived of this bundle is a piece of the wrapping paper with an LNWR 'insured goods' label affixed.

A month later, Collin had had second thoughts and the notice was withdrawn on 14 November. As recently as 10 November he had reported good progress with ballasting, the track was being aligned, telephone wires and poles had been erected, point interlocking was in hand, and buildings and sheds were being erected.

More finishing tasks in evidence during November were recorded by the WLLR directors. Check rails were to be added to the track over the Lledan brook and a hydraulic ram and tank were to be installed at Dolrhyd to supply locomotive water to Llanfair. A cheque for £40 5s was to be issued for payment to the ram's maker, W. H. Bailey & Company, in January 1903, but Collin asked for it not to be sent 'until it is found how the ram works.'

Apart from the finishing off that was needed, another issue had become manifest. While Strachan had been using the new wagons there had been two cases of couplings breaking.

Jones had written to Denniss on 11 November and then to the company on 24 November; the points that he made have been merged in the following paragraphs. He denied that the couplings had broken and that they were unsuitable. Following investigation on the Festiniog Railway, Glyn Valley Tramway, Corris Railway, Abergynolwyn [Talyllyn] Railway, and the North Wales Narrow Gauge Railways he determined that the coupling used by the last was the most satisfactory. He had originally specified an automatic, sprung, centre coupling for the passenger stock, intending to use a curved buffing plank with link and hook on the goods stock, an arrangement that would have caused 'very unpleasant shakings to the passengers' when the slack was taken up on mixed trains. The manufacturer was so convinced that using the same buffer on all the stock was the best thing to do that it had been installed on the goods stock without charge.

The GWR's 1937 plan produced in
connection with the cattle dock extension.
National Archives

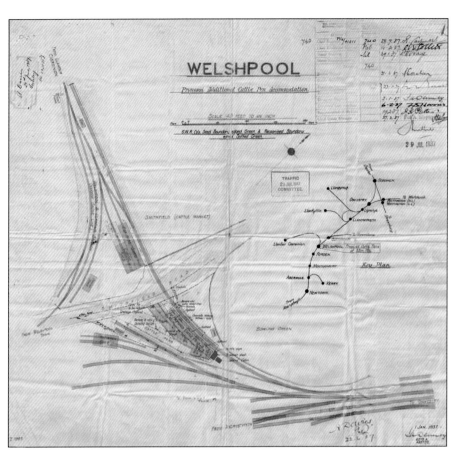

The first case involved two wagons separating from the loco 20–30 yards after starting, and he had found no evidence that they had been coupled properly. If that man who should have been riding on the last wagon had been in place, and not riding on the engine because it was raining, the damage would have been minimised.

In the second case, on 10 November, six wagons had run away from the loco. Jones was convinced that they had not been properly fastened and that the wagons were attached by a chain that was found broken, part on the loco and part on the first wagon, afterwards. One of Strachan's men said that the chain had been used for lashing round the couplings as an added precaution and it had broken after the couplings broke apart, but Jones did not accept that.

On 19 November he had taken a train comprising an engine, four wagons and brake van to Castle Caereinion and in the presence of representatives from the maker, the contractor and the engineer, had failed to 'break' a coupling on the sharpest curves or the steepest gradients. Propelling the train back to Welshpool at low speed, however, the wagon next to the loco derailed several times owing, he thought, to a combination of the track and the weight of the leading brake van. 'On no occasion did the derailments cause the couplings to become detached or loosened.' In many places it was not safe to go faster than 2mph.

A proper trial of the rolling stock could not be made due to the incomplete state of the track. He was satisfied that the stock was superior as regards to design, materials and workmanship than any to be found on other narrow gauge lines. He had contacted the VRLR which used a similar coupling and said that it was satisfactory with no cases of 'break loose'. In view of the WLLR's gradients and curves, however, he thought that the wagons should be fitted with side chains as an extra precaution. Pickering would supply them for 17s 6d per set.

Of the track, Jones said that several curves were sharper than the three chains specified, much of it was unballasted and the appropriate super-elevation had not been set. He could not tell if the maximum 1-in-30 gradient had been exceeded.

Denniss asked Collin for his observations on 14 and 24 November, but he did not visit Welshpool until 28 November, replying on 29 November 1902. He could not make an inspection because both of Strachan's engines had broken down. After discussions with Strachan's son and Eric Byron, the resident engineer, he had concluded that with satisfactory weather the line should be ready for opening by 1 January 1903. Two days had been lost to weather during the current week.

Regarding the track, he did not agree that it was in rough condition except in two places where Strachan had temporary sidings connected. He admitted that the rails were not as true as on an established line, but there was nothing to cause derailments which had occurred on straight sections as well as on curves. Strachan had gangs straightening and adjusting the rails who would be adjusting the vertical alignments where the gradient changed as well. Since 'the new engine' had been running he had found it impossible to keep the track to gauge on curves up to 10 chains radius despite adding extra spikes on the outside rails. The WLLR company had therefore approved expenditure on his recommendation to fit tie bolts and bars on curves of up to six chains.

He was reassured, Denniss told Jones on 1 December, but required confirmation that the minimum curvature was not less than three chains and the gradient was not steeper than 1 in 30. He continued: 'Your remarks about the new engine and its effect upon the permanent way are ambiguous. Do you intend to infer that its wheelbase is too long? If this is your opinion will you please say so.'

Replying on 8 December, Jones was insistent that the locomotives could work on three chain curves, they had a certain side play that would increase with use. They had been used on the partially completed railway without derailing despite some of the curves being sharper than three chains, one being as tight as two chains. If the curves were kept to three chains and the gradients did not exceed 1 in 30 he was confident that the locomotives would be satisfactory.

Writing on the same date, Collin said that he had had the curves and gradients checked 'in small lengths'. Some of the curves were slightly under three chains and there would be no difficulty in correcting them when the final adjustments were made. Short lengths of gradients steeper than 1 in 30 were due to settlement; they would be adjusted in due course and would require more attention for some months after the railway was opened. The locomotives had a 10ft wheelbase and checking with other narrow gauge railways, the longest he had found was 6ft 1in on the North Wales Narrow Gauge Railways. Denniss had already, on 29 November, told the WLLR that he thought the wagon chains should be adopted.

The entrance to Welshpool station yard in 1954. The main line station is out of the picture to the right. *Adrian Gray collection*

On 8 December 1902 Collin had informed the Cambrian directors that three miles of top ballast, metalling of station yards, point interlocking at two stations, and completing final track alignment were still required.

Returning to the rolling stock situation, on 12 November 1902 Jones reported that 36 goods wagons and the brake vans had been delivered. The carriages and the rest of the stock were ready but he had deferred delivery because the carriage shed was not ready and it would get in the way.

When Collin told the directors on 22 December 1902, that the line would be ready for inspection in January they decided that a preliminary inspection should be conducted by the Cambrian's officers, accompanied by representatives of the locomotive and rolling stock builders, on 20/21 January 1903, followed by the Board of Trade inspection the next week. Collin, in the meantime, should explain why his final certificate of £25,350 varied from the estimate of £24,636 he had given in April. He did not respond to the request and it was to take some considerable effort to obtain clarification.

Payments to Strachan 1901-2

1	29 June 1901	£663 19s 6d
2	29 August 1901	£1,502 9s 6d
3	26 September 1901	£1,161 4s 6d
4	31 October 1901	£1,050 1s 6d
5	28 November 1901	£1,858 7s
6	20 December 1901	£1,696 10s
7	23 January 1902	£1,469 6s 6d
8	20 February 1902	£661 1s
9	26 March 1902	£821 18s 6d
10	24 April 1902	£1,748 3s 6d
11	22 May 1902	£754 13s
12	11 July 1902	£1,281 3s
13	11 July 1902	£1,720 17s 6d
14	28 August 1902	£960 7s 6d
15	25 September 1902	£1,107 12s
16	23 October 1902	£877 10s
17	27 November 1902	£672 15s
18	17 December 1902	£697 2s 6d
		£20,705 1s 6d

The preliminary inspection had been postponed by 13 January 1903, because Collin had decided that he was unable to certify the track as fit for use. Bad weather during December, including heavy rain, floods and frost, had stopped work for most of that month. He was to produce the certificate with the least possible delay, as the directors would view with displeasure any application for a further extension of time. Such a step would not only entail further expense but seriously prejudice the company's interests. On 23 January he replied that the line would be ready for the Board of Trade inspection from 31 January.

Druitt submitted his report on 6 February. The width at formation level was 10ft 6in on embankments and 9ft in cuttings. The deepest cutting was 15ft deep and the highest embankment was 29ft high. The sharpest curves were three chains radius and the steepest gradient 1 in 30, in one place continuously for one mile.

The flat-bottomed rails were in 30ft lengths, weighing 45lb per yd secured by dog spikes; sole plates were used at the joints where the rails were secured by three dog spikes. The rails were joined by fishplates with four bolts. The sleepers were of creosoted Baltic fir, 6ft x 9in x 4½in laid 3ft centre to centre. The ballast was broken stone and river gravel laid to a depth of 5in below the sleepers.

In Welshpool, along the Lledan brook some unclimbable iron fencing had been used. There were 15 underbridges and one overbridge. Of the underbridges, that over the Banwy had three 40ft spans on the skew with masonry piers and abutments with steel girders under each rail. That over the Shropshire Canal had one span of 33ft 4in on the skew made of steel plate girders and iron rolled joists. Three underbridges were of brick arches with an 8ft span or less, and 10 were formed by timber baulks under each rail with spans varying from 4ft to 10ft 6in. There were also wooden baulks carrying the rails across the gaps forming the cattle guards at either side of the roads where gates had not been provided at public level crossings.

There was one masonry viaduct with six 22ft 6in spans and three viaducts over the Lledan brook, the line being carried directly along the course of the brook for some little distance by means of longitudinal rail beams supported by cross girders (rolled joists) which in turn rested on the masonry sides of the stream. There were about 45 of these joists of varying span, the longest being 17ft 3in. There were two culverts of 3ft and 4ft diameter respectively.

All the steel girders, baulks, joists etc had sufficient theoretical strength and proved fairly stiff under test load, but a

A short mixed train prepares to leave Welshpool in the first years of GWR control. Although *The Earl* has been numbered 822 it retains its original boiler fittings and chimney; its worksplate is still affixed to the smokebox. The train's solitary wagon has been lettered 'GW'. The photograph shows the terminus after alterations authorised by the Cambrian's 1913 act had been implemented (*see* p138). *Adrian Gray collection*

few of the rolled joists over the Lledan brook needed their bearings attended to.

There were 11 public road level crossings and the railway ran along the side of Smithfield Road for the first three chains of its length. Of the level crossings, three were provided with gates shutting across the railway but not across the road and the remainder had cattle guards. The usual notices were positioned on the roads, but notice boards had still to be provided for Bebb's Passage, Bushalls Lane near Raven Square, and the road adjoining Cyfronydd station. With the exception of the roads in Welshpool across which the corporation of Welshpool had fixed the speed of 4mph under the powers conferred on them by Clause 52(3) of the order, the only important road crossed on the level was that adjoining Castle Caereinion station, where gates were provided so the train would stop on each side of it. Over the rest of the level crossings a speed of 10mph was to be allowed.

The gates across the railway at Castle Caereinion were hung to close inwards and not across the high road. It would have been an improvement if they were hung to open across the road which is on a fairly steep gradient as they would have then be visible to cyclists or people in charge of vehicles, and also the person opening the gates could attract the attention of such people.

There were stations at: Welshpool, commencement; Welshpool [Severn Stars], 0m 33ch; Raven Square, 1m 0ch; Golfa, 2m 66ch; Castle Caereinion, 4m 66ch; Cyfronydd, 6m 57ch; Heniarth Gate, 7m 54ch; Llanfair, termination. The first and the last had booking offices and waiting rooms, Castle Caereinion, Cyfronydd and Heniarth had shelters. All had gravel platforms at rail level.

Sidings and loops worked from two-lever ground frames controlled by the train staff were at: Welshpool, exchange siding points; the goods yard, double frame, four levers working the up facing points of the loop siding and the point leading to the goods yard; Standard quarry siding, not yet connected; Golfa loop; Sylfaen siding, points facing to up trains; Castle Caereinion, loop; Cyfronydd, loop; Heniarth, loop; Llanfair

station, facing points at loop; the points at the end of the line for the engine run round were worked by hand.

The interlocking of the 15 ground frames was correct. The quarry siding was not ready; the left-hand tongue of the facing points needed to be removed and the right-hand one clamped to the stock rail if passenger traffic was commenced before the siding was ready. There was also not quite sufficient clearance between the main line and the siding opposite the trap points at Sylfaen, Heniarth and Llanfair stations. The sidings needed to be slewed further away from the line at these points. A buffer post was required at the termination of the line at Llanfair. At Cyfronydd station the pit of the cattle guard at road adjoining station required draining.

Requirements were: check rails on all sharp curves situated on high banks; wheel guards on the bridges over the Banwy and the Lledan brook; the top ballast required breaking up; sleepers required additional packing in places; gauge widening was required on some curves to allow the engines with a fixed wheelbase of 10ft to get round without throwing considerable strain on the outer rail and grinding heavily against it; all sharp curves of three chains needed to be tied to their proper gauge by steel ties. The speed of train on the sharp reverse curves below Golfa station was not to exceed 5mph 'at present'.

The rolling stock was: two six-coupled engines, gross weight 19½ tons with a weight of between 6 and 7 tons on each axle; passenger carriages were on 4ft 6in wheelbase bogies, the total length over headstocks was 35ft. They had entrances at both ends with side steps and appeared suitable. They and the goods trucks are fitted with centre buffer couplings with Norwegian hooks, but no sideplay had been given to the couplings on the engines or on the trucks, although some had been given on the carriages.

Druitt had been unable to see the couplings in use so could not say if the hooks would make a satisfactory coupling, but thought that it would be dangerous to use the couplings as fitted owing to the want of side play, as they would be very liable to cause derailments when a train was on the sharp curves, which are very numerous on the line. Some modification by which the rigid outer buffer couplings would be quite free to move when the train was on a curve was considered absolutely necessary.

He concluded: 'Under these conditions I do not feel able to recommend the Board of Trade that the light railway has been completed to their satisfaction, although with the requirements completed the permanent way would be fit for traffic. But in any case, the conditions regarding the payment of the balance of the free grant would not be fulfilled until the line has been opened for public traffic. Until the couplings above mentioned have been modified I consider the opening of the railway would be attended with danger to the public using it.'

No explanation was provided for Druitt not having seen the couplings in use. He was satisfied with them when he returned to Welshpool at the company's request on 20 February. This time a train was laid on for him. It comprised a locomotive, a carriage, two covered trucks, three open trucks and a brake van to represent what was expected to be a typical mixed train. Seeing that most of his requirements had been attended to he conducted a formal inspection to save another visit.

The only outstanding issues were the check rails on the three-chain curves, the wheel guards on the Lledan and Banwy bridges, the gauge ties, gauge widening and the 'proper super-elevation' on the sharp curves; the last had not been mentioned previously. He recommended that as soon as Collin had certified that they had all been done the Board of Trade should sanction the line for passenger traffic subject to the following speed restrictions:

- A maximum speed of 15 miles an hour on any part of the line. This restriction could be revised at the discretion of the company's engineer when the formation has consolidated.

- The further restrictions of speed laid down in Clause 52 of the order.

- A speed of 5 miles an hour on the sharp reverse curves south of Golfa, and at Dolrhyd Mill.

Druitt pointed out that before opening for traffic it would be necessary to ensure that all the facing and trap points of the sidings were connected to the ground frames as they had been disconnected for Strachan's convenience. The company should pay attention to Clause 28(4) regarding the gates at level crossings. He had asked the Cambrian to apply for the usual permission to run mixed trains.

Receiving Druitt's report, the directors met on 27 February and heard the resident engineer report his opinion that the requirements could be completed by 'next Tuesday night', 3 March. They hoped that Collin's certificate would be in the post the same day and started to make plans for an opening ceremony on 31 March.

During February the company had, incidentally, made it clear that it was not always going to be a pushover for every claim made against it. Denniss had asked it to provide wagon sheets, ropes, barrows and the other accoutrements required to run a railway. After a letter from the solicitor, he agreed that the Cambrian would supply them.

Collin had submitted a report on Druitt's visit dated 21 February to Denniss. Not mentioned by the inspector, the journey had not been without a little excitement. On straight line near Cyfronydd the brake van had derailed. Collin had checked the gauge and found it correct but a joint near the point of derailment had been slack. This, and the light weight of the van, he thought was responsible for the derailment. The vehicle was quickly re-railed. Returning through the curves near Golfa, three wagons had derailed. After they had been re-railed and the train moved forward, Druitt had checked the gauge, ½in wide as required, and the curve, exactly three chains. Collin could offer no explanation for this derailment, telling Druitt that he would have all the three-chain curves checked for alignment.

On his previous visit Druitt had asked for the check rails to be laid with 3in clearance, which had been done. However, it was found that because the wagon wheels were narrower than those of the locos, the clearance was too great. Druitt's fresh recommendation of making the flangeway 2½in was put in hand.

Denniss submitted a special report containing copies of the correspondence with Collin and the Board of Trade to the Cambrian directors on 28 February. Collin had recommended opening the line for goods traffic on 9 March. Denniss had inspected the line himself and was satisfied with the couplings and saw that 'the engine went round the curves satisfactorily.' Taking into account the condition of the track and the possibility of subsidence [on the embankments], they thought that the goods service should be run 'for a short period' before passenger services were started, Denniss recommending the Cambrian directors agree to 31 March too. He added that Collin would have to pay close attention to the permanent way for a few months after opening.

A hidden drama accompanied the start of the goods train service on Monday, 9 March 1903, for it was the day after the extension of time expired. Was a further extension required? The solicitor sent a telegram to the Parliamentary agent asking the question on 7 March. Without further ado, explanation or questioning, an extension of two months was granted by the Board of Trade on 9 March.

Strachan still had work to do, and on 17/18 March his men worked through the night. In the early hours of the second day a train hauled by one of his locos set off from Welshpool with several workmen riding on the front of it. At Severn Stars one of them, John Williams, jumped off, falling under the loco as he did so and dying from his wounds. The inquest recorded a verdict of accidental death. Neither the Cambrian nor the WLLR made any recorded comment about the incident.

Outwards	14 March 1903			21 March 1903			28 March 1903		
Description	Tons	cwt	£sd	Tons	cwt	£sd	Tons	cwt	£sd
Merchandise	28	18	£15 8s 3d	17	12	£9 8s 8d	18	3	£13 13s 1d
Grain etc.	40	11	£7 10s	28	11	£5 0s 8d	16	10	£4 7s 8d
Manure	17		£3 4s 4d	40	6	£7 1s 5d	87	8	£14 7s 8d
Slag	16	7	£3 14s 10d						
Coal and coke	109	18	£13 9s 6d	124	8	£15 5s 5d	83	10	£9 18s 3d
Other minerals	41	15	£5 7s 10d	35	17	£5 8s 1d	34	15	£4 10s 7d
Sawn timber							4	8	£1 2s
Total	254	9	£48 14s 9d	246	15	£42 4s 3d	254	15	£47 19s 3d
Inwards									
Merchandise				1		10s	5	8	£1 12s
Grain				7	10	£1 5s			
Total				8	10	£1 15s	5	8	£1 12s

Running without nameplates, No 822 crosses Smithfield Road on 21 June 1936. The loco has a Swindon boiler and a copper-capped chimney. Steam from the safety valves is diverted from the cab by a deflector that projects above the cab roof.
F. M. Gates/Author's collection

The first three weeks' goods traffic, reported by Denniss to the Cambrian directors, is shown in the table. For the first week he calculated the average income per mile as £5 8s.

The grand opening was deferred until 4 April, a Saturday, in order that Powis could be present. He had been in India. Rain fell at first, clearing later. In Welshpool, the streets were decorated with streamers. On the Cambrian, a special train from Oswestry brought that company's directors and officers. The WLLR loco, *The Countess*, was decorated with red and green muslin, red rosettes with yellow centres and daffodils, the Prince of Wales' feathers mounted on each end of the loco were surmounted by leeks, the slogan 'Success to the W&LLR' was displayed in white letters on the tank sides. Amongst the guests were representatives from the Shrewsbury & Welshpool joint line, the Shropshire Union Railways & Canal, and the Corris Railway, the last in the form of Dix.

The inaugural train's passage through Welshpool was a noisy affair. Fog detonators marked its departure and charges of dynamite were set off in the Standard quarry as it passed. More detonators marked its arrival at Llanfair Caereinion, where three evergreen arches had been erected, one of them over the track. Speaking at Llanfair Caereinion, Powis said that of the £50,000 spent on the railway so far little had been contributed from the Llanfair area, appealing for support in raising the £2,000 still required, explaining that shortage of funds prevented the installation of signalling and restricted the railway to 'one engine in steam' operation.

The only negative aspect surrounding the jubilation had been a threat by Llanfair traders to boycott the line over the rates charged to use it. Denniss explained that the railway was being run as a commercial undertaking and dividends were anticipated. More facilities were still required, the accommodation at Llanfair was limited and the yard could be bigger. The rates set were authorised and would be reviewed in the light of experience.

Returning to Welshpool, the party gathered for lunch at the Royal Oak Hotel, where more speeches followed. Tribute was paid to the railway's predecessor, 'Johnny Jones and the Llanfair bus'; Jones had often been seen perspiring while leading four horses hauling a heavy load and was not enjoying the best of health. Denniss had said that the Cambrian hoped to look after him now his business had been removed.

Ordinary passenger services started on 6 April. There were four mixed trains daily, with no Sunday service. Despite the lack of accommodation, passenger stock must have been left overnight at Llanfair Caereinion. The Monday/Tuesday/Wednesday 5.5am goods to Llanfair returned mixed at 6.45am, for example, except on Llanfair fair days when the outward journey was mixed and its return was goods only. The 7.5pm mixed from Welshpool returned as a passenger train leaving Llanfair at 8pm except on Saturdays when it ran mixed an hour later. Trains stopped at all stations and those from or to Welshpool stopped at Dolarddyn crossing on Mondays, when passengers paid as if joining or leaving the train at Cyfronydd.

Finances were considered under several headings when the WLLR directors met on 7 April. Two shareholders were to be asked to adhere to their conditional promises to subscribe to more shares; depending on the outcome, public support was to be canvassed. The final instalment of the Treasury grant was still awaited so the company was dependent on the goodwill of suppliers prepared to wait for payment. The overdraft stood at £6,260 12s 5d and about £2,000 was owed. Payments totalling £541 5s 5d to the investing authorities were approved. The opening ceremony had cost £38 19s 9d, an expense that could not be 'properly charged against the company', so donations were to be solicited from the directors.

The first two weeks' traffic was reported as shown in the table. It equated to £6 11s 3d per mile per week.

Goods	11 April 1903			18 April 1903		
Description	Tons	cwt	£sd	Tons	cwt	£sd
Merchandise	16	2	£8 19s 11d	29	10	10 11s 4d
Grain etc.	23	7	£3 16s 5d	12	12	£2 1s 4d
Manure	45	2	£7 15s 1d	37	16	£6 6d 10d
Coal and coke	51	19	£6 9s 2d	48	6	£5 16s
11d						
Other minerals	19	15	£2 13s 4d	46	4	£6 7s 1d
Total	156	5	£29 13s 4d	174	8	£31 3s 6d
Passengers						
	1,274		£32 13s 10d	864		£31 3s 6d
Parcels			14s 8d			
Total			£63 1s 10d			£56 13s 4

On 21 April, Denniss reported that if these figures were maintained then the railway would be a commercial success. He noticed that the traffic had dropped in the fourth week and attributed the reduction to traffic being held for the railway's opening. The LRO permitted the goods rates to be 25% higher than the equivalent Cambrian rates for five years, he reminded his directors. They had been set high because it was easier to reduce them to attract traffic if necessary. Following the traders' complaints the class rates had been reduced and special rates quoted for heavy groceries, drapery, hardware, packed manure, grain and oil cake. There was scope for

Left: **Transhipment of coal in progress on 26 June 1951.** *Brian Hilton/ Adrian Gray collection*

Below: **A view of the yard on 26 March 1956. Both brake vans and four cattle vans are present.** *J. A. Peden/ Adrian Gray collection*

further adjustment if required.

The Treasury grant balance of £10,250 had been received by 5 May, when the company was £3,194 13s 4d in credit. Half of Strachan's retention, £1,267, was approved for payment. Other payments authorised were £289 15s to Beyer, Peacock; £943 6s 4d to Pickering & Company; £685 8s 6d to the Cambrian, and the 21st payment due to Strachan. The solicitors were to sell the £1,000 India stock deposited in court as soon as it was released – it had been sold for £1,016 3s 7d by 7 July. Additional shares to the value of £750 had been spoken for, although £500 was

conditional on £1,357 being subscribed to trigger the authorised debenture issue.

Within a few weeks of the opening, problems had arisen at the interface between the locomotives' fixed wheelbase and the three-chain curves. Collin submitted a detailed report on 7 May, describing the problem locations and possible mitigation measures (*see table below*).

He estimated that the alterations described could be carried out for £1,000 without buying more land. There would still be five three-chain curves and 12 of 4 and 4½ chains. He

Location	Comment
Smithfield	Cannot be altered without taking a portion of the Smithfield.
Canal approach	Can be improved to 4½ chains without taking additional land.
Vicarage grounds	Route kept to Lledan brook due to cost of land. Curves can be eased to 4½ chains by building dwarf retaining walls to support embankments.
Llanfair side of Church Street	Three-chain curve necessary to follow Lledan brook; cannot be altered without purchasing property.
Hall Street	Severn Stars purchased to obtain three-chain curve; it might be improved to four chains by encroaching on the road.
Tannery	Curve might be improved to 4½ chains by widening the bank and building a short retaining wall.
Allotments at rear of armoury	Curve cannot be improved without taking land.
Armoury – Standard quarry	Two curves which can be altered to 4½ chains by widening cuttings and banks and building a short retaining wall.
Golfa curves	Curves adopted to reduce the amount of Pughe's land required. Can be improved to four and five chains by widening cuttings, making slopes steeper, widening an embankment, and building a short retaining wall.
Dolrhyd	Curve cannot be altered without taking more land

Scheme	Proposed alteration	Time	Cost per engine	Where done	Comments
1	Convert to 4-4-0T	14 weeks	£195	Welshpool	Inside bearings on bogie, 1½in side play, rigid wheelbase reduced to 5ft 10in, bogie unsatisfactory due to position of frames and cylinders, steadiness of loco would be diminished, tractive effort reduced, weight increased, brake power reduced, capability reduced.
2	Convert to 2-4-0T	7 weeks	£80	Welshpool	Remove leading coupling rods, substitute sliding axle boxes on leading axle to give 1in side play, rigid wheelbase reduced to 5ft 10in, leading wheels would have no radial action, engine would be more unstable, brake power and adhesion reduced.
3	Reduce wheelbase	16 weeks	£225	Manchester	Reduce wheelbase by 9in between leading and driving axles and by 1in between driving and trailing axles, cost out of proportion with possible merit.
4	Remove driving flanges	1 week	Nominal	Welshpool	Would be unsafe and make little difference on the track, increasing wear on leading and trailing tyres.
5	Additional play in axle boxes	3 weeks	£10	Welshpool	Increase side play by in in the leading axleboxes and by ¼in in the trailing axleboxes, the equivalent of shortening the rigid wheelbase to about 8ft 6in, would increase wear and tear on the loco, no structural alterations required, haulage and brake power unaltered.

recommended accepting Jones's suggestion of altering the locomotives to give extra side play on the leading and trailing axleboxes. Ideally, he said, the minimum curve should be six chains, but that would cost up to £5,000 to achieve.

Jones's report had been submitted the day before. He had consulted with Beyer, Peacock and between them they had produced five options, as shown in the table (*above*).

The final option was chosen and was completed on 15 May. By 10 June, Collin reported that the engines were running much better and not affecting the curves although 'there are two or three curves … when the engine … still moves the spikes a little.' He had arranged for soleplates to be used and for extra sleepers to be inserted to stiffen up the track.

In June, Denniss produced details of the WLLR's revenue for the first eight weeks. The average income of £7 1s 1d per mile per week was compared with £24 13s 6d earned by the Cambrian. He made no comment about the big dip after 9 May.

Week ending	Passenger	Goods	Total
11 April	£33	£30	£63
18 April	£41	£34	£75
25 April	£25	£45	£70
2 May	£34	£36	£70
9 May	£44	£31	£78
16 May	£24	£28	£52
23 May	£28	£27	£55
30 May	£20	£35	£55
	£249	£266	£515

By the end of June, the gross receipts had reached £1,007 4s 5d, 40% (£402 17s 9d) of which was to be paid to the company. The cost of working had been £532, leaving £72 profit for the Cambrian, Denniss commenting: 'You will no doubt consider [it] is not unsatisfactory.'

Nearly three years after closure, on 31 March 1959, the yard is still full of wagons, including a brake van, two goods vans, two cattle vans and several sheep wagons.
F. A. Wycherley/ Adrian Gray collection

Capital account expenditure to 26 June 1903	
Legal and preliminary expenses	£1,002 4s 5d
General and office expenses	£110 9s 3d
Engineer – payments on account	£1,350
Board of Trade – fee on application for amendment order	£50
Bank charges	£119 19s 9d
Deposit with Board of Trade	£1,000
Salaries – secretary and auditors	£83 7s 4d
Land claims and compensation	£5,739 0s 4d
Expenses cutting first sod	£22 10s 9d
Construction – payments paid per Cambrian Company	£23,874 4s
Permanent way materials	£5,236 17s 8d
Locomotives and rolling stock	£5,906 6s 1d
Shropshire Union Railway & Canal Company for stoppage of navigation	£10
Costs re loans	£269 11s
Rates and taxes	£3 4s 1d
Rent charges	£18
Signalling and telegraphs	£350
Engine and carriage shed	£280
Stations and buildings	£400
Weighbridge	£60
Water supply	£117 16s 8d
Severn Stars cottage	£106 7s 4d
Interest on loans	£455 5s 2d
Income tax on loan interest	2d
	£46,565 4s

July was a month of extreme contrasts so far as the company's finances were concerned. The overdraft was down to £46 11s 6d and unsecured borrowing of £1,000 had been arranged. The remaining share capital had been subscribed and steps were taken to issue the debentures. On the positive side, surplus land at Castle Caereinion and a house in Church Street, Welshpool, were to be sold.

Just as the directors must have thought they were close to getting the company's finances into a state of equilibrium, on 7 July Collin submitted certificate No 23 for £2,850 18s, followed by a note on 16 July saying that £800 was due for extras. This was £3,560 3s 5d above the estimate he had given in January, which was itself higher than forecast. Collin was asked to explain the discrepancy. The 'missing' certificates, Nos 19-22,

would have been for works undertaken outside the contract, buildings, for example.

The comment made on 4 April about inadequate facilities at Llanfair Caereinion was duly followed up, Collin estimating that it would cost £215 to enlarge the yard. On 11 August, Denniss informed the company that the Cambrian would do the work, including installing a siding, for 4½% interest, repayment being due when the debentures had been issued. He was informed that the debenture capital could not be used for this purpose and repayment would have to await the availability of funds from other sources. On 11 December, Dennis was informed that until Collin produced his final certificate to justify Strachan's claim, no further expenditure would be incurred.

A severe storm on 8 September 1903 that had washed out 200 yards of ballast was reported in the *Manchester Guardian* two days later. Until the damage was repaired trains terminated at Heniarth and passengers were transported to and from Llanfair by road.

The terms for issuing the debentures had been agreed on 1 September at 20 years at 4½% although the directors reserved the right to redeem them at 103% after 10 years, giving six months' notice. A prospectus was issued on 28 November and applications for £1,550 had been received by 22 December.

Addie's position as a director was terminated on 22 December 1903, when his successor as mayor, Charles T. Pugh, replaced him. During the year, David Davies, the son of the contractor of the same name, had been appointed to the board. Addie continued to act for the company as its valuer and on 20 April 1904 the directors were to pay tribute to his efforts on the company's behalf. He was to be reappointed to the board on 11 July 1905.

It was thanks to Addie that the directors eventually received information about Strachan's claim, several requests to Collin having been effectively ignored. His 15-page typewritten report had been dated 19 April 1904. Collin had also written with explanations on 28 July 1903 and 26 March 1904. Some of the additional costs had arisen because the work carried out had been re-surveyed, establishing that more had been done than first calculated. Specific explanations from Collin's first report have been tabulated (*overleaf*).

Below left: **Leaving the Welshpool depot area on 16 April 1938 there is an accumulation of permanent way trolleys on the ground between the WLLR and the corporation's Smithfield siding, including a pump trolley.** *Author's collection*

Below: **Climbing to the bridge over the Montgomery Canal on 20 October 1956. The bridge remains in situ; the area to the left of the train has been developed for a major supermarket that opened in March 2011.** *H. F. Wheeller/Adrian Gray collection*

Item	Increase	Explanation
Earthworks	£700	£215 for widening and lowering road to Heniarth station; £300 to remove slips in cuttings following rain; balance for extra excavations in various cuttings.
Drains	£460	Following the landslips it was necessary to install drainage in the cuttings concerned.
Track	£870	Installing check rails on the three-chain curves, gauge-widening, fixing ties and extra soleplates; installing an extra siding at Llanfair Caereinion requested by Denniss.
Metalling	£170	Surfacing the road at Heniarth after alterations.
	£135	Altering stiles at district council's request; fencing riverside to keep cattle from the track, the river having proved to be an inadequate barrier; fixing mile and quarter posts as required by the Board of Trade inspector.
	£90	Concrete footings to protect railway formation from scour at Dolrhyd.
	£40	Pulling down culvert over Lledan brook.
Stations	£635	Partly work carried out by Strachan previously estimated separately; increased works required installing water supply at Dolrhyd and extra gas supply at Welshpool.

Right: **Passing the vicarage wall, right, as the train approaches the Church Street crossing.**
J. A. Peden/Adrian Gray collection

The Board of Trade requirements could not have been foreseen, Addie thought, but 'it is difficult to explain why [the other items] should not have been taken into consideration by the engineer in previous reports.' The works at Heniarth were unauthorised. The Dolrhyd water supply cost £398 14 10d, 'the importance of this work was not properly realised at the commencement.' Druitt's permanent way requirements, the gauge widening, the check rails, moving the check rails, the tie bars and adjusting the cants where a 5mph speed limit had been imposed, had cost £1,066.

In his second report Collin concluded that he considered the cost of the contract works to be £29,253 2s 11d plus £1,907 10s 10d for extras, in round figures a 20% increase on the £25,350 he had given in January 1903. The extras included £238 for felling trees, which Addie thought was unreasonable. He said, however, that he had no reason to doubt the figures that Collin had submitted, but that the engineers should have obtained approval for works not included in the contract and queried whether the charges for the slips were properly chargeable to the company.

With Strachan's own claim for extras totalling £19,723 4s 6d the directors were happy that Collin could only justify £1,907 10s 10d, but were about to discover that Strachan was a very determined man who would not give up easily. No complete breakdown of Strachan's claim has been found; neither railway company thought it necessary to record details of it. Where details were mentioned, it is clear that he was trying his luck in some instances. He had been charged for the repair of some WLLR wagons that his men had damaged and tried to reclaim the expenditure, for example.

With £360 4s 5d in the bank, commitments totalling £672 17s 3d, the knowledge that there were still outstanding claims on the construction account to be met and a full subscription list for the debentures exhausting the company's ability to borrow, the directors decided to return to the Treasury for further assistance. Writing on 20 April 1904, Powis requested a further free grant of £3,500 and a loan of £5,800, to clear existing liabilities and to effect certain improvements. Strachan's claim was judged to be exaggerated and was expected to be settled for the amount certified by Collin. The proposed improvements were as shown in the table.

Improvement	Estimated cost
Additional sidings and enlargement of yard at Llanfair	£215
Altering signalling and provision of passing places so that more than one engine in steam can be run	£880
Platforms, goods sidings and metalling station yard at Castle Caereinion	£270
Timber wagons	£440
A third engine	£1,600
Additional passenger carriage	£235
	£3,640

Above: **The Church Street crossing in the 1950s.** *Frith/Adrian Gray collection*

Left: **The problem with the crossings was not so much with the trains but the failure of motorists to keep the crossings clear. No 822 on 12 October 1951.** *F. W. Shuttleworth/Author's collection*

No 822 at Severn Stars. The former waiting room has been taken over by an undertaker. *Adrian Gray collection*

Right: **Unlike any other, this photograph demonstrates the obstacles overcome by the WLLR to secure its route through Welshpool. On 25 March 1947 No 822 is seen on the Lledan brook having passed through Severn Stars.** *R. E. Tustin/Author's collection*

Below: **No 823 has a well-loaded train in tow as it crosses Raven Square in the early 1950s.** *Michael Whitehouse collection*

Bottom: **The advent of car-owning photographers in the 1950s made photographs of the halts more likely. This is Golfa with No 822 on 4 April 1956.** *G. F. Bannister/Author's collection*

Following an investigation into the company's situation, a reply was sent on 4 August, saying that an addition to the free grant was not justified but that a loan of up to £5,700 at 3¼% could be made if the remainder of the capital required could be found. The company was not informed that the reason the grant was refused was because it was making a profit and might pay dividends. Considering the matter on 13 September, the directors resolved to apply for an amendment to the light railway order to permit the loan to be taken and to increase the ordinary borrowing powers to £4,000.

Before the order application was submitted the company's Parliamentary agent informed the treasury that the loan would be sufficient to pay the cost of the works already carried out and put the company on a sound financial footing. The additional works would therefore be deferred until the money to pay for them could be raised. The application was advertised on 14 November 1904 and the Welshpool & Llanfair Light Railway (further borrowing powers) Order 1905 was to be made on 1 May 1905.

Despite the lack of funds for additional works, a siding had been installed at Tanllan, near Llanfair Caereinion, to handle timber traffic for E. O. Jones & Sons. It had been requested by Denniss on 18 April 1904. The merchant had purchased a large quantity of timber and was willing to load it if suitable facilities were provided. The work had been carried out by the Cambrian for £130, £70 of which would be repaid by the customer at a rate of 3d per ton loaded. The remaining £60 had been charged to the WLLR. The

Board of Trade had been asked to inspect it on 30 June and Druitt submitted his report on 25 November. The siding, which faced trains from Welshpool, was controlled by a two-lever frame locked by the train staff. He recommended approval subject to the traffic being worked with the loco at the lower end of the train due to the gradient.

Provision of wagons for timber traffic had been a saga that had started in July 1903, when Denniss had requested 10 or 12 wagons for it. Jones said that he wanted paying to specify and procure them, the WLLR replying that they had been included in the list of stock required by the Cambrian to equip the railway and that although their purchase had been deferred, they were included in the fee already payable to him.

The directors eventually gave up on dealing with Jones and took over the order themselves, Addie visiting Pickering on 11 November 1903. He was told that wagons without springs or central couplers could be supplied for £25 each, but that they would be unsuitable for the WLLR. Wagons that complied with the Cambrian's requirements could be supplied for £44 each or at £10 8s 10d per wagon per annum for five years. By 4 March 1904, six Cambrian-specification wagons had been ordered on a five-year lease contract, a nominal payment of 1s per wagon to be paid at the end of the term to complete the purchase. The wagons were delivered by 20 April but awaited acceptance by the Cambrian at that date. The lease with the Scottish Waggon Company Limited was to be sealed on 13 September.

Left: **Having a roadside location might explain why the GWR put some effort into making Sylfaen quite presentable. The sign to the left of the shelter reads 'GWR Sylfaen Halt'.** *Adrian Gray collection*

Below: **Bound for Welshpool, No 822 passes the little-used signalbox at Castle Caereinion.** *Adrian Gray collection*

Bottom: **This view of Castle Caereinion shows the station's waiting shelter. If the angle of the turnout is not distorted by perspective it is hard to see that either the mechanical or the permanent way engineers would be happy for it to be regularly used by locomotives. This is No 822 on 1 June 1956.** *Hugh Ballantyne*

In April 1904 Strachan had given notice that his claim should be put to an arbitrator. The contract nominated Collin, or the Cambrian's engineer for the time being, to deal with any disputes. Collin had started to handle the case only to resign from the contract on 6 May and from the Cambrian for health reasons the next day.

He later explained to Denniss that as a receiver had been appointed to the Tanat Valley Light Railway, of which he was also the engineer, he stood to lose 'what is to me a very large sum of money', or would have to wait for many years before he was paid. The WLLR had applied for further assistance from the Treasury and if it did not get all that it wanted there was also a possibility that a receiver would be appointed. As the WLLR had owed him money for about 12 months he had a personal stake in the arbitration so he had to withdraw. £225 was to be paid on account of his claim for £324 11s on 12 April 1905.

Strachan's solicitors initially refused to accept Collin's successor as the Cambrian's engineer, G. C. McDonald, as arbitrator because Collin had resigned but, after threatening to apply to a judge to make the appointment, they accepted him in July. Denniss and the Cambrian's solicitors decided that the remainder of Strachan's retention should be paid to prevent him from issuing a writ on that account; £1,355 5s 6d had been paid by 13 September 1904.

On 19 September 1904, Strachan wrote to the WLLR objecting to the repayments being made to the investing authorities 'considering the very large amount' due to the Cambrian. When the Cambrian directors met on 11 October, Denniss reported that not only had Strachan issued a writ for £1,509, he was also claiming damages for breach of contract, claiming that Collin had been dismissed to prevent him from issuing the final certificate. The solicitor expected the action to be dismissed with costs and recommended the WLLR pay £975 18s 6d into court against the final certificate. The WLLR had recently paid £1,000 to the Cambrian and only had £200 to hand. If the Cambrian would pay the money into court, and the remaining £1,850 18s owed, it would be settled when the Treasury loan was received.

On 10 August 1904, Collin reported that one of the Banwy bridge piers had been 'dangerously undermined by the water.' He had put repairs in hand immediately at a cost of about £50. 60 years later this pier or its fellow nearly brought about the permanent closure of the WLLR.

The train service was accelerated by 10 minutes from 3 December 1904. Denniss had obtained the approval of both the locomotive and the civil engineers to this move, the journey time now taking 55 minutes. The Cambrian's working expenses for the half-year were £898 14s, 56.47% of the £1,592 7s 10d gross receipts. 'Considering the amount of ballasting and other attention with the permanent way has required I consider this by no means unsatisfactory' Denniss was to report in May 1905.

The Cambrian was reimbursed the £3,068 17s 5d by the WLLR on 8 July 1905. The company had been charged 5% compound interest of £264 10s 11d, on capital expenditure incurred on its behalf as permitted by the working agreement. In view of the difficulties caused by Collin, it asked if the Cambrian would consider charging a lesser rate on the simple basis. The difference was £11 8s 4d.

The deposit against the final certificate should not be paid into court, Strachan's solicitors had written on 29 October 1904, because they were intending to apply to have the matter referred to arbitration. If it was paid into court it would be as if the action had been started and their claim for arbitration would not be heard.

Despite the earlier agreement over McDonald's appointment, the choice of arbitrator was prolonged. Eventually, Denniss recommended Charles Langbridge Morgan of the London, Brighton & South Coast Railway and Strachan put forward Walter Armstrong, new-works engineer of the Great Western Railway. In February 1905, Denniss agreed to the final selection being 'by means of drawing a piece of paper from a hat' and Armstrong was chosen. Addie had told Denniss that he had tried to negotiate a settlement with Strachan but had found him impossible to deal with. He had, however, established that Strachan was prepared to accept £6,000 in settlement of his claim.

Armstrong accepted the appointment and a preliminary hearing was held on 18 April. Strachan attempted to launch his case only for an objection to be upheld that he had not submitted his statement of claim. His original claim of £19,636 13s 9d had been reduced to £9,876 14s 5d. He was also claiming £17,893 17s 3d from the Tanat Valley Light Railway. Engineers for each side were to discuss the claim and produce lists of agreed and disputed items by 18 May. The Cambrian's counterclaim would be presented on the same date.

Agreement was reached on items valued at £1,574 6s 11d, but the statement of differences was not produced 'owing to Strachan's obstinacy in regards to proposed meetings.' The value of the counterclaim was £1,685 15s 11d, mostly represented by £50 per week for the 30 weeks the railway was incomplete after the date specified, 1 September 1902; the remainder represented locomotive hire, repair of wagons and other lesser items.

Left: **A train of at least two passenger carriages arrives at Llanfair Caereinion. The loco's running number is painted to the right of its coupling.** *Ian Allan Library*

Below: **Shunting the yard at Llanfair Caereinion, c1955. By this time, No 822's steam heating equipment had been removed.** *A. W. V. Mace/ Adrian Gray collection*

Collin probably saw the arbitration as an opportunity to recoup some of the money that he was fearful of losing. He had refused to return or give access to the contract documents that he had taken when he left the Cambrian's employment, and now he made what were perceived as extravagant demands to act as a witness against Strachan; 25 guineas retainer, 4 guineas a day for office work and 20 guineas a day to appear. Denniss approved of the retainer and offered 5 guineas a day to attend, including office work and producing any plans. In his accounts of the arbitration, Denniss did not refer to any contribution being made by Collin so possibly no agreement was reached.

The hearing was resumed on 4 August, when Strachan 'resumed his case in a very excited manner.' He had subpoenaed Denniss and questioned him about a letter he [Denniss] was supposed to have written on 17 December 1902, refusing to take delivery of rolling stock. When Denniss denied having written such a letter Strachan 'completely lost control of himself', claimed that the letter had been supressed and demanded an adjournment for it to be produced. When he refused to behave, the Cambrian's counsel walked out. Investigation established that the letter related to the wagons being fitted with chains that had been dealt with by the WLLR directors on 17 December.

Concerning Strachan's behaviour, the Cambrian wrote to Armstrong, copied to Strachan via his solicitors, on 10 August 1905. 'Reckless expenditure', 'waste of time', 'considerable inconvenience', 'quite unprecedented' and 'emphatic protest' were amongst the phrases used, calling upon Armstrong to use his influence 'to ensure the reasonable expeditious conduct of the proceedings with due regard to the expenditure and to avoiding the waste of time, both of which hitherto have been so recklessly incurred by Mr Strachan's action.' Armstrong replied: 'I quite concur with your expressions, and hope Mr Strachan will try to conduct his case in a more reasonable manner. His conduct at the last sitting was very objectionable.'

When the hearing was continued on 23 November, Strachan's counsel took two days to read letters that both sides agreed had no bearing on the case, but which revealed an 'unfortunate interference' by Byron, the resident engineer, in matters being dealt with by Strachan and the WLLR. 'It is unfortunate that so many letters on this

subject were written' Denniss informed the Cambrian directors, adding that the exercise had cost about £300 in fees.

Resuming the arbitration on 15 December, Strachan's solicitors made an informal offer to settle for £5,000, each side paying its own costs, which was refused. Strachan put up Arthur Cameron Hurtzig as his expert witness. It soon became apparent that his knowledge of the WLLR was limited to what he had been told by Strachan with the consequence that Strachan withdrew £1,200 of his claim because his witness was unable to support it. Denniss was cross-examined on 16 December, a Saturday, for 2½ hours about allegations that the Cambrian had not treated Strachan properly, none of which were relevant to his claim.

On 18 December evidence for the WLLR was given by Morgan. Proceedings were not resumed on 19 December as expected, because Armstrong was ill. Two more days were taken for closing speeches on 5/6 February 1906. Awaiting the decision, Denniss reported that he thought that Strachan's claim was based on feeble evidence. His claim had been reduced to £6,600 and 'would probably be substantially reduced by the award.'

Indeed, Armstrong awarded Strachan £4,251 10s 4d, and allowed the counterclaim, on 14 June. The WLLR, with only £1,200 available and unable to borrow from its bank without directors' guarantees, asked the Cambrian to advance the remainder which it did grudgingly to stave off more threats of action from Strachan. The Cambrian also paid the arbitrator's charges of £321 17s 6d, to avoid them being included in Strachan's expenses claim and thereby saving £8 in taxation fees.

One item that Strachan succeed with related to spoil removal, his contractual responsibility. However, he had made a verbal agreement with Collin to load it into Cambrian wagons so

Another view of the yard, on 15 March 1952. The 1905 complaint that it was inadequate and that wagons were left under load for want of space to empty them seems to be illustrated here. The coal merchant's scales are in the centre foreground.
R. E. Tustin/Author's collection

that it could be used to widen the embankment near Forden in preparation for doubling the track there. He had used his loco to transport the spoil to site and had unloaded it, charging £348 11s 5d for doing so. The WLLR directors thought that they should not be responsible for the entire charge as the spoil benefited the Cambrian, suggesting that they be credited with £300. The Cambrian offered £200. It appears that neither the Cambrian nor the WLLR thought to claim against Strachan in respect of his unfulfilled obligation to maintain the railway for twelve months after its completion.

Overall, a better result would have been obtained by accepting the settlement offer, for the costs incurred, including Strachan's expenses, amounted to £2,847 12s 9d. As precedents established during the hearings simplified the handling of Strachan's complaint against the Tanat Valley Light Railway, the WLLR thought that company should stand some of the expenses. The sum of £134 11s 1d was agreed upon.

In 1906, Pickering enquired about the outstanding order for four timber wagons. When Denniss said that the Cambrian could work the traffic without them, a request was made for the order to be cancelled. On 24 September 1906, Pickering wrote that the order could only be cancelled if it was replaced by orders for other rolling stock. A decision was deferred and nothing more was said.

The question of capacity at Llanfair Caereinion arose again at the end of 1906. W. H. Thomas, an Oswestry timber merchant, had bought timber in the area which was being transported to Welshpool by road. Enlarging the yard at a cost of about £170 would attract this traffic, some of which would be bound for destinations beyond Welshpool, and provide coal storage space, avoiding keeping wagons under load.

More timber traffic was responsible for an examination of the facilities at Castle Caereinion, reported on 2 January 1907. Jabez Barker, a Shrewsbury timber merchant, had bought an estimated 1,400 tons of timber in the locality which could be hauled to Llanfair and then to Welshpool. At 5s per ton gross revenue would be £550, 40% of which would be £140. On a Sunday, when the railway was closed, a successful trial had been

undertaken with some 60ft timbers and trucks connected with chains acting as bolsters; the timber's length prevented it from being carried in the ordinary (mixed) trains. Therefore two-train running, requiring the installation of signalling and a siding for the local traffic, was required to handle the traffic. The cost of the alterations and installing signalling was estimated at £160.

The WLLR directors agreed to the work being carried out on 23 March 1907 and on 4 June Samuel Williamson, Denniss's successor as secretary in 1906, gave notice to the Board of Trade that the station was ready for inspection. Submitting his report on 15 June, Druitt said that a small signalbox had been equipped with a 10-lever frame; one lever was spare. He explained that one-engine-in-steam working was to be replaced by train-staff-and-ticket combined with absolute block telegraph except that the telephone would be used instead of block instruments. He saw no objection to this, requiring only to see a copy of the working instructions and a fresh undertaking as to the method of working, signed by both companies, to approve its use.

The regulations were dated 23 September 1907. Of note was the requirement that when any train was assisted by a second engine it was to be attached to the rear of the train, no double-heading. Sending Druitt the regulations on 18 September, McDonald explained that it was only intended to use the crossing for a month or two at a time, 'chiefly for ballasting or maintenance purposes' and that at other times the points would be disconnected from the signalbox and re-connected to the ground frame. Druitt required that the staffs for the system not in use be locked up.

The company's liabilities had been the subject of a report that Addie submitted on 18 March 1907. Including £100 as working capital, the total was £4,145 5s 2d. He suggested issuing the remaining £200 debenture stock and borrowing by mortgage or a fresh debenture issue a further £3,850. The Treasury was to be asked to remit the interest due to it for five years and on 7 August 1908 the local authorities were to be requested to forego redemption payments due to them for seven years.

The corporation had become concerned about the rail deck on part of the Lledan brook, writing on 17 May 1907 to suggest that following work undertaken in Brook Street, the section near the tannery be covered in concrete. A contribution of £5 towards the estimated £10 cost was approved. On 19 July, the corporation asked for help in carrying out a 'further small portion to make the improvement complete.' Referring to the 'present dangerous open space', the request was passed to the Cambrian.

It was some two years after Castle Caereinion station had been altered to accommodate the passing of trains and timber loading that the WLLR directors discovered that it was not being used as they expected. On 30 July 1909, they resolved to ask the Cambrian to relieve the company of the interest being charged on the £190 expenditure until it was. The loop had not been used because the railway could keep up with the pace of timber delivery without it, Denniss was to explain to Conacher. The timber had been carried either before or after the ordinary service, the longest lengths being about 73ft. 2,113 tons had been carried, earning £587 16s 11d, £235 2s 9d of which accrued to the WLLR. In addition, the Cambrian had earned £412 3s 8d from timber despatched to destinations beyond Welshpool. Druitt's requirement for a repeater of the distant signals to be located in the signalbox, not mentioned in his report, accounted for the £30 increase in the cost over the estimate. The Cambrian offered to reduce the interest charged to 2½% until the crossing was brought into use, or to cancel the interest when the WLLR cleared its debt. If the WLLR had been unable to accommodate this traffic it would have been hauled to Dinas Mawddwy for conveyance via the Mawddwy Railway.

Barker's timber had been loaded at Tanllan but in May 1909 he was given notice to quit by E. O. Jones & Sons, owners of the loading dock, so alternative arrangements were required. With minimal alterations the timber could be loaded at Heniarth or it would be lost to the railway; about 300 tons was still expected.

The status of the WLLR's debt of £3,174 13s to the Cambrian had been reported on 2 March 1909. The operating company was the largest creditor. The investing authorities had agreed to interest-only repayments and the extra money would be used to reduce the debt over the seven years. Williamson calculated that unless the WLLR's finances improved considerably, it would still owe the Cambrian £2,569 17s 10d in seven years' time.

A 10-year-old boy no doubt rued the day that he decided to use the WLLR as a playground in 1909. He placed a length of timber across the line, 'to see what would happen.' The driver of the next train was able to stop and remove the obstruction without any damage being caused. The Cambrian's solicitor prosecuted the child at the magistrates' court where he was ordered to be birched.

It appears that the Castle Caereinion crossing might have seen more use than the WLLR directors and possibly some Cambrian management knew about. On 2 May 1910, McDonald reported that the Standard quarry had in stock a large quantity of chippings that he wished to use as ballast on the WLLR. He had used this material before but the quarry did not have enough stone in stock for the work to be finished. He raised it with the directors because to work the ballast trains at the same time as the 'ordinary' trains the Castle Caereinion signalbox and loop would have to be brought into use. 'This was done on the previous occasion, but I understand that there may be some question of policy involved in re-opening the crossing place for this purpose.'

The transport of livestock was the subject of correspondence between the WLLR and the Cambrian in 1911. Conacher, the Cambrian's chairman but acting as traffic manager at this time, wanted to modify six wagons for the purpose. After obtaining more information the WLLR approved £18 10s 10d expenditure on 20 February 1911.

Increasing timber traffic at Heniarth in 1911 prompted Conacher to ask for the siding to be lengthened at a cost of £27. The WLLR offered £20 on the basis that part of the work was maintenance. In October 1912, Barker's timber traffic warranted the entrance at Cyfronydd being widened. The railway companies were to share the £2–3 cost of a crane.

A cottage at Severn Stars had been bought when the railway was being built, modified to accommodate the railway and retained, being rented to the Cambrian which rented it to a guard. In 1903 Collin had certified that repairs valued at £106 7s 4d had been carried out. By 1912, the building was in a very poor state, the front and rear first floor walls were leaning, the floorboards were rotten, the entire first floor wanted taking down and rebuilding at a cost of up to £40. The WLLR directors thought that the work could not have been done properly in the first place and wanted a contribution from the Cambrian. On 24 June, it gave notice to quit but wanted to keep a section of land attached to the property as a site for a waiting room, replacing the room in the cottage allocated to that purpose. By 14 October 1912, the building had been sold to a builder for £70 and a tender for £24 17s accepted for the construction of a waiting shelter.

A protracted correspondence about the right to stop trains at Dolrhyd, between Heniarth and Llanfair Caereinion, during 1912, had its origins in the railway's construction, when the conveyance gave the former owners the right to erect 'a shelter as a waiting place for passengers by the railway', but no right to stop, join or leave trains. In 1903, permission had been given to stop trains at both Dolrhyd and Eithnog boathouse, 120 yards closer to Llanfair, and in 1908 the WLLR directors had approved the erection of a platform at Dolrhyd by the occupants. When the

No 823 shunting a loaded cattle wagon at Llanfair Caereinion on 2 April 1951.
W. T. Baldwin

137

The end of the road. No 822 could not get much closer to Llanfair Caereinion , c1954. *H. F. Wheeller/Adrian Gray collection*

The last BR train arrives at Llanfair Caereinion on 3 November 1956. *Adrian Gray collection*

locomotive water stop was moved from Dolrhyd to a point closer to Llanfair Caereinion in 1911/2, trains were sometimes delayed by having to stop three times within a short distance. Neither the shelter referred to in the conveyance nor the platform approved in 1908 appear to have been built.

A 1912 request for a platform and shelter at the boathouse prompted the Cambrian to review the number of stopping places in the locality with the intention of reducing them, but the proposal had been dropped by August 1913.

The Cambrian Railways' 1913 act that, amongst other things, sanctioned its amalgamation with the Vale of Rheidol Light Railway, contained a clause concerning the WLLR, too. With royal assent granted on 4 July 1913, the act approved the laying of a WLLR siding with its rails interlaced with those of the corporation's Smithfield siding. Sub-clause 16(3) revealed its purpose. Without the corporation's consent, the siding was only to be used for livestock traffic to or from the Smithfield market. The corporation granted an easement over the land for 50 years backdated to 4 April 1913. The WLLR had agreed to it on 2 May providing that all expenditure was devolved to the Cambrian. Set in concrete, the section of track alongside the cattle dock is all that remains of WLLR track in Welshpool.

A clause entitled 'for the protection of Welshpool Corporation' also affected the railway, for it required the company to reconstruct 136yd of the line at the Welshpool terminus, to remove it from Smithfield Road, and to erect a fence along the boundary. Cartwright (see Bibliography)

records that the corporation had been seeking the change for seven years so now it must have been the price paid to secure its agreement to the easement. The reconstructed track was within the original limits of deviation, on the alignment of the edge of the (former) platform building, so could have been undertaken without fresh powers. It was not a relocation into the goods yard as sometimes stated.

W. A. Jehu, a shareholder, had complained to the Cambrian about the inadequacy of the carriages in February 1913. On Welshpool fair days, the first and third Mondays of each month and every Monday from June until September, there was considerable overcrowding. The three carriages in use had a nominal capacity of 100 although in practice, they were overcrowded with 90 passengers. The WLLR directors had rejected the Cambrian's proposal to obtain another carriage on 2 May. When Williamson pursued the idea 'an estimate of the additional income that might reasonably be expected' was requested on 12 September but nothing more was done.

Complaints about the carriage oil lighting were eventually considered by the Cambrian on 13 February 1914, when it was reported that acetylene lighting equipment could be purchased for £25 14s. Installation would cost about £5. This minute is rather strange, because the WLLR had already rejected a proposal to adopt acetylene lighting on 2 May 1913.

The 1899 LRO exempted the railway from being assessed for rates beyond the land's original value for 10 years from its opening, with allowance made for an extension. The Forden Union must have had a good filing system, for on 3 April 1913 its clerk wrote to ask if the WLLR intended to apply for an extension. In December, the Board of Trade agreed to a five years' extension backdated to 4 April 1913, applicable to all the authorities. On 2 May 1913, the WLLR directors resolved to apply for a further extension of the time allowed for the repayment of the loans.

The Cambrian's negotiations for a motor service between Llanfair Caereinion and outlying districts were referred to Williamson for a further report on 8 May 1914. Without the forthcoming war's intervention preventing the implementation of this development the end of the WLLR's passenger service might have been hastened.

The locos in store at Oswestry Works, waiting for the preservation society to raise the money to buy them; seen on 15 June 1958. *Brian Hilton/Adrian Gray*

On the same occasion approval was given to extend the Llanfair Caereinion goods shed by 50ft, at a cost of £120, and to spend £15 improving the siding space there. The Cambrian directors were feeling quite generous, for they agreed to fund the work, have the repayments spread over five years and not charge interest. Meeting on 15 April 1914, the WLLR directors agreed to pay £50 from balances and asked for 10 years to repay the remainder. The work was reported as completed on 21 June 1915.

Work at other stations saw facilities at Sylfaen enhanced by the provision of a shelter at the same time and in 1916 facilities for handling milk traffic at Heniarth were improved at a cost of £1 10s.

A crisis occurred in May 1914, when axles on both locomotives broke within three weeks of each other. Williamson informed the directors 'by special letter' and Jones was asked to explain. The trailing axle of *The Earl* had broken on 4 May and the loco was still at Oswestry being repaired, when the driving axle of *The Countess* broke on 25 May. One of *The Earl's* wheelsets was sent to Welshpool and, by dint of working overnight, *The Countess* was ready for service at 6am on 26 May. The locos had a history of broken axles as shown in the table (*below*).

All the breaks had occurred in the same place, about ¼in inside the wheel boss, where they could not be seen. Jones commented that the original axles had been the best but did not explain why they had been replaced. He thought that the WLLR's sharp curves with excessive super-elevation and steep gradients 'set up severe and unusual strains on the axles.' The

failures occurring at similar mileages, with one exception, suggested the steel quality was consistent. Apart from the axles, he said, the engines had given very little trouble and had been quite satisfactory. The fireboxes were getting worn but did not need replacing for the present.

When the cost of coal used by the WLLR was increased in 1915, Williamson asked for an explanation and was told that it was due to price increases. Further investigation revealed that actually consumption had increased, to 455 tons from 393 tons. Jones was unable to offer an explanation and further investigations were put in hand without a recorded output.

In 1916 the Cambrian incurred its biggest loss in running the WLLR to date. Williamson explained that the increased costs were due to payment of war bonus and the higher cost of coal and materials, rates and taxes and wages. Coal consumed was 467 tons. Costs continued to rise during the war and the Cambrian's losses increased.

A timber merchant, Boys & Boyden, started trading in Welshpool in 1915. On 6 April, Williamson informed the WLLR directors of proposals to realign a WLLR siding in order to accommodate a standard gauge siding being laid into the woodyard. He emphasised that the Cambrian would receive little benefit from the arrangement because most of the traffic was expected to be routed over the joint line to Shrewsbury. The WLLR directors gave their approval, but nothing more was said or done about this scheme.

An alternative proposal arose out of the county council's complaint to the Ministry of Transport about damage being

Loco	Date	Axle mileage	Comment
The Earl	June 1908	73,161	Original axles, steel cast by Beyer, Peacock, replaced with carriage axles from stock, made by Patent Shaft & Axletree Company and machined to Beyer, Peacock dimensions.
	April 1911	39,488	Driving and leading axles broke, replaced with new Patent Shaft & Axletree Company axles with diameter at wheelseat increased by ⅛in.
	4 May 1914	77,429	Trailing axle broke. Nickel chrome steel replacement obtained from Thomas Firth & Sons, Sheffield. Wheel bosses bored out to accommodate wheelseats increased by ¼in. Replacements for the other axles ordered for fitting when received.
The Countess	July 1908	73,862	Original axles, steel cast by Beyer, Peacock, replaced with carriage axles from stock, made by Patent Shaft & Axletree Company and machined to Beyer, Peacock dimensions.
	January 1911	32,109	Driving axle broke, replaced with new Patent Shaft & Axletree Company axle with diameter at wheelseat increased by ⅛in.
	July 1911	38,202	Trailing axle broke, replaced with new Patent Shaft & Axletree Company axle with diameter at wheelseat increased by ⅛in.
	25 May 1914	40,825	Driving axle broke. Nickel chrome steel replacement obtained from Thomas Firth & Sons, Sheffield.

done to roads by the timber's haulage in 1920, the railways still being under government control. At issue was 5,000 tons of timber still to be carried. On this occasion, the response involved extending a WLLR siding into the timber merchant's yard at Welshpool, the provision of further wagons and minor alterations at 'one or two' WLLR stations.

The ministry did not think the matter was of sufficient importance to justify it covering the £140 expenditure required, although it would pay 5% interest if the expenditure was incurred on the WLLR's capital account. The merchant was prepared to pay half of the cost but as the WLLR had no funds it was asked if the Cambrian would be prepared to advance the £70 to the WLLR. The Cambrian did not want to advance any more money to the WLLR, which was no worse off than it ever had been, proposing instead that it paid for the work and was reimbursed 7d per ton from the extra traffic until it was recouped. As the extra wagons would have cost an estimated £400 the whole idea was not as worthwhile as represented. It must have been cheaper to have repaired the roads.

The return made to the Light Railways (Investigation) Committee in 1920 provides an insight into the railway's operation. There were two drivers, two firemen, one cleaner, one passenger guard, one porter guard, one stationmaster, one clerk, one porter and two goods porters. Standard conditions of service, rates of pay and hours of duty, applied. The track was maintained by two gangs of four platelayers working under the supervision of a Cambrian inspector.

There were no through rates for passengers, 53,449 of whom had been carried in 1913 and 55,227 in 1919. Goods rates were 25% higher than the equivalent Cambrian rate. Wagon capacity at stations was: Welshpool, 45; Sylfaen, 4; Castle Caereinion, 10; Cyfronydd, 8; Heniarth, 20 and Llanfair Caereinion, 45. Only the first and the last could handle cattle and sheep.

The issue of trains stopping near Dolrhyd was raised again in June 1920, because the owner, Anwyl, the WLLR director, wanted to sell Eithnog with the right to stop trains. Now called Eithinog Hall, the house was being offered with three reception rooms, eleven bedrooms, one bathroom, with stabling, garage and adjoining cottage. Williamson pointed out to Anwyl that whilst the conveyance gave the right to erect the shelter it left out the obligation to stop trains, 'It is easy to be wise after the event', he should have insisted on it. Anwyl made much of the point that the land occupied by the railway at Dolrhyd had been given to it by his wife without charge. He received the assurance he required on 22 October. The previous day instructions had been given that trains should only stop at the boathouse and not at Dolrhyd.

The unexpected consequence of his efforts of 1920 had Anwyl writing to the Cambrian again on 23 December 1921, because he had sold Dolrhyd to its occupant who was no longer allowed to stop the train. He now went to Welshpool by road. 'Would it not be a gain to the company to get the fares, as the train goes so slowly?' The Cambrian offered to allow the Dolrhyd owner and his family to stop trains at the boathouse, 120 yards away. Being told of this, the owner, D. O. Jones, coal and corn merchant, wrote that he did not see why the trains should stop at the boathouse and not at Dolrhyd. He used to look out for passengers stopping the train there to avoid it having to stop twice, someone from Dolrhyd used the train every week but the boathouse stop had only been used three or four times since Eithnog had changed hands, 'but I don't regret your offer.' That was the end of it.

Suspension of the loan repayments had allowed the WLLR some respite on its outstanding capital commitments. It had reduced its liabilities by £2,777 2s 2d since 1904 but it still owed the Cambrian £2,437 15s 1d. Resumption of the

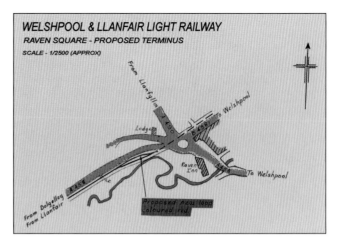

A 1962 sketch showing the proposed layout of a Raven Square terminus. *National Archives*

repayments was due in 1922 and Llanfyllin RDC had written on 12 November calling for payment to be resumed with immediate effect. The directors resolved to meet the authorities to plead their case for a further extension, and on 27 January 1922 Powis caused comment by attending on Welshpool Corporation to make a successful appeal on the railway's behalf. The county council and the treasury had also agreed to the extension by 31 March and responses from Llanfyllin and Forden were awaited. It was, in any event, an academic exercise as the consequences of the Railways Act, enacted on 19 August 1921, meant that the company's future was very limited.

The act provided for the grouping of railway companies and the distribution of £60 million compensation for the losses incurred by the railways while they were under government control from 1914 until 1921. On 22 March 1922, the WLLR directors resolved that the company should be represented by the Association of Smaller Railway Companies and claimed a total of £2,296 9s 10d under three headings, 'arrested growth of traffic', loss of income because of traffic being diverted to road transport, and loss of income because of the increased cost of administration and taxes. After a modified claim of £3,636 9s 10d had been submitted the company was awarded £2,667 7s.

Concerning the Grouping, a meeting that took place with the GWR on 21 June resulted in a cash offer of £19,345 being made. This was based on the net revenue for 1913 of £1,915, less rent charges and interest payable on the Cambrian's advances (£131), being capitalised to produce 5½%. Writing on 27 June, the GWR explained that it recognised that the sum offered did not represent the nominal value of the debenture stock or the loans, implying that they were worth less and that if they were scaled down for less than their face value the company would be able to make a distribution to its shareholders. The GWR pointed out that the Lampeter, Aberayron & New Quay Light Railway's investing authorities and the treasury had accepted a third of their advances in 2½% GWR debenture stock; a cash offer should improve the scope for negotiation.

The directors, however, thought that the offer was too low and resolved to ask for more. The negotiations appear to have been taken over by Davies's agent, W. Burdon Evans at Llandinam, which might explain why, considering the poor state of the company and small size of the undertaking, the appeal was successful. The cash offer was increased to £20,000 and the GWR would take over responsibility for the £2,387 15s 1d owed to the Cambrian and the rent charges payable. The company would retain all of the compensation and the balance of the net revenue account on 31 December 1922, producing £23,236 7s for distribution.

Payments of 80% to the investing authorities and 90% to the debenture holders would permit 5s per share for shareholders. The Treasury, however, wanted 90% as none of its loan had been repaid while the local authorities had been repaid 5% of theirs. It settled for 81%. This change, and a deduction for income tax due on the traffic receipts that had been overlooked, cost the ordinary shareholders 1d per share. The money was handed over to the GWR to make the distribution on the WLLR's behalf.

The WLLR directors met for the last time on 14 December 1922. Apart from the corporation's nominees, and Addie and Davies, the same men, Powis, Pryce, Anwyl and Hilton, had served throughout the company's existence. Addie, who had worked tirelessly on the railway's behalf, had retired on health grounds at the general meeting on 6 August 1920. Davies had been very much a figurehead director, rarely attending the board meetings. John Evans, the WLLR's secretary since its inception, had died on 9 March 1922, the directors minuting a tribute to him on 31 March. Appointed on 22 March, his successor was Isaac Watkin of Oswestry, one of the company's auditors.

The shareholders also met for the last time on 14 December, 12 in person and 30 by proxy. They approved the resolution required for the company to participate in the absorption scheme and gave thanks to the Davies's agent for negotiating their compensation and to the solicitor for negotiating the settlement with the investing authorities. They also resolved that 'in view of the great loss of traffic owing to the delay, inconvenience and expense attending the transhipment of goods, the Great Western Railway Company be urged to consider the desirability of converting the line from narrow gauge to standard gauge', before thanking the directors for the care and attention they had given to the company during its existence. Few companies could have had such a send-off. From 1 January 1923 their enterprise was a part of the GWR. Having taken control of the Cambrian from 25 March 1922, the GWR was already been responsible for the WLLR's operation.

As an independent concern the WLLR had been hampered on several fronts. The grant qualification, that the railway be built and operated by an existing company was intended to save money, the cost of administration being absorbed by the existing company, but it probably increased costs too, for the employees were paid the same as their main line counterparts. There was no local manager to canvass for business and to ensure that operating patterns reflected changing demands. It is notable that of the three railways dealt with in this book, the WLLR was the only one not to cater for tourists – there must have been a market for the residents of Welshpool, Oswestry and Shrewsbury to visit Llanfair Caereinion at the weekend or on holidays, if only someone had thought to develop it.

The lack of capital and Strachan's claim for extras prevented the WLLR from being fully equipped, but the provision of the enhancements sought in 1904, and the fourth carriage later, is unlikely to have had much influence on the outcome. Judged by the almost straight line of annual income, the WLLR's traffic levels varied little and there is no evidence that it was unable to meet the demands placed upon it, except that passengers on market days would have appreciated more space.

As an investment, the WLLR was marginally successful. Loan interest was always paid and most of the loans were repaid, but that was more by luck than judgment. The ordinary shareholders did less well but that is always the case. Without the free grant, though, the situation would have been very different, for the railway could not have been built. With the continued existence of the railway it could be argued that the Treasury is still seeing the benefit of the grant.

The WLLR was a marginal enterprise for the Cambrian, too. Over the years until 1914, the accumulated loss was a mere £36. During the following five years the losses amounted to another £5,343, no doubt largely due to the government's policy of not allowing the railways to increase charges in line with increasing costs.

There was a measure of tidying up required before the company's affairs were disposed of. In January, Lloyds Bank in Welshpool was instructed to change the name on the WLLR's account to that of the GWR. Watkin, the secretary, was awarded a cash payment of £60 for his loss of office by the GWR in March 1923.

Under GWR control, the WLLR carried on much as before. As a part of a much larger organisation less information about its operation remains in the public record.

The locos were renumbered 822 and 823, standard GWR-style cast numberplates being mounted on the tank sides. They

On 6 April 1963 the re-opening train was captured passing over the Lledan brook, carrying passengers without the approval of the railway inspector. *Michael Whitehouse collection*

Disaster. The Banwy bridge, 14 February 1965. The river waters are not always as calm or as low as shown here. In 1999 it was discovered that the pier had not been founded on rock.
F. J. Hastilow/Ian Allan Library

retained their names, but *The Countess* was shortened to *Countess* in order that the nameplate could be relocated to the cabside. They were repainted into GWR livery and received some Swindon features. Some of these changes were probably made when the locos were overhauled at Welshpool in 1924/5. *The Earl* returned to traffic on 10 January 1925 after 12 weeks out of service. *Countess* then received repairs that took 7½ weeks. Other changes, notably the copper-capped chimneys and brass safety valve bonnets, probably appeared when they were fitted with Swindon-designed boilers at Oswestry in 1929/30. The carriages and wagons were also painted in GWR livery and renumbered.

The WLLR's closure was recommended in the GWR's 1926 branch line review. The figures for 1924/5 are given in the table (*below*) although a complete comparison was not published.

During 1925 the railway had handled 5,639 tons of minerals, 2,579 tons of merchandise, 1,368 cans of milk, and 344 trucks of livestock. Reducing the train service to single-shift, eight hours, and abolishing the [non-existent] post of stationmaster at Llanfair Caereinion were proposed as economy measures, but complete closure would save £6,502 annually. This figure was actually the annual expenditure and took no account of any residual expenses or consequential losses arising from closure.

An unusual incident must have occurred with *Countess* in August 1928, for it was stopped for five days for light repairs carried out at Heniarth. The location suggests that it must have failed in traffic and been in such a condition that it could not be moved.

The locomotive committee approved the expenditure of

£147 to replace the wooden water tank near Llanfair Caereinion by one of iron on 25 April 1929. Still in situ although disused, this tank gives the appearance of having been manufactured from an old locomotive tender.

On 12 February 1931, the traffic committee accepted the general manager's report recommending the withdrawal of the WLLR's passenger services 'as from 9th instant', a decision taken after the event. On 28 March 1946, the committee was to approve the expenditure of £90 for the conversion of 10 narrow gauge timber trucks into open-side wagons for the WLLR.

A train was in a collision with a car 'at the Castle Caereinion level crossing' on 17 June 1932, the *Manchester Guardian* reported. Only one of the four occupants was detained in Welshpool hospital with unspecified injuries. The car was destroyed.

The locomotive history sheets show that both locos required heavy maintenance during the 2nd World War and afterwards. From 23 October 1941 *The Earl* was out of traffic to 20 weeks whilst an intermediate overhaul was carried out at Welshpool although the history card indicates an input from Swindon, too. Two weeks after it had returned it required another 19 days at Oswestry.

Countess was out of service for 15 months from 12 November 1946 whilst it was overhauled at Oswestry. These were the first recorded repairs it had received since 1930 and also required an input from Swindon. When *The Earl* failed and required 11 days to repair at Welshpool from 30 November 1947 the train service had to be cancelled until it was returned. On 1 March 1948, just in the nationalisation era, it was sent to Swindon for a general

Traffic department staff	Expenditure		Receipts					
	1924	1925	1924	1925	Passengers	Parcels	Goods	Total
Welshpool	£435	£435	£1,129		£750	£298		£1,048
Llanfair	£356	£382	£3,537		£501	£417	£2,544	£3,462
	£791	£817	£4,666		£1,251	£715	£2,544	£4,666

Loco department, engine and train running expenses	£3,557
Engineering department, maintenance and renewal	£1,930
Signal department	£138
Clothing	£10
Fuel, lighting, water and general stores	£5
Rates	£45

	Local to branch	Through Outwards	Inwards	Local to branch	Through Outwards	Inwards
Parcels		257	3,405		£27	£582
Freight	Tons	Tons	Tons			
Merchandise	5	62	812	£6	£109	£1,607
Coal			3,155			£1,659
Other minerals			2,647			£2,283
Total	5	62	6,614			
Wagons	Wagons	Wagons				
Livestock	109	148	18	£92	£837	£30
Tenancies and transhipping charges at Welshpool				£572		
Total				£670	£973	£6,161
					£7,804	
Increases from May 1950						£1,27
					£9,082	

overhaul that took until 24 June to complete.

Nationalisation on 1 January 1948 had no immediate effect on the WLLR beyond repainting the locos and fixing LMS-style Oswestry shed plates to them. The only records to survive from this era relate to closure proposals.

The British Transport Commission sanctioned the WLLR's closure twice. The Railway Executive's first proposal to close the line, to save £2,729 annually, was approved on 25 November 1950, although no explanation was recorded for not putting the policy into effect. Cartwright (*see Bibliography*) states that the corporation submitted a motion asking for the policy to be reconsidered but that in itself was unlikely to have caused a reversal. The 1955 'case for closure' was to state that none of the local authorities had objected to the 1950 proposal. The report recommending closure included details of the traffic carried during the year ended 31 August 1949 (*See table above*).

The Road Haulage Executive would arrange an alternative road service at an annual cost of £2,900. To facilitate the transfer of traffic from rail to road vehicles the standard gauge transfer siding at Welshpool would be extended by 80 yards at a cost of £270. Recovering the assets, mainly the track, would cost £768 more than they were worth. The land and redundant buildings were valued at £357. Re-sleepering in 1905/1 was expected to cost £5,000.

During the early 1950s the WLLR became a magnet for enthusiasts attracted by a goods-only narrow gauge steam railway being run by BR. Indeed, on 2 July 1949, the Birmingham Locomotive Club had been the first of several organisations to arrange for the operation of special trains where the passengers travelled in open wagons. The enthusiasts received a warm welcome with many riding in the brake van, either officially, having signed an indemnity, or unofficially.

The second and final closure proposal was approved on 20 July 1955 although the railway was to continue operating until 5 November 1956. Traffic carried in the year to 30 June 1954 formed a part of the case for closure.

	Forwarded	Received	Revenue
Parcels	106	2,280	£712
Merchandise	27 tons	2,612 tons	£4,875
Coal		3,263 tons	£3,535
Livestock	45 wagons		£95
Total			£9,217

Revenue likely to be lost to rail was calculated at £1,400, but if 1,000 tons of slag and fertilizer and 2,000 tons of coal destined for Llanfair Caereinion were diverted to road haulage throughout then a further £3,110 would be lost. Savings would be £3,764 employment, £3,095 maintenance and £2,489 interest. The railway employed two goods porters at Welshpool, one goods checker at Llanfair Caereinion, one ganger, two lengthsmen, one driver, one fireman, and a guard. As a sign of inflation, extending the standard gauge siding at Welshpool would now cost £550.

Permanent way renewals, including 3¼ miles of re-sleepering, over the next three years were expected to cost £7,100. Locomotive repairs estimated at £1,600 had been deferred pending a decision on the line's future. *The Earl* had been at Oswestry receiving a heavy intermediate repair since 20 July 1953, returning to Welshpool on 15 March 1956, just in time for the line's closure. Out of service since 1 February, *Countess* was taken to Oswestry for storage on the same date. Their nameplates had been removed in 1951.

Several special trains ran during the last few months, the Stephenson Locomotive Society running the last one on 3 November 1956. It was accompanied by the Newtown Silver Band at Raven Square and Castle Caereinion. Returning to Raven Square at dusk, the train exploded detonators, fireworks were let off, car drivers sounded their hooters and flashed their lights. On arrival at Welshpool the sound of *The Earl's* whistle was answered by those of locomotives on the main line. Then there was silence as the band played Handel's funeral march. Some of those present had seen the first train in 1903, and very likely the first sod being cut, too.

After clearing wagons and equipment back to Welshpool, *The Earl* was stored in the loco shed until 7 May 1958, when it too was sent to Oswestry. Applications to purchase nameplates and a chimney were recorded on the loco history sheets.

Preservation of the WLLR had first been suggested in 1952 and a society was formed shortly after the line was closed. The Welshpool & Llanfair Light Railway Preservation Company was registered as a company limited by guarantee on 4 January 1960, taking over the society's objectives and assets.

The BR file dealing with the sale has not been preserved. The Welsh Office file dealing with matters arising from the transfer of ownership was lost before a record of its contents had been completed. There remains in the National Archives a file dealing with the transfer order and one of the railway inspectors'.

At the time of the WLLR's closure, there were only the Talyllyn and the Festiniog Railways operating as preserved lines, with the involvement and support of volunteers. No-one had taken over a branch line from BR and officialdom was not quite certain how seriously it should treat such proposals.

In the face of increasing traffic, the corporation made it quite clear that it was no longer prepared to tolerate the Church Street crossing. An editorial in the *County Times* of 21 June 1958 supported the corporation, saying that 'with the great increase in road traffic the time has gone past for permitting the Llanfair narrow gauge trains to go trundling through the town and across Church Street, one of the busiest thoroughfares in Mid Wales ... there is also the conclusive fact that the area near the main line station is required for municipal development and there is no space there for a Llanfair train terminus.' The paper also objected to the railway's supporters being from London, Birmingham and elsewhere, and objected to them thinking 'it possible to make a nuisance ... by bringing the Llanfair trains through the town.' It was stated that the corporation should not talk to them about it.

The county council and the Ministry of Transport (trunk roads division) became concerned about the Raven Square crossing. Bearing in mind that the only facilities for storing or maintaining rolling stock were in Welshpool and the main source of traffic was expected from the town, the preservation company wanted to retain as much of the route as possible.

It seems to have given up on Church Street quite early on but fought to retain the Raven Square crossing so that a terminus could be established in the Standard quarry although British Railways Western Region accepted the corporation's offer of £2,350 for the WLLR up to Raven Square in Welshpool, on 17 February 1961. The corporation wanted to increase its car parking provision near the cattle market, but also took the remainder of the WLLR land and undertook to recover the redundant assets, mainly rail, at its own expense, saving BR £380. The sale was not to be completed until 1963.

At some unspecified date in the future the county council wanted to widen Brook Street and in 1960 the ministry said that it was considering adopting it as the trunk road when 'the proposed Welshpool bypass is constructed.' When the application for a Light Railway (Leasing and Transfer) Order was made in November 1961, the railway was described as 'situate between a point on the north west side of Brook Street near the Standard quarry Welshpool where the railway ... diverges from Brook Street aforesaid and Llanfair Caereinion ...'

The Raven Square crossing had not been the source of any recorded problems before the line had closed, yet now the authorities were determined to prevent the company using it. In an internal minute dated 4 January 1962, Colonel J. H. Robertson of the railway inspectorate said that he could not see the crossing being acceptable to the local and road authorities and he did not think that the company would be willing to incur the cost of a public inquiry to force the issue. If the company was to succeed at a public inquiry then the inspectorate would insist on 'at least full flashing red light control' of all the roads approaching the crossing, 'the cost of which ... would be considerable'. It could be, he speculated, that the road use was so heavy that 'something more elaborate (and costly) would be necessary.'

Objections to the proposal to re-open the line across Raven Square were made by Montgomeryshire County Council, Welshpool Engineering Company, based in the quarry, and Mid-Wales Motorways Limited, the last a coach operator, the company was informed on 14 February 1962. The nature of the objections and the company's response to them did not affect the outcome so will not be analysed here. Earlier, on 24 November 1961, the company's managing director, F. S. Mayman, had written to the divisional road engineer following a site meeting and agreeing to a proposal that the question of the crossing could be reviewed in five years, 'by which time the

Despite obstacles and setbacks, the WLLR survived to celebrate its centenary in due style on 4 May 2002. The Earl of Powis (right) and Ken Fenton, company chairman, posed at Raven Square with the spade and wheelbarrow used by Lord Clive to cut the first sod in 1901. *Author*

railway will have given an indication of its potential ...'

The road engineer had left the meeting with a different impression, writing on 12 January 1962 that 'It seemed to be clear that Mr Mayman expected and accepted that the crossing over Raven Square in perpetuity could never be agreed.' Faced with the loss of the buildings and sidings in Welshpool and accepting that the company did not have the resources to re-open or operate the complete line at once, the company had already said that re-opening would occur in stages, starting from Llanfair Caereinion, so it was quite clear that it would be several years before WLLR trains returned to Welshpool.

All the authorities were happy for the terminus to be to the west of Raven Square, a location resisted by the company due to restrictions it placed on the layout. When the terminus was eventually built there additional land was obtained and the stream diverted to improve the site's usefulness.

The application placed the minister in an awkward position, a highways official noted on 14 February 1962. One the one hand he was expected to deal with the LRO application impartially, on the other, he would want to object to it on highways grounds. The existence of the other objections could save him the embarrassment of making a formal objection, though.

A high-level meeting was held at the ministry with both railway and highways divisions represented on 27 March 1962. Its purpose was to co-ordinate views and to decide on a common course of action. The 'west of Raven Square' terminus was reasonable; the future possibility of widening the adjacent trunk road should not be used as a bar to it. The meeting's chairman felt that the company was not aware of the 'very strong objections' the ministry had and Robertson confirmed that, having met company officers, he thought that they expected the order to be made as it stood.

Before consulting the Treasury solicitor on the propriety of the minister holding an enquiry where he would be making an objection, it was agreed to make another approach to the company. By 4 April 1962, however, the highways branch had decided 'to take a rather more positive line than hitherto.' It would point out that there were strong trunk road objections to the idea of a level crossing, any level crossing was a serious impediment to the free flow of traffic, and new impediments could not be permitted. The previous existence of a level crossing, its low usage and 'that the trunk road is relatively lightly trafficked' were not material. Mayman was to be told in person at the meeting which took place on 10 May 1962, when he stood his ground.

Officials took the view that their objection to the crossing would prevail at a public inquiry, but felt that it would be wrong to put the company to the trouble and expense of an inquiry if the result was a foregone conclusion. The Treasury solicitor had given his opinion on 9 April 1962. The minister could refuse the application or amend its provisions to ensure public safety. He was not bound to hold an inquiry if he was in possession of such information as was material or useful to determine the application. If an inquiry was held the agent authority, Montgomeryshire County Council, could present the minister's objection as its own.

On 6 June 1962, the ministry informed the company's solicitor that the minister would be recommended to modify the order, eliminating the crossing, that there should be no difficulty in terminating the railway to the west of Raven Square, and that the ministry and the local authorities would cooperate as much as possible. The company was invited to submit any further information or arguments that the minister

should consider before making up his mind. If it required a public inquiry to be held it would be responsible for the costs.

The company had made its first formal contact with the railway inspectorate on 28 June 1961, explaining its ambition to run passenger services over part of the line from April 1962, and requesting a site meeting to so the company could be informed of likely requirements.

Robertson carried out an informal inspection on 26 July 1961, producing a two-page report of requirements and observations. During the course of the afternoon, he did not arrive at Welshpool until after 2pm, he produced a straight-line diagram of the railway, with all crossings, underbridges and other features noted. At Welshpool, he saw the carriages and wagons the company had acquired from the Admiralty's Chattenden & Upnor Railway in Kent.

The Chattenden line was unusual amongst 2ft 6in gauge military lines in having run a passenger service. Its closure on 29 May 1961 made its stock available just at the right time for the WLLR. More stock was to be obtained from the same source in November.

The WLLR locomotives had been offered to the company for £654 each in 1960. Despite not being formally withdrawn from stock until 17 August 1961, *The Earl* had been returned to Welshpool and company ownership on 28 July. While at Oswestry it had been stripped down and given a light overhaul by the apprentices. *Countess* was to be condemned on 27 July 1962, sold on 28 September and delivered to Welshpool on 6 October. Some repairs, including retubing, were carried out at Oswestry; a bargain if included in the purchase price.

Delivery of the new stock and materials to Welshpool

A mark of the WLLR's maturity is its ability to operate trains of 'original' rolling stock. In GWR livery, *Countess* stands at Llanfair Caereinion with two Ffestiniog Railway-built Pickering carriages on 22 May 2008. *Author*

provided the company with several opportunities to run trains through the town before the tracks were lifted. The first transfer had actually taken place in 1959, when a member hired a pair of horses to pull stock purchased from BR to Raven Square.

Robertson's report had included a requirement for a stop block to be placed on the Llanfair side of the Raven Square crossing 'at once' to protect it from runaways. On 3 August 1961, Mayman explained that the company had arranged to take a lease on the line to a point beyond the quarry entrance that included the crossing. He argued that the Raven Square site was narrow and passengers leaving and joining the train there would be at a greater danger than any hazard caused by trains using the crossing. From a commercial perspective, the terminus needed to be as near to the town as possible and at a location where vehicles could park without causing inconvenience.

If the LRO was made in time, re-opening between Llanfair Caereinion and Castle Caereinion was to be on 19 May 1962, Mayman told Robertson on 31 January. The latter was to conduct an unofficial inspection on 20 March and an official inspection on 1 May.

Robertson was in hospital when he sent Mayman two pages of handwritten observations on the company's proposed rules in May – Mayman sent them to Robertson's office saying that he could not read them, 'no doubt he was writing under great difficulty', and asking for a typewritten version to be produced, 'you are probably used to his style.'

Although the company had given in to the ministry's pressure to abandon the Raven Square crossing Mayman was clearly unhappy about the situation when he wrote to Robertson on 25 July, asking for help in getting the county council to provide signs for the level crossings without charge. After telling the company that it [the company] would have to pay for the signs the council had ignored all letters. A colleague of Robertson's was able to persuade the council to cooperate.

The British Transport Commission (Welshpool and Llanfair) Light Railway (Leasing and Transfer) Order 1962 was made on 3 October 1962, effective from 10 October. It provided for the lease or transfer of the railway from the south west of Raven Square to Llanfair Caereinion on such terms and conditions as could be agreed, and required the approval of the minister in writing before any part of the railway was used for the carriage of passengers. Cartwright states that the lease was for 21 years with no renewal option. The annual charge was £100 for the first five years, increasing in stages thereafter.

Subject to certain conditions, provisional written permission to carry passengers between Llanfair Caereinion and Castle Caereinion was given on 5 October 1962. An inspection was subsequently arranged to take place on 26 March 1963.

With the opening date set for 6 April 1963, an invitation was sent to Robertson. He returned it on 11 March, pointing out that the intended operation of trains between Welshpool and Castle Caereinion would be illegal and he could have no part of it. The inspection took place as arranged and Robertson submitted his report on 2 April. Subject to attention being given to some points before the opening and to others as soon as possible thereafter, he recommended that the provisional approval given for the carriage of passengers between Llanfair Caereinion and Castle Caereinion be confirmed.

Notwithstanding Robertson's comment about its legality, the reopening train ran from Welshpool on 6 April, 60 years since the WLLR was opened. Once, again the Earl of Powis, the 5th earl, was the principal guest. At Llanfair he drove *The Countess* through a ribbon before the loco returned the train to Welshpool where the guests took lunch at the Royal Oak Hotel, another link with the past.

Completing the purchase of the route through the town on 4 April, the council gave notice that it could not be used after August. On 17 August the final last train was run and track lifting was started two days later.

Unlike the TR and the FR, the WLLR had no facilities for storing or maintaining its rolling stock. With passenger services having finished in 1931 there was no background of a market in tourism to draw on. Finding out if a business could be made was going to be a long and difficult process. As soon as 1964 the company was going to find out just how difficult life could be.

The season started off well, with services extended to Sylfaen on 6 June. Looking to the future, a loop was installed at Raven Square. Then in August, the difficult decision was taken to cut back services to Castle Caereinion because the track beyond was inadequate.

The hardest blow came in December, with the discovery that heavy rain on 12/13 December had increased river levels so much that one of the piers on the Banwy bridge was undermined. Evidence of scouring had been found in 1963, when a repair using bagged concrete had been implemented. It was, of course, just over 60 years since Collin had first dealt with a problem there. With financial support from members and the public, and the practical support of the Royal Engineers the bridge was repaired although it was to 1997 before the underlying problem was identified, and 1999 before an effective repair was completed.

Services to Castle Caereinion were resumed on 14 August 1965 and to Sylfaen again on 15 July 1972. As a series of members' specials to Welshpool to mark the 10th anniversary of reopening were being arranged for 12/13 May 1973, BR offered to sell the line, a price of £8,000 being agreed. The Wales Tourist Board offered at 15-year loan of £3,500 and Welshpool Borough Council contributed £1,000 to the appeal fund. The sale was completed on 12 March 1974. After a four-year rehabilitation project, the first public trains ran to Welshpool on 18 July 1981 and the 6th Earl of Powis performed the official opening on 16 May 1982.

For locomotives and rolling stock, the company acquired locomotives from Austria, Antigua, Sierra Leone and Finland, and carriages from Austria, Sierra Leone and Hungary, the trains gaining a very cosmopolitan appearance as a result. Between 2003 and 2010 a rake of Pickering carriages was added to the fleet.

As the company's position stabilised, a programme of building work was carried out to provide facilities and accommodation for all parts of the business. Charitable status obtained in 1990 opened the way to a £786,000 five-year programme supported by the Heritage Lottery Fund that started in 1997.

These works, including overhauling the original locomotives, were completed in time for the railway's centenary on 5 April 2003, when *Countess* hauled the commemorative train, just as it had done in 1903 and 1963. The 8th Earl of Powis participated in the celebrations, planting a tree at Raven Square station.

Earlier, the railway's achievements had been recognised with the presentation of the 'independent railway of the year' award by HRH the Princess Royal on 3 December 2002, the judges saying that the WLLR had 'made great strides and has after many years become a complete railway ... with good facilities at each end and plenty of interest in between.' Another royal accolade was bestowed on 19 July 2003, when HRH the Prince of Wales visited the line, travelling from Llanfair Caereinion to Welshpool.

With the benefit of some generous bequests, the WLLR has reached maturity in a manner unimaginable either to its original promoters or to those who fought so hard for its preservation.

Appendix 1

Locomotives

Corris Railway

No 1 0-4-0ST
Hughes 324/1878,
adapted to 0-4-2ST c1886,
rebuilt 1895

No 2 0-4-0ST
Hughes 322/1878,
adapted to 0-4-2ST c1886,
rebuilt 1898

No 3 0-4-0ST
Hughes 323/1878,
adapted to 0-4-2ST c1886, rebuilt 1900, condemned 25
October 1948, sold to Talyllyn Railway 1 March 1951;
recorded mileage when sold – 64,341

No 4 0-4-2ST
Kerr, Stuart 4047/1921; condemned 25 October 1948,
sold to Talyllyn Railway 1 March 1951;
recorded mileage when sold – 198,566

The returns recorded a fleet of four locomotives in 1921 and
1922, reducing to three in 1923. From the evidence of dated
photographs, Nos 1 and 2 were not used after No 4 arrived,
although one of them, probably No 1, was nominally available
for use until 1928. There are photographs of No 2 standing
out of use at Machynlleth from c1925. Not taken into GWR
stock, Nos 1 and 2 were scrapped by Peter Vaughan & Son of
Machynlleth in 1930.

The Board of Trade returns record a heavy locomotive
repair carried out in 1919 and 1920; Cozens (See
Bibliography) states that No 3 was rebuilt in 1920, so the
work was probably carried out over two years. Repair
expenditure of £238 in 1920 and £96 in 1921 is not
indicative of substantial work being undertaken.

Above: **Corris Railway No 2
stored out of use at Machynlleth,
c1928.** *Paul Ingham Collection*

Left: **No 3 shunting at
Machynlleth after 1930.**
Author's collection

Below left: **No 4 at Machynlleth
soon after the GWR took
control. The loco retains its
unmodified builder's plate, yet
has a GWR-style lamp bracket.
The wagon has also been
numbered in GWR stock.**
Paul Ingham Collection

Below: **Pulled out of Maespoeth
shed for the photographer, No
4's builder's plate has been
modified to incorporate its
running number.**
Paul Ingham Collection

Vale of Rheidol Light Railway

No 1 2-6-2T
Edward VII Davies & Metcalf 1902,
not numbered when new;
No 1212 from 1923,
scrapped 1935

No 2 2-6-2T
Prince of Wales Davies & Metcalf
1902,
not numbered when new,
scrapped c1924

No 3 2-4-0T
Rheidol Bagnall 1497/1897

No 7 2-6-2T
Swindon 1923,
named Owain *Glyndŵr* in 1956

No 8 2-6-2T
Swindon 1923,
named *Llywelyn* in 1956

No 1213 2-6-2T
Swindon 1924,
recorded as, but not actually,
a rebuild of No 2;
No 9 from 1948,
named *Prince of Wales* in 1956

Top: **Vale of Rheidol Light Railway No 1** *Edward VII* **as delivered by Davies & Metcalf in 1902.** *Ian Allan Library*

Middle top: **No 2 as rebuilt by the Cambrian Railways and seen at Devil's Bridge. It has wider coal bunkers and grab handles on the leading edge of the water tanks, and now carries a re-railing jack as standard equipment.** *Author's collection*

Middle bottom: **No 3** *Rheidol* **at Aberystwyth on 28 June 1909, by which date it had a traditional chimney.** *H. L. Hopwood*

Bottom: **Representing Nos 7 and 8, the latter was photographed at Swindon before delivery in 1923. Although based on the Davies & Metcalfe locomotives there were many detail differences.** *Author's collection*

Above: **After it was overhauled by the GWR it seems that No 1/1212 rarely saw service on the VRLR. The photograph was taken at Swindon while the loco was awaiting its fate.** *A. W. Croughton/Michael Whitehouse collection*

Middle: **No 9 at Swindon in 1959.** *Author's collectiont*

Bottom: **Returning from Swindon on 20 April 1960, No 9 being unloaded at Plascrug provides entertainment for a young observer.** *John Reeves/Ian Allan Library*

Welshpool & Llanfair Light Railway

No 1 0-6-0T
The Earl Beyer, Peacock 3496/1903,
No 822 from 1922;
mileage when sold – 213,887

No 2 0-6-0T
The Countess Beyer, Peacock 3497/1903,
No 823 *Countess* from 1922;
mileage when sold – 223,162

These locos were not numbered in Cambrian Railways' stock.

Below: **No 1** *The Earl* **became No 822 under GWR management. It was photographed with its new number, and lettered GW whilst retaining its Beyer, Peacock boiler fittings and chimney. The loco is coaled from a wagon stabled on the Smithfield siding.** *Author's collection*

Bottom: **Renumbered No 823, No2** *The Countess* **became** *Countess* **to fit its name on to the cabside. The location of the WLLR numberplate is discernible above the nameplate.** *Author's collection*

Above: **No 822 with its GWR boiler and accoutrements.** *H. Norman/Author's collection*

Right: **Similarly altered, No 823 was photographed on shed on 10 April 1946.** *R. E. Tustin/Author's collection*

Below: **Because there was usually only one loco in use at a time, both were rarely seen together. This scene, from the early 1950s, must have been set up for an enthusiast party. The photographer was so overcome that the picture is slightly out of focus.** *Adrian Gray collection*

Welshpool & Llanfair Light Railway

estimate 1887

Length of line				10m 2f 8ch
Construction of line	Cu yd	Price/yd	£ s d	£ s d
Earthworks				
Cuttings – rock	13,950	1s 9d	1,220 12 6	
Cuttings – soft soil	158,800	10d	6,616 13 4	
Total	174,050		7,902 5 10	7,902 5 10
Embankments, including roads – 151,800 Cu yd				
Accommodation bridges and works (9)				2,750 0 0
Culverts and drains				900 0 0
Metalling of roads and level crossings				300 0 0
Gatekeepers houses at level crossings				90 0 0
Permanent way, including fencing: – cost per mile: 10m 2fg 8ch @ £1,083 0 0				11,210 0 0
Permanent way for sidings and cost of junctions				800 0 0
Stations				2,000 0 0
				27,152 5 10
Contingencies at 5%				1,357 14 2
Total for construction				28,510 0 0
Land and buildings – 45 acres				2,700 0 0
Total cost of construction and of acquisition of land and buildings				31,210 0 0

23 December 1886
Simpson, Davies & Hurst
Engineers

Welshpool & Llanfair Light Railway

estimate of proposed light railway 1897

Railway No 1				9m 1f 1½ch
Gauge				2ft 6in
Construction of line	Cu yd	Price/yd	£ s d	£ s d
Earthworks				
Cuttings - rock	3,880	3s	582 0 0	
Cuttings - soft soil	37,551	1s 4d	2,503 8 0	
Roads	160	2s 6d	20 0 0	
Total			3,105 8 0	3,105 8 0
Embankments, including roads – Cu yd	33,720			
Accommodation bridges and works				275 0 0
Viaducts				800 0 0
Culverts and drains				614 0 0
Metalling of roads and level crossings				567 0 0
Gatekeepers houses at level crossings				
Permanent way, including fencing and heavy permanent way through streets: – cost per mile: 9m 1fg 1.5ch @ £950/mile				8,682 0 0
Permanent way for sidings and cost of junctions				1,275 0 0
Stations				1,390 0 0
				16,690 8 0
Contingencies at 10%				1,669 0 0
Land and buildings				2,950 0 0
Total cost of construction and of acquisition of land and buildings				21,309 8 0

Calthrop & Ward
Engineers

Appendix 4

Welshpool & Llanfair Light Railway

amended estimate 1901

Railway No 1				9m 1f 1 1/2ch
Gauge			2ft 6in	

Construction of line	Cu yd	Price/yd	£ s d	£ s d
Earthworks				
Cuttings - rock	3,000	3s 6d	525 0 0	
Cuttings - soft soil	61,000	1s 4d	4,066 13 0	
Total			4,591 13 0	4,591 13 0
Embankments, including roads – Cu yd				
Accommodation bridges and works				3,973 11 0
Viaducts				1,899 12 6
Culverts and drains				1,350 0 0
Metalling of roads and level crossings				600 0 0
Gatekeepers houses at level crossings				
Permanent way, including fencing and heavy permanent way through streets: – cost per mile: 9m 1fg 1.5ch @				10,926 10 0
Permanent way for sidings and cost of junctions				1,500 0 0
Stations				2,000 0 0
				26,841 6 6
Contingencies at 10%				2,688 13 6
Total for construction				29,530 0 0
Land and buildings				2,950 0 0
Total cost of construction and of acquisition of land and buildings				32,480 0 0

Appendix 5

Welshpool & Llanfair Light Railway

Statement as to total cost showing increases on statement furnished to HM Treasury in May 1902

Railway No 1		9m 1f 1½ ch
Gauge		2ft 6in

Construction of line	Estimate 1902 £ s d	Actual cost £ s d
Earthworks	7,240 0 0	8,990 0 0
Accommodation bridges and works	3,854 0 0	2,224 0 0
Viaducts and bridges	2,683 0 0	5,100 0 0
Culverts and drains	1,070 0 0	1,650 0 0
Metalling of roads and level crossings	785 0 0	730 0 0
Permanent way, including fencing, interlockings and telegraphs Permanent way for sidings and cost of junctions	15,554 0 0	17,212 0 0
Stations	1,575 0 0	2,664 0 0
Land and buildings	6,300 0 0	6,753 0 0
Sum expended on house retained		105 0 0
Rolling stock	5,500 0 0	5,500 0 0
Expenses, engineers fees, legal and other expenses	3,400 0 0	3,630 0 0
Miscellaneous, including interest on loans during construction and costs of local authorities in connection therewith and other incidental expenses	1,900 0 0	1,386 0 0
	50,271 0 0	59,345 0 0
Value of land given by landowners	2,400 0 0	2,400 0 0
	52,671 0 0	59,345 0 0
Additional works required not yet executed		3,540 0 0
Total cost of railway and equipment		62,985 0 0

Welshpool & Llanfair Light Railway

Capital account 1902-3

Income

	To 31 December 1902 £ s d	To 26 June 1903 £ s d	Total £ s d
Share capital – cash received	13,546 10 0	232 5 0	13,778 15 0
Bank interest allowed	111 8 11		111 8 11
Sundry receipts for registration fees etc.	15 0	7 6	1 2 6
Rents received	17 17 6	5	22 17 6
Sale of timber, hay etc.	38 0 6		38 0 6
Loans (less instalments of principal repaid)	15,350 0 0	101 1 6 cr	15,248 18 6
Law costs recovered	4 16 0	1 0	4 17 0
Treasury free grant	7,250 0 0	10,250 0 0	17,500 0 0
	36,319 7 11	10,386 12 0	46,705 19 11
Lloyds Bank Limited (General a/c) amount at debit			4,715 3 1

Outgoings

	To 31 December 1902 £ s d	To 26 June 1903 £ s d	Total £ s d
Legal and preliminary expenses – payments made	1,002 4 5		1,002 4 5
General and office expenses	110 9 3		110 9 3
Engineer – payments on account	1,350 0 0		1,350 0 0
Board of Trade – fee on applying for amendment order	50 0 0		50 0 0
Bank charges	119 19 9		119 19 9
Deposit with Board of Trade	1,000 0 0		1,000 0 0
Salaries – secretary and auditors	77 2 4	6 5 0	83 7 4
Land claims and compensation	5,295 3 2	443 17 2	5,739 0 4
Expenses cutting first sod	22 10 9		22 10 9
Construction – payments made per Cambrian Company - £23,837 5 6			
Construction – other payments - £36 18 6	20,705 2 0	3,169 2	23,874 4 0
Permanent way materials	5,202 8 7	34 9 1	5,236 17 8
Locomotives and rolling stock	3,669 10 9	2,236 15 4	5,906 6 1
Shropshire Union Railway & Canal Company – for stoppage of navigation	10 0 0		10 0 0
Costs re loans	269 11 0		269 11 0
Rates and taxes	6 5	2 17 8	3 4 1
Signalling and telegraphs	200 0 0	150 0 0	350 0 0
Engine and carriage shed	280 0 0		280 0 0
Stations and buildings	350 0 0	50 0 0	400 0 0
Weighbridge	60 0 0		60 0 0
Seven Stars cottage		106 7 4	106 7 4
Interest on loans		455 5 2	455 5 2
Income tax on interest	15 15 5	15 15 3 cr	2
	39,875 5 6	6,689 18 6	46,565 4 0
Lloyds Bank Limited (Construction a/c) amount at credit – 4,775 6 10			
North & South Wales Bank Limited amount at credit – 67 9 9			
Secretary – cash in hand – 13 2 5			4,855 19 0
			£51,421 3 0

Appendix 7

Corris Railway

Revenue 1872-1915, 1920-30

	1872	1873	1874	1875	1876	1877	1878	1879	1880	1881	1882	1883
Passenger traffic			£90	£290	£372	£414	£523	£74				£417
Mail, parcels &c												£7
Merchandise						£157	£198	£235	£310	£343	£320	£36
Minerals	£1,648	£1,594	£1,512	£1,726	£1,816	£1,818	£1,467	£1,225	£1,561	£1,516	£1,563	£1,845
Miscellaneous									£262	£5	£4	£3	£3
Traffic revenue	£1,648	£1,594	£1,602	£3,742	£2,188	£2,389	£2,188	£1,796	£1,876	£1,863	£1,886	£2,657
Total expenditure	£662	£785	£813	£1,064	£840	£844	£891	£1,518	£1,483	£1,338	£1,394	£1,688
Net receipts	£986	£809	£789	£952	£1,348	£1,545	£1,297	£278	£393	£525	£492	£949

	1884	1885	1886	1887	1888	1889	1890	1891	1892	1893	1894	1895
Passenger traffic	£925	£991	£925	£943	£1,023	£954	£1,058	£1,058	£1,034	£1,156	£1,490	£1,263
Mail, parcels &c	£40	£53	£49	£50	£64	£65	£98	£137	£130	£130	£130	£153
Merchandise	£388	£444	£408	£390	£467	£399	£386	£384	£379	£377	£393	£399
Minerals	£1,719	£1,839	£1,637	£1,690	£1,727	£1,526	£1,462	£1,439	£1,893	£2,020	£1,958	£1,886
Road services							£125	£138	£154	£193	£249	£317
Miscellaneous	£4	£6	£4	£6	£6	£124	£14	£156	£172	£221	£24	£344
Traffic revenue	£3,076	£3,333	£3,023	£3,079	£3,287	£3,068	£3,026	£3,174	£3,608	£3,904	£3,995	£4,045
Total expenditure	£2,130	£2,338	£2,399	£2,397	£2,581	£2,506	£1,802	£2,613	£2,847	£2,693	£2,721	£2,96
Net receipts	£946	£995	£624	£682	£706	£562	£1,224	£561	£761	£1,211	£1,274	£1,078

	1896	1897	1898	1899	1900	1901	1902	1903	1904	1905	190
Passenger traffic	£1,278	£1,393	£1,518	£1,432	£1,331	£1,252	£1,261	£1,172	£1,187	£1,027	£901
Mail, parcels &c	£159	£160	£163	£174	£174	£173	£177	£159	£189	£174	£178
Merchandise	£387	£416	£451	£445	£445	£390	£432	£382	£419	£377	£392
Minerals	£1,839	£1,915	£1,791	£1,819	£1,916	£1,913	£2,019	£1,857	£1,536	£1,192	£1,070
Road services	£335	£321			£424	£436	£433				
Miscellaneous	£364	£35		£367	£16	£23	£23	£492	£430	£469	£460	£490
Traffic revenue	£4,027	£3,919		£4,290	£4,310	£4,325	£4,184	£4,381	£4,000	£3,800	£3,230	£3,031
Total expenditure	£2,796	£3,082		£3,263	£3,132	£3,105	£3,113	£3,250	£2,841	£2,932	£2,818	£2,73
Net receipts	£1,231	£837		£1,027	£1,178	£1,220	£1,071	£1,131	£1,159	£868	£412	£301

	1907	1908	1909	1910	1911	1912	1913	1914	1915
Passenger traffic	£888	£917	£809	£809	£850	£819	£865		£689
Mail, parcels &c	£169	£169	£162	£159	£168	£177	£185		£184
Merchandise	£347	£319	£236	£367	£414	£347	£115		£380
Coal, coke &c							£83		£81
Minerals	£753	£742	£757	£767	£789	£743	£632		£572
Road services				£248					
Miscellaneous	£351	£340	£294	£9	£527	£713	£29		£16
Traffic revenue	£2,508	£2,485	£2,258	£2,200	£2,748	£2,799	£1,909		£1,648
Total expenditure	£2,426	£2,375	£2,468	£2,308	£2,672	£2,689	£2,031	£2,360	£1,817
Net receipts	£82	£110	-£210	-£108	£76	£110	-£122	-£430	-£169

	1920	1921	1922	1923	1924	1925	1926	1927	1928	1929	1930
Passenger traffic	£1,281		£1,389	£1,251	£1,276	£1,196	£1,247	£1,350	£1,221	£1,080	£390
Mail, parcels &c	£243		£236	£225	£205	£215	£236	£349	£321	£325	£130
Merchandise	£732		£220	£331	£467	£283	£209	£143	£133	£188	£63
Coal, coke &c	£229		£260	£230	£196	£191	£144	£236	£236	£225	£89
Minerals	£490		£369	£588	£619	£1,030	£1,152	£891	£826	£813	£363
Miscellaneous	£2		£6	£15	£12	£12	£6	£6	£5	£7	£1
Road services net	-£72		£165	£191	-£264	£53	£200	£399	£592	£48	£370
Gross receipts	£2,978		£3,106	£3,652	£6,997	£8,532	£8,876	£8,968	£9,291	£8,775	£2,975
Expenditure	£3,309		£4,025	£4,296	£7,995	£9,096	£9,059	£9,011	£9,128	£9,440	£3,557
Net receipts	-£404	-£1,703	-£919	-£644	-£998	-£564	-£183	-£43	£163	-£665	-£582

Appendix 8

Vale of Rheidol Light Railway

Revenue 1903-13

	1903	1904	1905	1906	1907	1908	1909	1910	1911	1912	1913
Passenger traffic	£3,703	£3,903	£3,913	£3,838	£3,935	£3,753	£4,012	£4,185	£4,201	£4,207	£976
Mail, parcels &c	£82	£98	£31	£42	£90	£93	£97	£92	£123	£194	£85
Merchandise	£143	£191	£371	£560	£465	£386	£346	£250	£330	£475	£150
Livestock				£9	£10						
Coal, coke &c											£52
Minerals	£662	£745	£627	£662	£547	£613	£374	£316	£393	£308	£144
Miscellaneous	£113	£188	£211	£119	£99	£61	£67	£22	£21	£22	£
Traffic revenue	£4,703	£5,125	£5,153	£5,230	£5,146	£4,906	£4,896	£5,431	£5,068	£5,206	£1,408
Total expenditure	£2,807	£3,398	£3,659	£3,646	£3,826	£3,871	£3,617	£3,177	£3,798	£4,038	£1,822
Net receipts	£1,896	£1,727	£1,494	£1,584	£1,320	£1,035	£1,279	£2,039	£1,270	£1,168	-£410

Appendix 9

Welshpool & Llanfair Light Railway

Revenue 1903-22

	1903	1904	1905	1906	1907	1908	1909	1910	1911	1912	1913
Passenger traffic	£1,167	£1,352	£1,365	£1,406	£1,323	£1,84	£1,265	£1,239	£1,226	£1,213	£1,318
Mail, parcels &c	£108	£219	£177	£180	£176	£170	£184	£189	£182	£184	£17
Merchandise	£852	£1,057	£735	£723	£824	£871	£936	£922	£1,016	£883	£782
Minerals	£521	£566	£631	£640	£669	£548	£557	£551	£520	£714	£674
Livestock	£9s	£12	£10	£15	£19	£30	£35	£54	£94	£88	£90
Rent and miscellaneous	£1	£1	£1	£2	£2	£3	£3	£4	£5	£7	
	£2,659	£3,209	£2,920	£2,967	£2,913	£2,907	£2,981	£2,960	£3,046	£3,088	£3,049
Working expenses	£1,595	£1,925	£1,752	£1,780	£1,748	£1,744	£1,788	£1,776	£1,828	£1,853	£1,829

	1914	1915	1916	1917	1918	1919	1920	1921	1922
Rent and miscellaneous	£1	£1	£1	£1	£2	£36	£17	£10	£46
Share of operating revenue	£1,188	£1,232	£1,234	£1,235	£1,234	£1,240	£1,239	£1,235	£1,236
Received by company	£1,189	£1,233	£1,235	£1,236	£1,236	£1,276	£1,255	£1,245	£1,282

Cambrian Railways

Personnel employed on narrow gauge railways – Locomotive department (RAIL92/142)
Aberystwyth

	Date of birth	Joined		Wages/day	
Richard Humphreys Edwards	18 October 1895	15 March 1914	Fireman VRLR	5 May 1919 – 3s 8 August 1919 – 9s 6d 16 May 1921 – 10s 6d	On strike 26 September – 6 October 1919
John Edward Davies	22 November 1887	21 December 1902	Fireman VRLR	7 July 1914 – 3s 8d (4s 6d when driving) 18 August 1919 – 12s	On strike 26 September – 6 October 1919
Joseph Probert Salmon	12 November 1865	April 1907	Cleaner VRLR	3s	On strike 26 September – 6 October 1919
Edward Griffiths	2 December 1870	8 January 1912	Fitter VRLR	5s 8d 24 August 1916 – 6s	Died 15 August 1917
William Joseph Evans	13 June 1867	1 May 1902	Joiner VRLR	4s 1d	On strike 26 September – 6 October 1919
Henry Milman	20 January 1863	1 May 1902	Assistant fitter VRLR	3s 6d	On strike 26 September – 6 October 1919 Died 25 December 1922
Evan Williams	31 May 1855	1 April 1870	Engineman VRLR	5s 4d – 2 December 1902	Left of own accord 12 December 1918

Employed from 22 December 1902, Evan Williams was the only engineman allocated exclusively to the VRLR by the Cambrian. He had been dismissed from Cambrian Railways' service on 4 November 1899 for passing a signal at danger at Talwrn Bach on 12 October, 'thereby causing fatal accident to Ganger Humphreys'.

Welshpool

	Date of birth	Joined		Wages/day	
George Owen	2 October 1882	18 August 1902	Cleaner Fireman Passed fireman	2s 4d 3s – 12s 17 December 1919 – 12s	Joined at Oswestry, fireman at Welshpool from 1910. Did not strike in August 1911. On strike 26 September – 6 October 1919
Frederick William Evans	6 January 1885	22 March 1904	Cleaner Passed cleaner Fireman (9 April 1910)	2s 4d 2s 4d – 2s 8d 2s 8d – 12s	Most of service at Welshpool with spells at at Oswestry and Kerry. Transferred to Kerry as passed fireman on 12 January 1922. Did not strike in August 1911. On strike 26 September – 6 October 1919
Parey Ernest Evans	9 July 1890	18 May 1908	Cleaner Passed cleaner Fireman	2s 2s 4d – 2s 8d 3s 4d 12s	Most of service at Welshpool, three years at Oswestry. Did not strike in August 1911. On strike 26 September – 6 October 1919
David Harold Humphrey	23 September 1890	16 July 1908	Cleaner Passed cleaner Fireman	2s 2s 4d 3s 4d – 11s	Most of service at Welshpool, two years at Oswestry. Did not strike in August 1911. On strike 26 September – 6 October 1919
William Henry Humphreys	24 July 1893	21 June 1910	Cleaner Passed cleaner Fireman	2s – 2s 4d 2s 4d – 2s 8d 3s 2d – 11s	All service at Welshpool. Did not strike in August 1911. On strike 26 September – 6 October 1919

These were the only loco crew based at Welshpool so might be assumed to have worked on the WLLR. Drivers were presumably rostered from Oswestry. Before 1910 George Owen's service as cleaner and passed cleaner alternated between Oswestry and Welshpool. While he was a passed cleaner at Welshpool in May 1904 he was suspended for two days 'for neglect of duty by failing to test gauge taps on their [sic] engine, thus causing boiler to be short of water and lead plus to drop', an incident which might, therefore, have occurred on the WLLR.

Outdoor staff – goods department (RAIL92/145)
Welshpool station – new appointment in connection with transhipment of Llanfair traffic

	Date of birth	Joined		Wages/week	
R. H. Parry	18 May 1873	10 March 1903	Goods porter	16s	Resigned 5 January 1904
David E. Davies	24 October 1884	20 May 1902	Goods porter	15s	Dismissed for pilfering 29 August 1904
William Waring	13 October 1885	23 August 1904	Goods porter	16s	Resigned 7 July 1905
John Evans	1 February 1875	14 April 1919	Temporary goods porter	£2 17s – £3 3s	Resigned 9 May 1921. Maximum pay £3 7s on 1 January 1921.
Donald McTavish	21 October 1888	11 July 1921	Temporary goods porter	£2 18s	Services dispensed with on 18 November 1921
John Eveson	18 May 1890	3 December 1919	Goods porter	£2 14s – £2 8s	Ellesmere 26 February 1923

Llanfair Railway – Welshpool station

	Date of birth	Joined		Wages/week	
George Griffiths	12 March 1875	19 January 1903	Transhipping goods porter	17s – 18s	Resigned 1 August 1904
Thomas Walker Jones	8 July 1883	9 November 1903	Transhipping goods porter	17s	Resigned 26 July 1905
Henry Edwards	28 September 1883	19 September 1904	Transhipping goods porter	17s	Resigned 12 May 1908
Albert R. Watkins	30 May 1884	16 July 1908	Transhipping goods porter	16s – 17s	Resigned 19 October 1909
George Griffiths	12 March 1875	19 October 1909	Transhipping goods porter	17s – 18s	Called up 9 November 1914
Walter A. Beedles	25 September 1892	9 November 1914	Goods porter	17s – £2 10s	Pay increased to £3 6s by 1 October 1920 then reduced
George A. Lloyd	12 November 1893	30 April 1919	Goods porter	£2 10s	Pay reduced to £2 8s on 1 July 1922

Llanfair Caereinion

	Date of birth	Joined		Wages/week	
H. Tudor	10 June 1879	5 November 1919	Temporary goods porter	£2 17s – £2 18s	Pay increased to £3 6s by 1 October 1920 then reduced. Services dispensed with on 3 December 1921.

Station staff uniform men (RAIL92/146)
Welshpool station, Llanfair staff

	Date of birth	Joined		Wages/week	
Charles Done	4 June 1882	7 May 1898	Train porter	18s	Services dispensed with 9 June 1905
Clement Lewis	9 June 1882	5 July 1899	Train porter	18s	Talgarth 1 February 1906
David G. Blockley	4 October 1883	April 1900	Train porter	18s – £1	Shunter 2 February 1912
W. F. G. Lloyd	3 May 1876	12 December 1904	Train porter	18s	Pool Quay 16 May 1912
Charles E. Preece	6 September 1890	2 April 1907	Porter guard	17s – 18s	Porter 8 July 1918, foreman 19 August 1919.
Fred E. Thomas	9 August 1894	14 June 1910	Porter	15s	Platform porter 13 February 1919
Edward Foulkes	22 November 1895	7 October 1914		16s – £2 9s	Pay peaked at £3 9s 6d on 1 January 1921
George J. Phely	28 July 1871	11 February 1886	Relief man	£1 – £1 1s	Porter, Pool Quay 7 November 1900
John George	8 September 1875	4 November 1890	Relief man	£1 3s	Machynlleth 14 March 1901
D. Gilbert Blockley	4 October 1883	April 1900	Booking porter	13s 5d – 16s	Train porter 1 February 1906
John Smith	18 July 1884	21 January 1901	Booking porter	16s	Incapacitated owing to ill health 5 February 1906
Richard Jones	19 November 1884	6 October 1902	Booking porter	16s	Resigned 1 November 1906
Richard J. Leighton	26 April 1887	2 April 1902	Booking porter	15s	Resigned 28 March 1908
William H. Roberts	27 November 1888	29 December 1905	Booking porter	14s	Incapacitated owing to ill health 20 August 1908

Llanfair Railway – Welshpool station

	Date of birth	Joined		Wages/week	
Evan H. Humphreys	11 June 1872	16 November 1892	Guard	£1 4s	Checker Oswestry 13 July 1903
John Pritchard	17 January 1863	1 July 1890	Guard	£1 4s	Talsarnau 3 December 1913
Henry Lewis	29 November 1872	1 October 1895	Guard	£1 8s – £3 5s	Pay peaked at £4 3s 6d on 1 January 1921

Llanfair Caereinion station

	Date of birth	Joined		Wages/week	
William R. Edwards	11 September 1879	8 July 1902	Porter	16s	Resigned 28 August 1906
George Roberts	2 February 1855	10 June 1873	Porter	17s	Llanfechain 18 January 1901
John L. Williams	9 March 1890	28 November 1907	Porter	13s – 15s	Resigned 28 January 1913
Frank Humphreys	20 December 1895	31 January 1913	Porter	15s	Resigned 31 January 1914
D. Richard Jones	21 September 1893	2 February 1914	Porter	15s	Resigned 7 July 1914
Edward Foulkes	22 November 1895	7 October 1914	Porter	15s	Welshpool 9 August 1919
James Herbert Brown	12 April 1898	4 August 1919	Temporary porter	15s	Resigned 10 September 1919
Humphrey Tudor	10 June 1879	3 November 1919	Temporary porter	18s	Transferred to goods 29 December 1919
Joseph George Hughes	10 April 1905	2 February 1920	Porter	10s – £1 5s	Maximum pay was £1 14s on 2 February 1921
Albert James	25 May 1886	23 March 1903	Junior porter	9s – 10s	Newtown 27 November 1907
John L. Williams	9 March 1890	28 November 1907	Junior porter	10s	Porter 1 February 1909
William Pritchard	22 May 1892	1 February 1909	Junior porter	10s	Bettisfield 11 August

A Select Bibliography

Booth, T.; The Corris Railway; *Railway Magazine*, June 1898

Boyd, J. I. C.; *Narrow Gauge Railways in Mid-Wales*; Oakwood Press, 2nd edition, 1970

Briwnant-Jones, G.; *Great Western Corris*; Gomer Press, 1994

Briwnant-Jones, G.; *The Last Days of the Old Corris*; Gomer Press, 2001

Burkhill-Howarth, David; *The Deadly Tablet – the Abermule Railway Disaster of 1921*; Tempus, 2007

Cartwright, Ralph & Russell, R. T.; *The Welshpool & Llanfair Light Railway*; David & Charles, 1972, 1981, 1989

Cartwright, Ralph I.; *The Welshpool & Llanfair*; RailRomances, 2002

Coleman, D .K.; J. R. Dix; *Journal of the Corris Railway Society*, 1985, 1986

Cozens, Lewis; *The Corris Railway*; Author, 1949, reissued with notes by the Corris Railway Society 1972, 1977, 1987 and 1992

Cozens, Lewis; *The Vale of Rheidol Railway*; Author, 1950

Cozens, Lewis; *The Welshpool & Llanfair Light Railway*; Author, 1951

Cozens, Lewis; *The Plynlimon & Hafan Tramway*; Author, 1955

Eade, Sara; *Ratgoed – a study in slate*; Author, 2010

Gasquoine, C. P.; *The Story of the Cambrian – a biography of a railway*; Woodall, Minshall, Thomas & Co, 1922

Gratton, Robert; *The Leek & Manifold Valley Light Railway*; RCL Publications, 2005

Green, C. C.; *The Coast Lines of the Cambrian Railways Volume 1*; Wild Swan, 1993

Green, C. C.; *The Vale of Rheidol Light Railway*; Wild Swan, 1986

Greenhough, Richard; Sir Clifton Robinson; *Journal of the Corris Railway Society*, 1990

Greenhough, Richard; The Corris Carriages; *Journal of the Corris Railway Society*, 1979

Greenhough, Richard; The Corris Railway Traffic in the 1920s and 1930s; *Journal of the Corris Railway Society*, 1988

Gwyn, David; *Gwynedd: Inheriting a Revolution – the archaeology of industrialisation in north west Wales*; Phillimore, 2006

Jones, Gwyn Briwnant; *Tales of the Old Corris*; Gomer Press, 2008

Lazard Brothers & Company; *Vale of Rheidol Railway Limited – invitation to tender*; Lazard Brothers & Company, 1988

Macfarlane, Harold; The Vale of Rheidol Light Railway; *The Railway Magazine*, September 1903

Metcalfe, Richard; *Davies & Metcalfe Ltd Railway Engineers to the World*; Senior Publications/Foxline Publications, 1999

Oxley, J. Stewart; *Light Railways Procedure*; Jordan & Sons/W. Hay Fielding, 1901

Rees, James; Our Newest Recruit – the Corris Railway; *Great Western Railway Magazine*, September 1930

Richards, Alun John; *Slate Quarrying at Corris*; Carreg Gwalch, 1994

Scott-Morgan, John; *Corris – a narrow gauge portrait*; Irwell Press, 1991

Vignes, Edouard (Translated by D. A. Boreham); *A Technical Study of the Festiniog & other narrow gauge railways*; P. E. Waters & Associates, 1986

Wade, E. A.; *The Plynlimon & Hafan Tramway*; Twelveheads Press, 2nd edition, 1997

Williams, Glyn; *The Welshpool & Llanfair Light Railway*; Wild Swan, 2010

Index

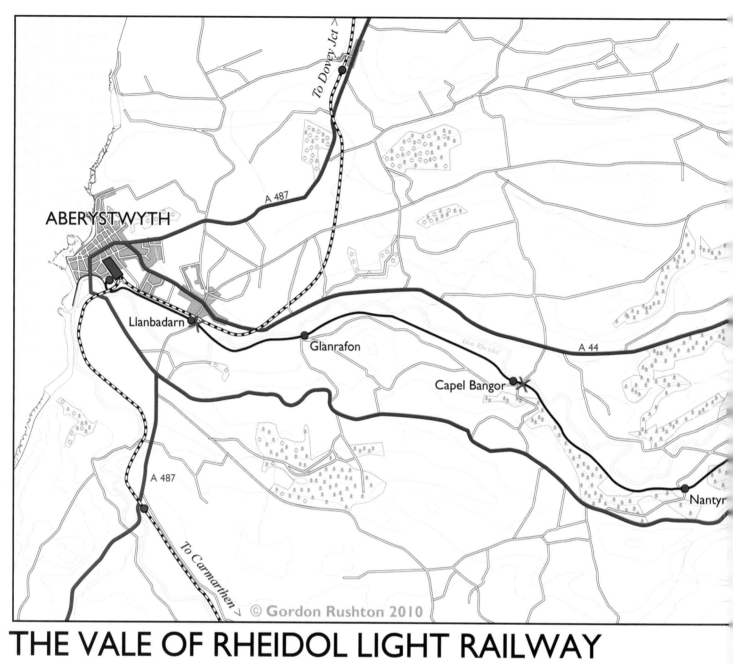

THE VALE OF RHEIDOL LIGHT RAILWAY

THE WELSHPOOL & LLANFAIR LIGHT

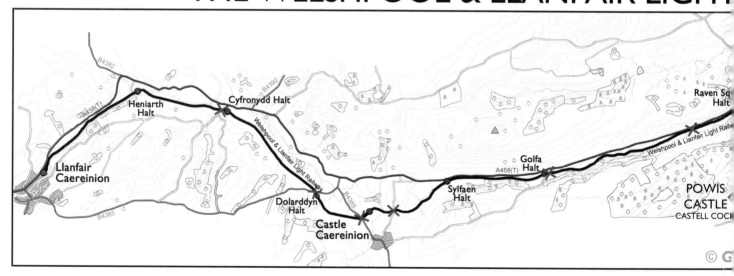